Murska Sobota

Maribor

Slovenj Gradec

Ptuj

Velenje

Celje

SOUTHERN AND
EASTERN SLOVENIA

Novo
Mesto

0 kilometres 20
0 miles   20

Ljubljana Area by Area

EYEWITNESS TRAVEL

SLOVENIA

EYEWITNESS TRAVEL

SLOVENIA

Main Contributors **Jonathan Bousfield, James Stewart**

DK | Penguin Random House

Managing Editor Aruna Ghose
Senior Editorial Manager Savitha Kumar
Senior Design Manager Priyanka Thakur
Project Editor Shikha Kulkarni
Project Designer Shruti Singhi
Editor Parvati M. Krishnan
Designer Rupanki Arora Kaushik
Senior Cartographic Manager Uma Bhattacharya
Cartographer Subhashree Bharati
Senior DTP Designer Azeem Siddiqui
DTP Designer Rakesh Pal
Senior Picture Research Co-ordinator Taiyaba Khatoon

Contributors
Jonathan Bousfield, James Stewart

Photographers
Demetrio Carrasco, Linda Whitwam

Illustrators
Chinglemba Chingtham, Sanjeev Kumar,
Arun Pottirayil, Shruti Soharia Singh

Printed and bound in Malaysia

First American Edition, 2012
17 18 19 20 10 9 8 7 6 5 4 3 2 1

Published in the United States by DK Publishing,
345 Hudson Street, New York, New York 10014

Reprinted with revisions 2015, 2017

Copyright © 2012, 2017 Dorling Kindersley Limited, London
A Penguin Random House Company

Published in the UK by Dorling Kindersley Limited.

A catalog record for this book is available from the Library of Congress.
ISSN 1542-1554
ISBN 978-1-4654-6028-8

Floors are referred to throughout in accordance with British
usage, ie the "first floor" is the floor above ground level.

**The information in this
DK Eyewitness Travel Guide is checked regularly.**
Every effort has been made to ensure that this book is as up-to-date as possible
at the time of going to press. Some details, however, such as telephone numbers,
opening hours, prices, gallery hanging arrangements and travel information, are
liable to change. The publishers cannot accept responsibility for any consequences
arising from the use of this book, nor for any material on third party websites, and
cannot guarantee that any website address in this book will be a suitable source of
travel information. We value the views and suggestions of our readers very highly.
Please write to: Publisher, DK Eyewitness Travel Guides, Dorling Kindersley,
80 Strand, London, WC2R 0RL, UK, or email: travelguides@dk.com.

Front cover main image: Bled Island with the Church of the Assumption, Lake Bled

◀ Picturesque valley with the Alps in the background

Beautifully painted exterior of
the Cooperative Bank, Ljubljana

Contents

The stunning Mount Triglav, Slovenia's
highest peak

Red-tiled roofs in Koper's main square, with the harbour in the background

Guided tour, Postojna Caves

Painted Attic cup, Tolmin Museum

Bogenšperk Castle

HOW TO USE THIS GUIDE

This guide helps you get the most from your visit to Slovenia. It provides detailed practical information and expert recommendations. *Introducing Slovenia* maps the country and its regions, sets them in a historical and cultural context and describes events through the entire year. *Slovenia Region by Region* is the main sightseeing section. It covers all the important sights, with photographs, maps and illustrations. Information on hotels, restaurants, shops and markets, entertainment and sports is found in *Travellers' Needs*. The *Survival Guide* has advice on everything from travel to medical services, telephones and post offices.

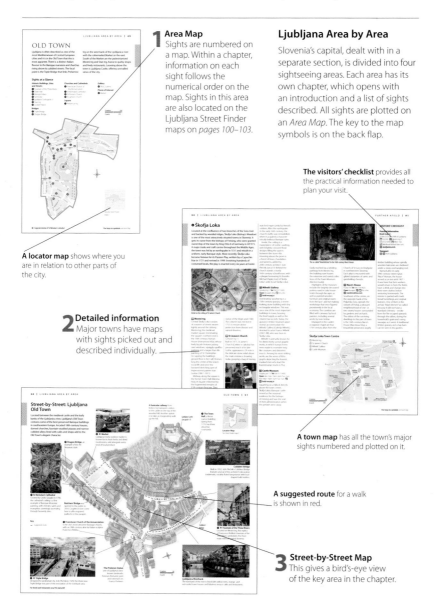

1 Area Map
Sights are numbered on a map. Within a chapter, information on each sight follows the numerical order on the map. Sights in this area are also located on the Ljubljana Street Finder maps on *pages 100–103*.

Ljubljana Area by Area

Slovenia's capital, dealt with in a separate section, is divided into four sightseeing areas. Each area has its own chapter, which opens with an introduction and a list of sights described. All sights are plotted on an *Area Map*. The key to the map symbols is on the back flap.

A locator map shows where you are in relation to other parts of the city.

The visitors' checklist provides all the practical information needed to plan your visit.

2 Detailed information
Major towns have maps with sights picked out and described individually.

A town map has all the town's major sights numbered and plotted on it.

A suggested route for a walk is shown in red.

3 Street-by-Street Map
This gives a bird's-eye view of the key area in the chapter.

Slovenia Region by Region

Apart from Ljubljana, Slovenia is divided into three regions, each with a separate chapter.

Sights at a glance lists the chapter's sights by category: Historic Streets and Buildings, Museums and Galleries, Parks and Gardens, and so on.

1 Introduction
The landscape, history and character of each region is outlined here, revealing how the area has developed over the centuries and what it offers visitors today.

2 Regional Map
This map shows the road network and gives an illustrated overview of the region. All the sights are numbered and there are useful tips for getting around.

3 Detailed information
Important places to visit are described individually. Addresses, telephone numbers, opening hours and other practical information are provided for each entry.

Each region can be identified by its colour codes, which are listed on the front inside cover.

Driving tours explore areas of special interest.

4 Major sights
Top sights and historic buildings are dissected to reveal their interiors, while museums have colour-coded floorplans to help find the most important exhibits. Stars indicate the main features visitors should not miss.

INTRODUCING SLOVENIA

DISCOVERING SLOVENIA

The following itineraries have been designed to include as many of Slovenia's highlights as possible, while keeping long-distance travel manageable. First comes a two-day tour of the country's small but sophisticated capital, Ljubljana. This is followed by a two-day itinerary of the Karst and coastal regions, with suggestions for places to visit around this unique limestone plateau, as well as the short but engaging Slovenian coastline. A

one-week tour of the Alps covers all the key sights contained within Slovenia's magical mountain landscape. Extra suggestions are provided for those who wish to extend their stay by another day or so. Lastly, there is a wonderful two-week itinerary of the whole country, which takes in all the sights of the one-week tour, and more besides. Pick one, or perhaps two or three, or just dip in and out and take things at your own pace.

Church of the Holy Trinity
The interiors of this Romanesque church in Hrastovlje are covered with beautiful frescoes.

Key

— Two Days on the Coast and the Karst

— One Week in the Alps

— Two Weeks in Slovenia

Two Days on the Coast and the Karst

- Amble around the medieval hilltop settlement of **Štanjel**, the archetypal Karst village.

- A show at **Lipica**, birthplace of the world-famous white Lipizzaner horse, is not to be missed.

- The world's largest subterranean canyon is the highlight of **Škocjan Caves**, Slovenia's greatest natural wonder.

- Admire Slovenia's finest medieval iconography – the *Dance of Death* fresco – in Hrastovlje's diminutive **Church of the Holy Trinity**.

- Get lost amongst the tangle of Venetian streets and squares in **Piran**, the coast's prettiest town.

- Learn how to pan for salt at the **Sečovlje salt pans** in the Gulf of Piran.

Peč Undergroun Min

Kranjska Gora

Vršič Pass
Vrata Valley
Bovec
Kobarid
Lake Bohinj
Triglav National Park
Tolmin
Most na Soči
Goriška Brda
Vintgar Gorge
Lake Bled
Radovljica
Kropa
Škofja Loka
Logarska dolina
Rob Kot
Velika Planina
Kamnik
Ljubljana

Predjama Castle
Štanjel
Postojna Caves
Lake Cerknica
Snežnik Castle
Adriatic Sea
Lipica
Škocjan Caves
Snežnik Plateau
Piran
Koper
Sečovlje salt pans
Hrastovlje
Kolpa V

Soča
Sava

One Week in the Alps

- Ramble through **Logarska Dolina**, a glorious alpine valley surrounded by toothy peaks.

- Spotted with shepherd's huts selling cheese, **Velika Planina** is also a great destination for hiking.

- Swim, fish or just take a stroll around **Lake Bohinj**, Slovenia's most scenic lake.

- Make your way over the 50 hairpin bends that comprise the spectacular, 1,611 m- (5,285 ft-) high **Vršič Pass**.

- Brave the bewitching **Soča river**, which runs through the equally awe-inspring Soča Valley.

- Compelling and sobering, the **Kobarid Museum** recalls the region's World War I mountain battles.

Two Weeks in Slovenia

- Take a walk around **Lake Bled**, Slovenia's showpiece attraction, thanks to its fairy-tale island church and clifftop castle.

- Bordering Italy, the sunny **Goriška Brda** region is just the spot in which to enjoy a few glasses of superb Slovenian wine.

- Hop aboard the cave train to reach the dazzling formations inside **Postojna**, a classic show-cave.

- Explore the **Krka River Valley**, stopping at ancient castles and an island village along the way.

- Seek out architectural and archaeological riches in **Ptuj**, Slovenia's oldest and prettiest town.

- **Prekmurje** stands in marked contrast to the rest of the country, a pancake-flat region home to pretty little churches and lots of storks!

Kostanjevica na Krki
This picturesque historic village, located on an island in the Krka river, dates back to the 13th century. One of the main attractions is the monastery, which houses an excellent art gallery that displays works by Božidar Jakac, as well as pieces by other 20th-century Slovenian artists.

Two Days in Ljubljana

Slovenia's elegant capital city is centred on its gorgeous Old Town, but there's plenty more to see and do beyond here.

- **Arriving** Ljubljana Airport is 23 km (14 miles) north of the city. Shuttle buses take around 30 minutes to get to the city centre; public buses take slightly longer.

Day 1

Morning Start at Prešeren's statue on **Prešernov trg** (see p52) before crossing Joze Plečnik's ingenious **Triple Bridge** (see p53), on the other side of which is the colourful **Central Market** (see p54), packed with deliciously fresh foodstuffs. Head to the funicular, which transports you up to **Ljubljana Castle** (see pp56–7), and visit the virtual museum, climb the clock tower, or just take in the majestic alpine views.

Afternoon After lunch in the Old Town, pore over the magnificent Baroque and Renaissance architecture, notably the **Fountain of the Three Rivers** (see p53) and the **Town Hall** (see p53) on Mestni trg. Cross the Cobbler's Bridge and head to Plečnik's extraordinary **National University Library** building (see p72), before winding up at the **Ljubljana City Museum** (see p73) for a fascinating insight into the city's history. In the evening, try to catch a live music performance in the atmospheric, open-air **Križanke** theatre (see p73).

Day 2

Morning Take a walk along Miklošičeva ulica, rampant with eye-popping Secessionist architecture, then pop in to **Metelkova Mesto** (see p81), the city's alternative cultural hub, which mixes historical heritage with contemporary cool. Close by, the imaginatively arranged **Slovene Ethnographic Museum** (see pp82–3) showcases a number of superb artifacts, both from Slovenia and further afield.

Afternoon Familiarize yourself with Slovenia's greatest painters at the **National Gallery** (see pp64–5); look out for the much-loved group of Impressionists, Grohar, Jakopič, Sternen and Jama. Afterwards, stretch your legs in **Tivoli Park** (see p78), and if you've got surplus energy, make for the wooded heights of **Rožnik Hill** (see p79). Finish the day with a glass of wine in one of the many convivial bars strung along the Ljubljanica river.

Two Days on the Coast and the Karst

The captivating Karst region manifests dry-stone villages and dramatic caves, while the short stretch of coastline stars elegant resorts like Koper and Piran.

- **Arriving** Arrive and depart from Ljubljana Airport, or Trieste Airport, just across the border in Italy.

- **Transport** A car is essential for this trip.

Day 1: The Karst

Morning Head south from Ljubljana into the arid limestone plateau of the **Karst** (see p23), famous for its spectacular rock formations. Don't miss **Predjama Castle** (see pp152–3), improbably situated in the mouth of a huge cavern – you might even catch some jousting. Continue west until you come to **Štanjel** (see p145), most appealing of all the Karst villages, a warren of crooked streets lined with brilliant bleached-white stone houses.

Afternoon At **Lipica** (see p141), you can view the stables housing the Lipizzaner horses, but better still, time your visit to coincide with a presentation by the Classical Riding School. A short drive away, the vast subterranean chambers of the **Škocjan Caves** (see pp142–3) make for an unforgettable visit. Back above ground, the protected nature reserve has some scenic walks.

Day 2: The Coast

Morning Heading towards the coast, call in at the little Church of the Holy Trinity in **Hrastovlje** (see p140) and pore over some of Slovenia's finest medieval frescoes, the standout being the macabre (but amusing) Dance of Death. Hit the coast at **Koper** (see pp138–9) and soak up the Venetian buildings and squares before a quick laze on the beach.

Afternoon It's a short journey down the coast to **Piran** (see pp134–5), strewn with gorgeous Gothic-Venetian architecture, and with a maritime heritage that still resounds today. Take coffee on Tartinijev trg, named after the famous composer, Tartini, who lived in a house just off the square. To the south of Piran are the **Sečovlje salt pans** (see p137), well worth visiting to witness a demonstration of the age-old salt-making process.

> **To extend your trip...**
> Visit **Portorož** (see p136), the coast's premier beach resort, with all its associated activities, before heading over to the cleverly conceived Forma Viva sculpture park.

The dramatically situated Predjama Castle

One Week in the Alps

- **Arriving** Arrive and depart from Ljubljana Airport.
- **Transport** A car is essential for this trip.

Day 1: Kamniško-Savinjske

From Ljubljana, head north to the picturesque **Logarska dolina** *(see p126)*, where you can inspect the sinuous Rinka waterfall, walk or cycle amongst flower-speckled meadows, or partake in horse riding or rock climbing. In the afternoon, turn your attention to neighbouring **Robanov kot** *(see p126)*, a more secluded but no less beautiful glacial valley.

Day 2: Kamnik to Lake Bled

Stop for an hour or so in **Kamnik** *(see pp124–5)*, before taking the cable car up to **Velika Planina** *(see p125)*, a lush alpine plateau spotted with shingle-roofed shepherd's huts; buy some cheese here and whip up a picnic lunch. Afterwards, drive to the timeworn village of **Kropa** *(see p115)*, where blacksmiths still ply their trade, before the short trip to **Radovljica** *(see pp114–15)*, home to one of Slovenia's more curious attractions, the marvellous **Museum of Apiculture** *(see p115)*.

Day 3: Lake Bled and around

Enjoy an early morning jaunt around **Lake Bled** *(see pp112–13)*, pausing along the way to visit the clifftop castle with its glorious views. Back down on the lake, take a gondola – or row yourself – across to **Bled Island** *(see pp112–13)*, where the Church of the Assumption sits in perfect isolation. In the afternoon, make the short trip to the **Vintgar Gorge** *(see p114)*, an impressive ravine with wooden gantries suspended from the precipitous rock face. Back in Bled, end the day with a fish supper by the lake.

To extend your trip…

Head for the thickly forested **Pokljuka Plateau** *(see p117)* with its magnificent gorge and nature trails.

Kayaking on the stunning Soča river

Day 4: Lake Bohinj and around

Entering **Triglav National Park** *(see pp116–17)*, carry on to **Lake Bohinj** *(see pp118–19)*, where you can swim or kayak, visit the Church of St John with its astonishing frescoes, or take the cable car up to Vogel for the best mountain views in Slovenia. It's a short trek both to Slap Savica, the country's most photogenic waterfall, and Stara Fužina, a beautifully preserved valley village much visited for its unique double hayracks.

Day 5: Kranjska Gora and the Vršic Pass

After a brief diversion up the **Vrata Valley** *(see p117)* to view Mount Triglav's massive north face, continue to **Kranjska Gora** *(see p120)*, where you can marvel at the head-spinning Planica ski jumps. This is also the starting point for the memorable trip over the **Vršic Pass** *(see pp120–21)*, which climbs to 1,611 m (5,285 ft) over the course of 50 hairpin bends;

Red rooftops in Kamnik, a regional capital in the Middle Ages

numerous points of interest along the way include the Russian Chapel, the **Alpinum Juliana** *(see p121)* and the source of the Soča River.

Day 6: Soča Valley

Prepare for some thrills and spills in **Bovec** *(see p122)*, Slovenia's premier adrenaline sports centre – take to the magnificent Soča river for some rafting or kayaking. After a well-deserved lunch, continue down the Soča Valley to **Kobarid** *(see p122)*, where the horrors of World War I mountain warfare are relayed in the superb Kobarid Museum. If there's time, undertake the Kobarid Historical Walk, which embraces a number of fascinating man-made and natural attractions. End the day with dinner in one of the town's many outstanding restaurants.

Day 7: Tolmin to Most na Soči

Continue south down the Soča Valley to **Tolmin** *(see p122)*, with its absorbing museum, and then the stunning Tolmin Gorge, where you can unravel the secrets of Dante's Cave. In the afternoon, conclude your tour with a stop in **Most na Soči** *(see p122)*, one of Slovenia's most important prehistoric settlements – a well-conceived trail marks out the town's rich tapestry of natural and historical sights.

To extend your trip…

Heading away from the mountains, take a tour of the gorgeous **Goriška Brda wine region** *(see p149)*, nestling against the Italian border.

Two Weeks in Slovenia

- **Airports** Arrive and depart from Ljubljana Airport.
- **Transport** A car is essential for this trip.
- **Tip** The Vršič Pass may be closed due to snow between November and April, so check conditions in Kranjska Gora before attempting a crossing.

Day 1: Ljubljana
Pick a day from the Ljubljana itineraries (see p12).

Day 2: Ljubljana to Lake Bled
As you head out of the capital, first stop is **Škofja Loka** (see pp90–91), one of Slovenia's loveliest towns, overlooked by a majestic Baroque castle. Explore the medieval **Mestni trg** (market square; see p90), pausing to admire the façades of the Homan House (Homanova hiša) and the Town Hall. Next, make your way towards the black-smiths' village of **Kropa** (see p115), whose history is relayed in the excellent **Iron Forging Museum** (see p115) and where you may still get to see master craftsmen at work. Better still is the **Museum of Apiculture** (see p115) in Radovljica (see pp114–15) and its wickedly amusing beehive panels.

Day 3: Lake Bled and Lake Bohinj
Begin the day at Slovenia's star attraction, **Lake Bled** (see pp112–13), where you can circumnavigate the lake on foot, or, if you've got surplus energy, row across to the magically picturesque island church. Following a lakeside lunch, it's a short drive into the **Triglav National Park** (see pp116–17) and **Lake Bohinj** (see pp118–19). Stand on the bridge at the head of the lake for glorious views, before popping inside the Church of St John to marvel at its dazzling frescoes – if there's time, catch the cable car up to Vogel to enjoy more breath-taking alpine views.

Day 4: Kranjska Gora to Bovec
Head northwest to **Kranjska Gora** (see p120), though not before a quick detour up the **Vrata Valley** (see p117) to size up the hulking north face of Mount Triglav, Slovenia's highest peak. From Kranjska Gora, prepare for a spectacular drive over the serpentine **Vršič Pass** (see pp120–21), stopping along the way to take in numerous points of interest, like the Russian Chapel and the source of the Soča. Arrive in the alpine town of **Bovec** (see p122).

Day 5: Soča Valley
After breakfast, the Soča river beckons you to its thrashing waters for some whitewater rafting, kayaking or some such other thrill seeking activity. Reinvigorated following lunch, continue down the awesome Soča Valley to **Kobarid** (see p122). Kobarid was the scene of horrific mountain warfare during World War I, which you can learn more about in the brilliant Kobarid Museum. Take dinner in one of the town's fine coterie of restaurants.

Day 6: Goriška Brda and the Karst
First stop is **Goriška Brda** (see p149), where you can sample some of Slovenia's finest wines, try some local produce, and wander around the fortified village of Šmartno. The Karst

Alpine meadows and rugged peaks, Kranjska Gora

region lies in wait further south. Here, take a walk amongst **Štanjel**'s stone houses (see p145), enjoy a performance of the world-famous Lipizzaner horses at **Lipica** (see p141), before the day's real highlight – a guided tour of the unforgettable **Škocjan Caves** (see pp142–3).

Day 7: The Coast
Spend the day on the short Slovenian coastline. In the morning, inspect the historic heart of **Koper** (see pp138–9), taking in the Venetian Gothic and Renaissance architecture and, if the weather's fine, pop to the beach for a quick dip. In the afternoon, head down the coast to the beautiful town of **Piran** (see pp134–5), where you can (and probably will) get lost amongst the warren of narrow streets and small squares. Time permitting, consider taking an excursion to the **Sečovlje salt**

Lake Bohinj in the southeastern corner of Triglav National Park

pans *(see pp136–7)*. Return to Piran for a fish supper down on the waterfront.

Day 8: Notranjska
Make your way from the coast to the stunning, stalagmite-filled caves at **Postojna** *(see pp154–5)* and the dramatically sited **Predjama Castle** *(see pp152–3)*. From here, it's not far to **Lake Cerknica** – the "disappearing lake" – *(see p157)*, which, depending upon the season, will either be there or it won't! In the afternoon, make the short journey south to **Snežnik Castle** *(see p158)*, surrounded by the forested **Snežnik Plateau** *(see pp158–9)*, where you might even encounter a bear or two.

Day 9: Kolpa Valley to Novo Mesto
Head south towards the **Kolpa Valley** *(see p165)*, whose river rapids are ideal for canoeing. Afterwards, seek out the sculpture of local folk hero Peter Klepec, and enjoy a riverside picnic. In the afternoon, walk through **Kočevski Rog** *(see p165)*, home to some of Europe's last virgin forests and some fantastic wildlife, including wolves and bears. **Novo Mesto** *(see p166)*, whose museum contains some of the country's richest archaeological treasures, is the day's last stop.

Day 10: Along the Krka Valley
The first port of call today is **Pleterje Monastery** *(see p168)*, where you can learn all about the Carthusian Order and try a homemade fruit brandy. From here, take a trip along the **Krka Valley** *(see p169)*, dotted with grand castles like **Otočec** *(see p169)* and **Mokrice** *(see p169)*, and pretty villages like **Kostanjevica na Krki** *(see p169)*, which sits on its own little island. At the end of the day, treat yourself to a soak or a splash at the **Terme Čatež** *(see p169)* spa and water park.

Day 11: Ptuj and around
Leaving the Krka Valley, make tracks for the **Bizeljsko-sremiška Wine Road** *(see p170)*,

Novo Mesto, southeastern Slovenia's largest city, located on the banks of the Krka river

visiting a cellar or two along the way, such as Istenič at Stara va, before a quick diversion up to the mist-swathed ruins of **Žiče Monastery** *(see pp178–9)*. Continue northeast to **Ptuj** *(see pp182–3)*, where you'll have plenty of time to admire this lovely town's remarkable Roman-era monuments, including the amazing Mithra Shrines. As the day draws to a close, have a quick tour of the sun-kissed hills of the **Jeruzalem** *(see p185)* wine region.

Day 12: Prekmurje
A bewitching, iron-flat landscape, the region of Prekmurje is characterized by lush fields, picturesque villages and roadside churches. Two churches not to miss are those in **Bogojina** *(see pp186–7)* and **Martjanci** *(see p186)*, while the one must-see village is **Velika**

Lush vineyards in the wine village of Jeruzalem, north of Ormož

Polana *(see p187)*, where you'll witness the remarkable sight of storks perched, improbably, atop telegraph poles. While in the region, be sure to sample some of the local specialities, typically *bograč* (a stew) and *gibanica* (a cheese pastry dish).

Day 13: Maribor and Koroska
Slovenia's second city, **Maribor** *(see pp180–81)*, offers exquisite Baroque and Renaissance architecture, alongside the world's oldest grape vine down in the riverside Lent district. After lunch, cross the Pohorje massif into Koroška, stopping at **Slovenj Gradec** *(see p176)* – where the prominent artist Jože Tisnikar lived and worked – and then the **Peca Underground Mine** *(see p177)* for an exhilarating subterranean train or bike ride.

Day 14: Kamniško-Savinjske Alps
Spend the morning exploring the twin glacial valleys of **Logarska dolina** *(see p126)* and **Robanov kot** *(see p126)*, the pearls of this glorious mountain range. Visit friendly **Kamnik** *(see pp124–5)* and explore the Little Castle or the Intermunicipal Kamnik Museum. Conclude your trip by taking the cable car up to **Velika Planina** *(see p125)*, where you can wander among shepherd's huts and soak up the views from these lush alpine meadows. From here it's a short drive back to Ljubljana.

Putting Slovenia on the Map

Slovenia is one of Europe's smaller states, with an area of 20,273 sq km (7,825 sq miles). It has borders with Austria to the north, Hungary to the east, Croatia to the south and Italy to the west. There is a short stretch of Adriatic coastline and the main mountain chains are the Karavanke and the Julian Alps. The principal river is the Sava, which rises in the Julian Alps before flowing southeast towards Croatia then Serbia, where it joins the Danube. The capital, Ljubljana, stands at the centre of the road and rail network. From here, even the furthest regional attractions can be reached in a couple of hours.

0 kilometres 20

0 miles 20

For keys to symbols *see back flap*

Central and Eastern Europe

A PORTRAIT OF SLOVENIA

Few countries pack so much variety into such a small geographical area as Slovenia. The landscape changes swiftly from the high Alps to arable plains, and from dense deciduous forests to the palm-fringed Mediterranean coastline. At the centre of the country is the capital Ljubljana, a vibrant city combining graceful architecture with a certain joie de vivre.

Outside the capital, characteristic alpine farmhouses and whitewashed hilltop churches are scattered across the landscape of central and eastern Slovenia. To the west, however, Mediterranean styles are more evident and coastal towns such as Koper and Piran have an instantly recognizable Venetian character. This diversity reflects Slovenia's geographical position at the junction of Central Europe, the Balkans and the Mediterranean.

The country has a population of just over 2 million, of which 83 per cent are Slovenians. Small but significant others include Albanians, Bosnians, Croats and Serbs, who came to Slovenia during the Yugoslav period. Slovenians themselves are descendants of the Slav tribes who settled here from the 6th century AD onwards. The Slovenian language is closely related to other Slav tongues such as Croatian, Serbian, Czech and Slovak, although it retains many unique characteristics.

Despite being ruled by foreign dynasties for much of their history, the Slovenians have proved to be remarkably resilient. Slovenia's status as a federal republic in Communist Yugoslavia after 1945 gave the nation stable borders for the first time in its history, although the country did not achieve full independence until 1991.

Lake Bohinj, against the backdrop of the fog-covered Alps

◀ Slovenians dressed in historical costumes parading the streets of Škofja Loka

Visitors enjoying a ride on a horse-drawn wagon, Logarska dolina

Society

Slovenia's culture is vibrant and maintains its bold, forward-looking approach. During the 1970s and 80s, the country emerged as a major centre of contemporary art, music and design, and even today, boasts the kind of film, newspaper and publishing industries that are the envy of its neighbours. Until the early 20th century, however, Slovenia was predominantly a peasant country, and traditional costume, folk music and village festivals remain an important part of life.

Given Slovenia's spectacular mountainous terrain, the great outdoors features prominently in the national psyche. Hiking and skiing are popular, and facilities for winter sports are of a very high standard. The primeval forests of Kočevski Rog and the vine-cloaked hill villages of the southwest are no less compelling in terms of unspoiled nature. Slovenia is also famous for its breathtaking limestone formations in the Karst region.

People

Slovenia's status as a cultural crossroad has also had an impact on its national character. Typical Central European traits such as honesty, hard work and cheerfulness are valued, although Mediterranean qualities such as style, sociability and a taste for good food also fit the nation's psychological profile. Slovenian attitudes to the Balkan regions to the southeast are more complex. Indeed, "Balkan" was considered an unpleasant word in the aftermath of independence in 1991, when Slovenians were eager to emphasize their complete break with former Yugoslav nations. Today, however, supposedly Balkan characteristics such as warmth, spontaneity and vivacity are viewed more positively by most Slovenians.

Slovenia is a predominantly Catholic country, although the tone of everyday life is secular. A third of all marriages end in divorce, which is somewhere near the European average.

Sculpture outside Gruber Palace, Ljubljana

Politics

Despite the dissolution of Yugoslavia in 1991, attitudes towards the Yugoslav heritage still remain complex. Pride in Slovenia's economic achievements often exists side by side with a feeling of nostalgia for a Communist system that offered more in the way of social justice

Exhibition on Communism at a gallery in Idrija

and job security. Even though the Yugoslavia of President Tito was a one-party state with limited political freedoms, the nation was still culturally open to the outside world.

The Communist-led partisan struggles of World War II are still seen by most as a genuinely heroic period in the nation's history; many streets and squares bear the names of partisan divisions and heroes. This is especially true in western Slovenia and Slovenian Istria, which would not have been part of the country today were it not for the partisans. Yet, at the same time, there is little nostalgia for Communism as a political system, and Slovenians are enormously proud of the "Slovene Spring" of the late 1980s, when citizens successfully challenged Communist authority.

Since 1990, Slovenia has been a parliamentary democracy with power passing fairly painlessly between right- and left-wing parties. The main planks of post-independence policy – membership of NATO and the EU, and acceptance of the euro as the national currency – were greeted positively by the majority of Slovenians and are widely recognized today.

Slovenia Today

Of all the former Communist countries of Europe, Slovenia has enjoyed the easiest transition to a capitalist democracy. Even during the Communist period, Slovenia was a highly educated society with competitive manufacturing industries, a modicum of private enterprise and a vibrant consumer culture. Post-independence, Slovenia has become a technocratic society in which young educated people are frequently employed in high positions. Most Slovenian professionals want to stay and work in their home country, and Slovenia has thus experienced little of the economic emigration suffered by other former Communist states.

Tourism is a major industry, with Slovenia's alpine terrain offering a wealth of hiking and skiing opportunities, as well as adrenaline sports such as rafting and canyoning. Ljubljana, Lake Bled and Lake Bohnj count among Central Europe's prime holiday destinations. Slovenia's reputation as a "green" destination of unspoiled countryside, ecological consciousness and organic food has only served to increase the country's appeal.

Grape harvest at a vineyard near Ljutomer

Landscape and Wildlife

Slovenia packs an extraordinary variety of flora and fauna into what is, by European standards, a relatively small country. The landscape changes swiftly from the snow-covered peaks and glacier-carved valleys of the alpine north to the rolling farmlands of the southeast and the palm-fringed Adriatic resorts of the southwest. The most distinctive part of the Slovenian landscape is the Karst, an arid plateau of porous limestone that stretches across the west of the country. Rich in caves and potholes carved by centuries of rainfall, the Karst makes for some of the most dramatic underground scenery in Europe.

Traditional salt pans in Sečovlje, coastal Slovenia

Alpine Slovenia

Northern Slovenia is dominated by mountains. The Julian Alps in the northwest boast the highest peaks, including Mount Triglav. Much of alpine Slovenia is covered in evergreen forest and its lush highland meadows are perfect for dairy farming.

Coastal Slovenia

Slovenia's short strip of coastline enjoys a warm Mediterranean climate – vines and olive trees cover the hills above the shore and palm trees line the seafront promenades. The waters of the Adriatic are rich in shellfish and crustaceans.

Alpine ibex roam the high-altitude pastures in the spectacular Triglav National Park.

Olive trees are grown on the slopes overlooking the coast for their highly prized oil.

Brown bears can be quite easily spotted in Slovenia's alpine region.

Bottlenose dolphins can be seen frolicking off the Slovenian coast.

The primula blooms in spring and can be found all over alpine Slovenia.

Vipava valley is an important vine-growing region famous for its dry white wines.

Forests of Slovenia

Over 50 per cent of Slovenia is covered with woodland, making it one of the most densely forested countries in Europe. The Julian Alps are carpeted with a mixture of spruce, beech and larch. Beech trees predominate in the deep, primeval forests of southern Slovenia, notably the Kočevski Rog area, which serves as an important habitat for wolves, lynx and bears. Common in all areas of Slovenia is the linden, a deciduous tree whose heart-shaped leaves are a national symbol.

Linden tree at the Lipica stud farm, where a tree is planted every time a foal is born

Forest-dwelling dormouse on the branch of a tree

The Karst

The limestone uplands of western Slovenia are famous for their subterranean cave systems, carved out over the millennia by underground rivers. The caves at Postojna and Škocjan are among the most-visited speleological attractions in Europe.

Bats, including the lesser horseshoe and the greater mouse-eared species, inhabit the caves in the Karst.

Human fish (*Proteus anguinus*) grow up to a length of 30 cm (1 ft) and can live for as long as 100 years.

The persimmon, with its succulent golden flesh, is the most common garden fruit in the western Karst.

The Pannonian Plain

The rolling lowlands of the Pannonian plain stretch from eastern Slovenia across much of Hungary, eastern Croatia and northern Serbia. It is a rich agricultural area with sunflower, rape, pumpkin and grape among the most important crops.

White storks spend late spring and early summer in the villages of eastern Slovenia, migrating southwards in August.

Pumpkins are harvested for their seeds, which yield delicious oil.

Sunflowers, which fill the fields during summer, are an important agricultural crop.

Architecture

Slovenia's location between Central Europe and the Mediterranean has placed it at the crossroads of architectural styles throughout history. During the Middle Ages, a wealthy and ambitious Church built monasteries throughout the country, frequently employing Gothic styles imported from Northern Europe. During the Counter-Reformation, Slovenia welcomed a wave of architects influenced by Italian Baroque. In the 20th century, Slovenia became a breeding ground for Modernist trends: Art Nouveau was eagerly adopted in the years before World War I, while more functionalist styles became popular in the years that followed.

Baroque fountain by Francesco Robba on Mestni trg, Ljubljana

Gothic

The medieval church was the organization most responsible for the spread of Gothic style in Slovenia, with its construction of churches and monasteries. Apart from major 12th-century projects such as the Carthusian Monastery at Žiče or the Cathedral of St John the Baptist at Maribor, there are a number of exquisite parish churches scattered throughout the country.

The Baroque belfry, added in the 18th century

The Church of St John *(see p119)* on the eastern shores of Lake Bohinj, is a typical example of a Gothic-era village church, with a rib-vaulted ceiling and well-preserved frescoes.

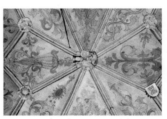

St James's Church *(see p90)* is a late-Gothic church in Škofja Loka that contains superb examples of complex rib-vaulting, with exuberant floral motifs filling the spaces in between.

Baroque

Through the 16th and 17th centuries, an influx of architects from Italy brought the best of Baroque to Slovenia's main towns. Prominent among them was Andrea Pozzo, architect of the capital's famous St Nicholas's Cathedral.

Maribor Castle's façade *(see p180)* showcases the Baroque taste for swirly decorative details with its crests and mouldings. The castle is also home to a spectacular Baroque staircase.

St Nicholas's Cathedral *(see p54)* boasts a typically ornate Baroque interior, with frescoes by Giulio Quaglio and statues by Francesco Robba.

Art Nouveau

The dominant architectural style in Ljubljana at the beginning of the 20th century was Art Nouveau. Many city-centre apartment blocks still bear the decorative details associated with the movement.

Centromerkur Building *(see p52 and p63)* now the Galerija Emporium, a fashion store, was built in 1903. Among its original features are a cast-iron canopy and a beautiful Y-shaped staircase.

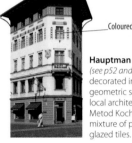

Coloured tiles

Hauptman House *(see p52 and p63)* was decorated in a lively geometric style by local architect Ciril Metod Koch, using a mixture of paint and glazed tiles.

Ljubljana's Cooperative Bank *(see p62)* was the work of architect Ivan Vurnik. He took Art Nouveau one step further, drawing on Slovenian folk motifs to produce this highly original decorative scheme.

Contemporary (20th Century)

The main currents of modern architecture all left their mark on Slovenia. The country's greatest 20th-century architect was Jože Plečnik, who combined modern styles with elements from the ancient world to create a unique personal style.

Ljubljana City Museum

Arched top-floor windows add decorative charm

Nebotičnik *(see p62)* is a stately Art Deco building, best appreciated by taking a trip to the top-floor café.

National and University Library *(see pp72–3)* is Plečnik's masterpiece, combining locally quarried marble with red brick to create a dappled façade.

Medieval Castles

Slovenia was, for centuries, a feudal society run by landowning warlords, and their castles are still scattered across the landscape. Although much altered in the intervening period, dramatically located hilltop castles at Ljubljana, Bled and Celje retain plenty of their original medieval features. Many castles were converted during the Renaissance and Baroque eras to serve as aristocratic dwellings – those at Ptuj, Predjama, Bogenšperk, Škofja Loka and Kromberk are popular museum destinations today, packed with fine furnishings and *objets d'art*.

Predjama Castle, pressed against the mouth of a cave in the Karst region

Folk Art and Music

Despite entering the 21st century as a modern and technologically advanced society, Slovenia has retained a good deal of its folk traditions. Each region has a distinct musical style, with age-old songs and dances kept alive by local societies and schools. Regional folk costumes no longer form part of everyday dress, but are still very much in evidence during Slovenia's busy calendar of festivals and fairs. The products of traditional craftspeople can be seen in ethnographic museums all over the country – one of the most characteristic folk arts being painted wooden beehive panels, featuring fanciful scenes with human and animal figures.

Folk dancers in the regional costume of the Dolenjska area

Traditional Dress

Each region has its traditional costume that is still worn on festive occasions. Intricate geometric or floral patterns on skirts, blouses and tasselled shawls were specific to an area and helped identify a person's village. Black ankle-length skirts are the most common attire for women. Typical for men are waistcoats, breeches and a hat.

The Slovenian bonnet called the *avba*, frequently decorated with lace, ribbons and embroidery, is an important national symbol.

The umbrella is a characteristic accessory, usually bright orange-red with coloured concentric stripes.

Folk Music

Slovenian folk music is still widely performed in rural areas, especially at weddings, feast days and local celebrations. The most widely distributed form of traditional music is the polka- and waltz-dominated style of the alpine region. Featuring an accordion backed by strings, it is joyful, melodic and ideal for dancing in couples. Its commercial music form, perfected by the Avsenik brothers from the Bled region, has enjoyed international success, selling millions of records in alpine Europe. Two current groups inspired by folk music are Terrafolk and Katalena, whose experiments in folk-rock fusion are contemporary in flavour.

Pan pipes or *trstenka*

Zither, a common musical instrument

The accordion is a key component in almost every folk group.

Live music is an important part of social life, especially during summer, when most towns and villages organize festivals and celebrations that often involve groups playing on an open-air stage.

Painting and Other Crafts

Painting, embroidery and lace-making added style, colour and spiritual symbolism to the traditional Slovenian home. Furniture was frequently painted to add brightness to living and sleeping rooms, while intricately patterned textiles created an aura of wealth and comfort. One widespread form of popular art involved the painting of religious images on glass panes.

Detail of Idrija lace   Traditional lace-making in progress

Intricate lace, from the town of Idrija *(see p150)*, is traditionally made by intertwining threads from a series of small bobbins, a complicated procedure that requires nimble fingers.

Beehive panels were highly decorative and were used to identify the hive and its owner. Seasonal agricultural activities usually formed the subject matter.

Painted Easter eggs are traditionally decorated with colourful pattens in melted wax, a custom that has been preserved in the villages of southern Slovenia.

Furniture, such as wardrobes, bedsteads and cradles, was frequently painted in bright colours. Flowers, geometric shapes and figures of angels were the most common decorations. Painted wooden chests played a ritual role in weddings and were part of a bride's dowry.

Gingerbread, made in various shapes and iced in bright colours, is a gift often given on festive occasions. The gingerbread heart *(lectovo srce)* is the traditional love token – although it is likely to be hung on a wall as a memento rather than eaten.

Folk Architecture

Folk architecture, with farmhouses and barns constructed from traditional materials, still survives in rural areas. In alpine Slovenia, timber housing with flower-decked verandahs is the dominant style, followed by modern house builders too. In the Karst and on the Adriatic coast, most houses were made from stone blocks, grouped around narrow alleys – this can be seen in Karst villages such as Štanjel. One of the characteristics of traditional houses was the black kitchen, consisting of an open hearth and no chimney. Smoke rose up through the beams of the house, curing grain and meats in the process.

Traditional timber-built house, common in Slovenia's highland region

Slovenian Art

Slovenia has long been a melting pot of European artistic styles, and has frequently been at the epicentre of major cultural movements. The history of Slovenian art closely follows that of the country's architecture, with Gothic art flourishing throughout the Middle Ages and a major explosion of Baroque art occurring during and after the Counter-Reformation of the 16th century. From the late 19th century onwards, art was often closely related to national politics, with the Slovenian Impressionists aiming to modernize national culture while remaining true to its traditional ideals. Slovenia's post-World War I generation eagerly embraced Cubism, Constructivism and other modern art movements.

Woman Drinking Coffee by Ivana Kobilca

The Medieval Period

Medieval Christianity provided a fertile ground for the growth of a rich artistic culture, with frescoes, stained glass and sculpture filling the country's churches and monasteries.

Dance of Death, Hrastovlje, was painted in 1490 by John of Kastav. This animated frieze is the best known of a series of frescoes that fills Hrastovlje's village church.

St George, Gabrska Gora, an anonymous mid-15th century wood sculpture, is a compelling example of late-Gothic art.

Baroque Art

The Counter-Reformation encouraged new styles in the arts, with an enhanced sense of spiritual drama visible in both painting and sculpture. Artists from Italy flooded Ljubljana, bringing with them the best in Baroque style.

Frescoes in the Seminary Library, Ljubljana *(see p55)*, were painted by Giulio Quaglio together with his son Raffaello in 1721. They depict a mixture of Christian figures and Classical deities. Clever use of perspective creates the illusion of added height.

Fountain of the Three Rivers by **Francesco Robba** *(see p53)* shows Slovenia's three main rivers symbolized by a trio of Tritons pouring water from jugs, with fish providing a playful touch.

The 19th Century

The early 19th century saw a growing middle class, in Ljubljana and other towns, who were wealthy enough to buy pictures for their homes, and frequently commissioned family portraits from local artists. Painters Matevž Langus, Jožef Tominc and Mihael Stroj mixed pictorial realism with domestic warmth and sentiment.

Julija Primic With Her Brother Janez by Matevž **Langus** was one of his many portraits of Primic, subsequently a celebrated beauty and object of unfulfilled desire for poet France Prešeren.

Impressionism

Taking their lead from the French Impressionists, Slovenian artists such as Ivan Grohar, Rihard Jakopič, Matija Jama and Andrej Sternen brought a new sense of colour and atmosphere to Slovenian painting. Choosing to depict local landscapes and rural subjects, the Slovenian Impressionists saw their art as a patriotic duty, creating truly Slovenian paintings for a Slovenian audience.

The Sower by **Ivan Grohar** was painted in 1907. This enigmatic depiction of a toiling peasant, face turned away from the viewer, has become something of a national icon.

Modernism

Slovenian artists enthusiastically took up new ideas after World War I, with Avgust Černigoj experimenting with Constructivism and Ferdo Delak publishing avant-garde magazine *Tank!* Expressionism and New Objectivity influenced the work of painters Veno Pilon and Tone Kralj.

In the Café by **Veno Pilon** is a 1926 work dating from Pilon's period in Paris. It illustrates the enduring fascination of Slovenian artists with Western Europe.

Postwar and Contemporary Art

Unlike some more strictly controlled Communist countries, Slovenia remained open to international art trends after World War II, and frequently stood at the forefront of the global avant-garde. The 1960s art group OHO (Marko Pogačnik, David Nez, Milenko Matanović, Andraž and Tomaž Šalamun) was one of the leading conceptualists of the era, performing "actions" and publishing theoretical texts rather than producing artworks as such. In the 1980s, the art collective IRWIN produced a provocative mixture of painting, political symbolism and performance art that still exerts a strong influence on artists elsewhere.

Big Bright Self-Portrait by **Gabriel Stupica**, painted in 1959, is an example of the versatile and prolific artist's use of mixed elements of Expressionism, Surrealism and Abstraction over a long and influential career.

Skiing in the Slovenian Alps

Slovenians have been skiing since the 18th century, so it is of little surprise that skiing is the most popular activity in the country and that Slovenia has produced several Olympic and World Cup champions. Most of the country's resorts lie in the alpine northwest or are strung along the Pohorje massif near Maribor. Although each has its own character and pistes for most levels, Slovenian resorts are small and relaxed compared to the more famous ones elsewhere in Western Europe. The resorts here are also far cheaper, even though they provide the same facilities as the more celebrated resorts in Austria and Italy.

Vogel is one of the most scenic skiing destinations in Slovenia. This mountain lies in the Triglav National Park (see pp116–17). There are pistes for beginners and mid-level skiers, while experts have the opportunity to go off-piste as well as to ski on one of Slovenia's best "black" runs, Žagarjev graben. There is a snowboarding park too.
Star attractions: *Spectacular views; off-piste skiing*

Kranjska Gora, Slovenia's oldest and best-known ski resort (see p120), is famous for its World Cup links and awesome ski jumps in Planica. It has everything from child-friendly runs to steep competition pistes in nearby Podkoren. Off-piste skiing is possible when conditions allow. There is also a wide variety of hotels, family activities and a range of après-ski activities.
Star attractions: *Alpine scenery; excellent holiday facilities*

0 kilometres   20

0 miles   20

Kobla is a modern intermediate-level resort above Bohinjska Bistrica, which has the distinction of being the only Slovenian ski destination that can be accessed by train.

Cerkno, a small resort in Primorska, is not as busy as those further north. It has 18 km (11 miles) of pistes that suit all levels of skiers, from children and novices to thrill-seekers.

Mount Kanin, at 2,300 m (7,546 ft), has Slovenia's highest pistes and its greatest vertical descent. The scenic mountain offers skiing late into spring as well as views of the Adriatic on clear days. It also allows the unique opportunity of skiing to the Italian resort, Sella Nevea.
Star attractions: *All ski slopes above 2,000 m (6,562 ft); long skiing season; skiing into Italy*

Mariborsko Pohorje, located next to Maribor *(see pp180–81)*, the second-largest city in Slovenia, is the country's largest ski resort and one of its most popular. With pistes spread over a 220-ha (544-acre) area, the resort caters best to intermediate and novice skiers, although there are challenging runs for experts too.
Star attractions: *Only 30 minutes from Maribor centre; 10-km-(6-mile-) long night-time piste; cross-country forest trail*

Velika Planina is popular with day trippers. The slopes are gentle for beginners and cross-country skiing is spectacular.

Kope is the highest part of the Pohorje range and enjoys one of the longest seasons.

Krvavec is very popular with the residents of Kranj *(see p124)* – the cable car to the ski base is just 17 km (11 miles) from Kranj's city centre. Krvavec's smooth alpine meadows permit skiing even under a thin blanket of snow and its pistes are well equipped for all activities, including snowboarding.

Rogla, popular with advanced skiers and snowboarders, is the training base for the Slovenian Olympic team. Most of its 12 km (8 miles) of pistes are ranked in the intermediate level.

Statistics

Kranjska Gora
Resort at: 810 m (2,648 ft)
Skiing altitude: 1,210–800 m (3,937–2,625 ft)
Pistes: 20 km (12 miles)
Maximum descent: 813 m (2,667 ft)
Ski lifts: 19
Cross-country trails: 40 km (25 miles)
Season: Dec–Mar

Mariborsko Pohorje
Resort at: 325 m (1,066 ft)
Skiing altitude: 1,150–325 m (3,773–1,066 ft)
Pistes: 42 km (26 miles)
Maximum descent: 1,010 m (3,314 ft)
Ski lifts: 20
Cross-country trails: 25 km (16 miles)
Season: Dec–Mar

Mount Kanin
Resort at: 460 m (1,509 ft)
Skiing altitude: 2,300–1,600 m (7,546–5,249 ft)
Pistes: 30 km (19 miles)
Maximum descent: 1,840 m (6,036 ft)
Ski lifts: 5
Cross-country trails: 16 km (10 miles)
Season: late Nov–early May

Mount Vogel
Resort at: 570 m (1,870 ft)
Skiing altitude: 1,800–570 m (5,905–1,870 ft)
Pistes: 18 km (11 miles)
Maximum descent: 1,231 m (4,039 ft)
Ski lifts: 8
Cross-country trails: 35 km (22 miles)
Season: Dec–mid-Apr

Key

△ Peak

▬ Motorway

▬ Major road

▬ Minor road

— Railway

▬ International border

Family Fun

Winter sports are family activities in Slovenia. Many children start to ski or toboggan as toddlers and most resorts have nursery slopes for youngsters. There are myriad activities to tempt younger skiers on to the slopes in places such as Kranjska Gora, Vogel or around Lake Bled. Here, pistes are set aside for those who want to toboggan on sledges or rubber rings, go snowshoe trekking, sleigh-riding, snowboarding or dog-sledding. Daring youngsters can sled at night on floodlit slopes.

Children playing at Krvavec

For keys to symbols *see back flap*

SLOVENIA THROUGH THE YEAR

A nation with distinct seasons, Slovenia has warm springs, long and hot summers, golden autumns and crisp, cold winters. Spring and early summer tend to be dry and warm but rarely stifling, making them ideal times to visit the country. July and August are the peak periods for holidaying on Slovenia's stretch of the Adriatic coast, while the winter sports season can last from mid-December right through to Easter. Whatever the time picked to travel, there are always plenty of events to plan a trip around, from seasonal celebrations of local folklore to major arts and music festivals, which attract a large number of big-name international participants.

Skiiers at the Golden Fox tournament, Maribor

Spring

Spring comes early to lowland Slovenia, with café tables spilling out on to the pavements. In the alpine parts of the country, however, snow can linger until Easter or beyond. By May, the weather is warmer and drier all over the country, heralding the first of the year's open-air cultural festivals.

March

World Cup Ski Flying *(mid-Mar)*, Planica, near Kranjska Gora. The winter sports calendar reaches a climax with international competitions at Planica *(see p120)*, the highest ski-jumping hill in the world.

April

Ljubljana Tango Festival *(mid-Apr)*, Ljubljana. This festival brings together dancers from Latin America and Europe. There are plenty of opportunities for audience participation.
Spring Festival *(2nd half of Apr)*, Ljubljana. This is a two-week season of electronic music concerts and avant-garde art exhibitions.
Salt Festival *(weekend closest to 23 Apr)*, Piran. The local salt-making industry is celebrated with a weekend of handicraft fairs, outdoor concerts and church processions, all in honour of Piran's patron saint, St George.

May

May Day *(1 May)*, nationwide. This is traditionally celebrated with the erection of the *mlaj*, a tall spruce trunk that is stripped of most of its branches except a few twigs at the top. Coloured ribbons and the Slovenian flag are hung from its tip.
Druga godba *(mid-May)*, Ljubljana. With concerts taking place in the open-air Križanke complex *(see p73)*, this is one of Europe's foremost world music festivals, featuring top-name participants from across the globe.
Cerkno Jazz *(mid-May)*, Cerkno. An eclectic selection of top-class jazz, jazz rock, jazz noise and ethno jazz, with internationally known names performing on Cerkno's main square, followed by after-party events around town.

Dancers at the Ljubljana Tango Festival

Average Daily Hours of Sunshine

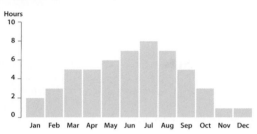

Hours
10
8
6
4
2
0

Jan Feb Mar Apr May Jun Jul Aug Sep Oct Nov Dec

Climate Chart
The greatest number of sunny days occur between May and September. The least occur from November to January, when the hours of daylight are shorter. Hours of sunlight pick up again in February and March when the winter scenery is at its best.

Magdalena *(May)*, Maribor. A prestigious festival for young designers and graphic artists, with exhibitions in the daytime and gigs along with DJ events in the evenings.

Summer

There is a rich and varied menu of festivals in the summer, with many towns organizing a season of open-air concerts.

June
Kino Otok Film Festival *(early–mid-Jun)*, Izola. A festival of international feature films and short films, often featuring a strong Third World angle, with screenings taking place on Izola beach.
SEVIQC Brežice *(Jun–Aug)*, various venues. A season of early music concerts, which take place in historic buildings throughout Slovenia.
Ljubljana Jazz Festival *(late Jun–early Jul)*, Ljubljana. A week of outstanding jazz performances from international stars, with concerts in Križanke and other venues around the capital city.
Summer in the Old Town *(Jun–Sep)*, Ljubljana. A summer-long series of classical and jazz concerts held in historical buildings and courtyards.
Medieval Festival *(last weekend of Jun)*, Škofja Loka. Pageants, jousts and feasting in one of the nation's best-preserved historic towns.
Rock Otočec *(last weekend of Jun)*, Otočec. This three-day festival is Slovenia's biggest outdoor rock event. Local and international bands perform in a field near the Otočec Castle.

Conductor at the Ljubljana Festival, featuring concerts and chamber music

Lent Festival *(late Jun–early Jul)*, Maribor. One of Slovenia's prime summer events, offering a fortnight of rock, jazz, theatre and folklore on outdoor stages on the riverbank and outside the town hall.

July
Ana Desetnica *(early Jul)*, Ljubljana. An international festival of street theatre with drama, circus acts and dance.
Bled Festival *(Jul)*, Lake Bled. A month-long programme of music and theatre in a range of venues around Lake Bled, featuring new contemporary work as well as the classics.
Ljubljana Festival *(Jul and Aug)*, Ljubljana. A season of major operas, symphonic concerts and chamber music using the Križanke outdoor stage.
Trnfest *(late Jul–late Aug)*, Ljubljana. A month-long series of open-air rock gigs and DJ events organized in the Trnovo district by the KUD France Prešeren Cultural Centre.

SEVIQC Brežice concert in progress at a historic building

Average Monthly Rainfall

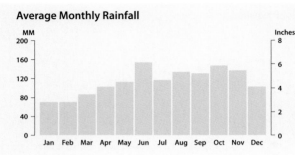

Rainfall Chart
The heaviest rainfall occurs in the summer months, although it is concentrated in the mountains. The lowland regions remain significantly drier. In winter, precipitation takes the form of snowfall, which can be dramatic, especially in the Alps.

August

Tartini Festival *(Aug and Sep)*, Piran. Outstanding classical soloists and chamber musicians perform in Piran's Minorite Monastery *(see p134)* and other historical buildings.

Radovljica Festival *(early Aug–mid-Aug)*, Radovljica. A three-week festival of early music, with concerts in Radovljica manor house (free bus for concert-goers from Ljubljana).

Kamfest *(mid-Aug)*, Kamnik. The centre of Kamnik is taken over by a two-week programme of concerts featuring rock, pop and world music.

Autumn

Autumn sees several major cultural festivals, with film and theatre featuring prominently. One massively popular seasonal activity is mushroom-picking, an all-the-family affair that gets into full swing by mid-September and can last until mid-November. The best harvests occur after a good period of rain.

September

Nagib Contemporary Dance Festival *(mid-Sep)*, Maribor. A week of challenging dance performances by international and local artistes. Performances take place in a variety of venues throughout the city.

The Cows' Ball *(2nd or 3rd weekend of Sep)*, Bohinj. A long weekend of feasting, drinking and folk dancing, celebrating the transhumance of the dairy herds from the alpine meadows to pastures on the valley floor.

Biennial of Graphic Arts *(Sep and Oct, odd years)*, Ljubljana. A major event attracting the world's best printmakers, designers and illustrators. Exhibitions are spread across several major galleries.

October

Slovene Film Festival *(early Oct)*, Portorož. A review of the year's best Slovenian feature films, short films and documentaries. Prizes are awarded to the best directors.

BIO (Biennial of Industrial Design) *(Oct, even years)*, Ljubljana. A prestigious international design festival, embracing product design, graphic arts and fashion, with exhibitions at Ljubljana's Fužine Castle *(see p85)*.

Onlookers and participants at the Cows' Ball festival, Bohinj

Average Monthly Temperature

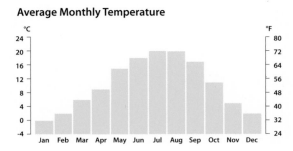

Temperature Chart
Summer is generally mild, with average temperatures peaking at 20° C (68° F) in July, although summers in the mountains can be significantly cooler. Winters tend to be harsh, with the temperature often dropping below zero from December.

Borštnikovo srečanje *(mid-Oct)*, Maribor. Slovenia's premier contemporary theatre event, repeating the outstanding performances of the previous year.

November
St Martin's Day *(11 Nov)*, nationwide. Traditionally the day on which the year's new wine is ready to be drunk, St Martin's Day is marked with drinking and feasting – roast goose is the traditional dish.
LIFFE International Film Festival *(mid-Nov)*, Ljubljana and Maribor. A 10-day showcase of recent art movies from around the world, with lectures by visiting directors.

Winter
The opening of the ski season in mid-December is marked with DJ parties at the main resorts. The main folkloric event of late winter is Shrovetide, when archaic Lenten rituals take place in Ptuj, Cerkno and the villages of the southwest.

Hand-painted clock sold at Advent

December
Advent *(Dec)*, Ljubljana. This market brings craft and delicatessen stalls on to the streets of the Old Town.
Living nativity scenes *(Dec)*, Postojna Caves. Local high-school students re-create scenes from the New Testament in Slovenia's most-visited cave.
Outdoor Film Festival *(last week of Dec)*, Bovec. This

Revellers dressed as Kurenti during Kurentovanje, Ptuj

innovative festival of films focuses on documentaries dealing with sports, nature and the environment.

January
Golden Fox (Zlata lisica) *(mid-Jan)*, Maribor. Women's world-cup skiing on the pistes of the Mariborsko Pohorje *(see p181)*.

February
MED (Maribor Electronic Destination) *(late Feb)*, Maribor. The Kibla Multimedia Centre in Maribor celebrates experimental electronic music with a weekend of concerts.
Kurentovanje *(Shrove Sunday)*, Ptuj. The most famous of Slovenia's pre-Lenten carnivals is held in Ptuj, where the Kurenti (traditional carnival figures) dance and leap through the town clad in animal skins and masks driving away the evil spirits of winter as they go.

Public Holidays

New Year's Day (1 Jan)
Prešeren Day (Day of Slovene Culture, 8 Feb)
Easter Sunday (variable)
Easter Monday (variable)
Day of the Anti-Fascist Uprising (27 Apr)
May Day (1 and 2 May)
Pentecost (7th Sun after Easter)
Day of Slovene Statehood (25 Jun)
Assumption Day (15 Aug)
Reformation Day (31 Oct)
All Saints' Day (1 Nov)
Christmas (25 Dec)
Independence and Unity Day (26 Dec)

THE HISTORY OF SLOVENIA

Located at the junction of the Central European, Mediterranean and Balkan worlds, Slovenia was, for a large part of its history, a marginal space squeezed between more powerful nations and cultures. That the Slovenians emerged as a coherent national group with a state of their own is a remarkable story of its people's resilience as well as survival.

Archaeological finds have suggested that Slovenia was already settled during the Paleolithic Age; however, evidence of the first well-established human culture in the area dates back to 4000 BC, when pile-dwellings were built in the Ljubljana Marshes, south of what is now the capital.

Constant migrations brought in new ethnic groups such as the Illyrian-speaking tribes that settled in the alpine region. By the 2nd millennium BC, a Bronze Age society based on hilltop fortresses was emerging in western Slovenia. The more sophisticated cultures of the 1st millennium BC were famous for their jewellery and situlae (ritual bronze vessels decorated with reliefs). The Vače Situla in the National Museum in Ljubljana is the finest example.

Migrating Celts arrived somewhere around 300 BC, bringing with them technical innovations such as the horse-drawn chariot and the potter's wheel. Celts assumed leadership of the existing population and carved out several states, of which the most powerful was Noricum, a tribal federation covering northern Slovenia and much of Austria.

The Romans

In the 2nd century BC, the Romans began to expand towards present-day Slovenia. This was a gradual and largely peaceful process in which the Romans extended their power through trade agreements and favourable alliances. It was under Emperor Augustus (63 BC–AD 14) that the region was fully absorbed into the Roman state and divided between the provinces of Italia in the west, Noricum in the northeast and Pannonia in the southeast. Roman legionaries were encouraged to settle in Emona (present-day Ljubljana), which soon became a thriving centre of trade and commerce. Celeia (Celje) and Poetovio (Ptuj) were the other main urban centres that developed during this period. Some of the best-preserved Roman ruins can be found around these towns.

By the middle of the 5th century AD, these Roman towns had been abandoned, with the populace seeking sanctuary in the hills from incursions by a succession of invaders. The Ostrogoths overran large parts of Slovenia in the 5th century only to be displaced by the Lombards several generations later.

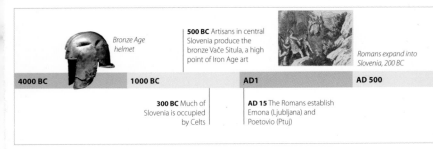

Bronze Age helmet

500 BC Artisans in central Slovenia produce the bronze Vače Situla, a high point of Iron Age art

Romans expand into Slovenia, 200 BC

4000 BC	1000 BC	AD1	AD 500

300 BC Much of Slovenia is occupied by Celts

AD 15 The Romans establish Emona (Ljubljana) and Poetovio (Ptuj)

◀ Fresco from the Besenghi degli Ughi Palace, Izola

Painting depicting the Magyars invading Central Europe, AD 896

Arrival of the Slovenians

The Slovenian nation has its origins in the great migrations of the 6th century AD, when Slav tribes from the east settled in what is now Slovenia and southern Austria. They became the dominant ethnic group and were briefly drawn into a tribal federation led by Frankish merchant Samo in the mid-7th century. After Samo's death in 658, the Slavs formed their own state, which came to be known as the Duchy of Carantania. The 8th and 9th centuries saw the gradual absorption of these territories into the Frankish Empire. Frankish control helped ease the progress of Christian-ization, a process largely carried out by missionary priests from Salzburg and Aquileia. Frankish rule was profoundly shaken in the 10th century due to raids by the Magyars, and the Holy Roman Empire (the name adopted by a confederation of German rulers) expanded into Slovenia to fill the vacuum. Priests and warlords from the German province of Bavaria were awarded lands, creating a German-speaking aristocracy that held sway in Slovenia until the end of the 19th century.

Habsburgs and Ottomans

Medieval Slovenian society was dominated by a small number of super-powerful landowning dynasties – notably the Spannheims and the Counts of Celje – who controlled central Slovenia in the 14th and 15th centuries. Apart from building castles, the Counts of Celje made donations to Pleterje Monastery and the pilgrimage church at Ptujska Gora. Another feudal family increasing its holdings in the region were the Habsburgs, and, by the late 15th century, Slovenia had effectively become a province of the Habsburg Empire. Throughout the period of the Habsburg reign, the language for politics and culture was German, and Slovenian was spoken only among the peasantry.

Italian culture exerted an influence over the western Slovenian lands, where

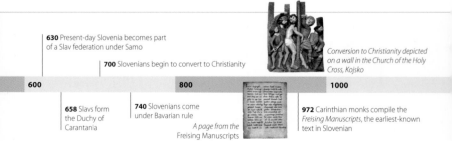

630 Present-day Slovenia becomes part of a Slav federation under Samo

700 Slovenians begin to convert to Christianity

Conversion to Christianity depicted on a wall in the Church of the Holy Cross, Kojsko

| 600 | 800 | 1000 |

658 Slavs form the Duchy of Carantania

740 Slovenians come under Bavarian rule

A page from the Freising Manuscripts

972 Carinthian monks compile the *Freising Manuscripts*, the earliest-known text in Slovenian

Slovene-inhabited villages were in close proximity to the largely Italian-speaking area along the Adriatic coast. Slovenians and Italians mingled in the multiethnic port city of Trieste, which became a Habsburg possession in 1382. The nearby towns of Capodistria (Koper) and Pirano (Piran), meanwhile, came under the rule of Venice.

The Ottoman conquest of Bosnia in 1463 suddenly made Central Europe vulnerable to a new and powerful enemy. The Ottomans immediately started raiding Slovenian territory, leading to the fortification of towns, villages and churches throughout the country. Slovenians fought in the Habsburg armies that defeated the Ottomans at the Battle of Sisak in 1593, removing the threat of invasion for several generations.

Artist's view of the addition of Trieste to the Habsburg Empire (1382)

Reformation and Counter-Reformation

Slovenian society was shaken by the emergence of Protestantism in the early 16th century. The preacher Primož Trubar became leader of the local Protestants, but was forced to leave for Germany in 1548 when the authorities clamped down on the new creed. Prayer books, published by Trubar in Tübingen, were the first books to be printed in the Slovenian language. Most of Slovenia's gentry and townsfolk accepted Protestantism by the 1560s, but the high aristocracy remained loyal to the Catholic

Bronze relief depicting the spread of Christianity, Ljubljana Cathedral

faith. The Jesuits arrived in Ljubljana in 1597 to spearhead the Counter-Reformation and, in 1628, the Habsburg emperor, Ferdinand II, enforced Catholic obedience on all high state officials. The Counter-Reformation won over the peasantry by encouraging new popular forms of worship, in which the cult of the Virgin Mary and mass participation in pilgrimages played increasingly important roles. The 17th century witnessed a renewed interest in Slovenian history and culture, led by geographer Janez Vajkard Valvasor. In 1689 he published his most important work, *Honour of the Duchy of Carniola*, on the natural history of his homeland.

Detail of Dance of Death *fresco*

1282 The Habsburgs gain a foothold in the region

1490 Janez of Kastav decorates Hrastovlje Church with his *Dance of Death* fresco

1515 A peasant revolt ruthlessly put down by pro-Habsburg aristocrats

1200	1400	1600

1365 The Habsburg ruler, Rudolf IV, founds Novo Mesto

Duke Rudolf IV

1456 Death of Ulrich II, last Count of Celje; lands acquired by Habsburgs

1597 Jesuits arrive in Ljubljana to spearhead the Counter-Reformation

1593 Habsburgs defeat the Ottomans at the Battle of Sisak

Slovenia's National Awakening

Intellectual life in Ljubljana began to take off at the turn of the 18th century, with learned societies such as the Academia Operosorum as well as the Academia Filharmonicorum encouraging literature, music and the arts. Renewed interest in the Slovenian language was promoted by the intellectuals grouped around Žiga Zois, an enlightened baron whose collection of minerals became the basis for the Slovene National Museum. Among Zois's circle were Valentin Vodnik, editor of the first Slovenian newspaper, and Jernej Kopitar, linguist and philologist.

Further impetus to Slovenian culture came from a brief period of French rule (1809–13), when Ljubljana became the capital of the "Illyrian Provinces", which included Slovenia and western Croatia. The Slovenian

Habsburg's coat of arms

language was introduced in schools, increasing the demand for Slovenian books. Even though Austria returned to power after the end of the Napoleonic Wars (1799–1815), interest in Slovenian culture continued. The epic verses of Romantic poet France Prešeren demonstrated that Slovenian language was fit for fine literature as well as the marketplace.

Social upheavals in 1848 raised hopes that the Habsburg Empire would be decentralized, leading to some autonomy for the Slovenians. However, the authorities in Vienna retained their grip on power, and the 1850s saw a return to absolutist rule. In 1867, the Habsburg Empire was divided into Austrian- and Hungarian-administered halves, creating the Dual Monarchy of Austria-Hungary. Most of Slovenia fell within the Austrian part, although the Slovenians of the eastern province of Prekmurje found themselves under Hungarian rule. Between 1868 and 1871 Slovenian intellectuals launched what became known as the Tabor Movement, a series of mass meetings calling for the reunification of Slovenians, nurturing a new sense of patriotism. Most Slovenians believed their country was too small to be a viable political entity on its own and campaigned for a self-governing Slav unit within Austria-Hungary. However, gaining ground by the close of the 19th century was the concept of Yugoslavism – the idea that those south-Slav peoples who shared similar languages (Slovenians, Croats and Serbs) should form a common state.

Poet France Prešeren's statue, Prešernov trg, Ljubljana

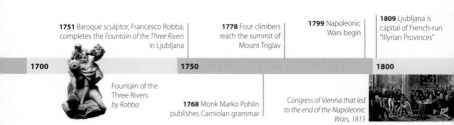

1751 Baroque sculptor, Francesco Robba, completes the *Fountain of the Three Rivers* in Ljubljana

1778 Four climbers reach the summit of Mount Triglav

1799 Napoleonic Wars begin

1809 Ljubljana is capital of French-run "Illyrian Provinces"

1700

1750

1800

Fountain of the Three Rivers by Robba

1768 Monk Marko Pohlin publishes Carniolan grammar

Congress of Vienna that led to the end of the Napoleonic Wars, 1815

An 1845 engraving showing an aerial view of Ljubljana

World War I and the Birth of Yugoslavia

During World War I, Slovenians were drafted into Habsburg armies and served on all fronts. Italy declared war on Austria-Hungary in 1915, hoping to conquer ethnic Slovenian territory in the Adriatic hinterland. Three years of bitter warfare along the Soča (Isonzo) river followed, with huge casualties on both sides. After the October 1917 breakthrough at Kobarid, the Austro-Hungarian forces won at the Soča Front but faced collapse elsewhere, leading to a disintegration of authority.

With the defeat of the Austro-Hungarian Empire in October 1918, Slovenia's leaders rushed to declare a union with their south-Slav neighbours, creating the Kingdom of Serbs, Croats and Slovenians. Trieste and its hinterland were awarded to Italy, disappointing Slovenians who considered it to be part of their national heritage. The Slovenians of Trieste soon became the target of Italian nationalist attacks and the Slovene Cultural Centre (Narodni dom) was burnt down by a Fascist mob in 1920. The German-Slovenian areas around Klagenfurt in Carinthia were subjected to a plebiscite

in October 1920, with the majority voting for incorporation into Austria. Slovenians initially thought that the new south-Slav state would be a loose federation in which they would enjoy a measure of autonomy. However, the Constitution of 1921 created a centralized country with a single parliament in Belgrade. Slovenian politicians tried to reform the system, but the new state remained politically unstable. After the fatal shooting of Croat leader Stjepan Radić in parliament (1928), Serbia's King Alexander established a royal dictatorship. The state was renamed "Yugoslavia" in the hope that officially enforced Yugoslav patriotism would end ethnic quarrels.

Political frustrations aside, Slovenian culture flourished in the interwar period, with the extension of local-language education, the founding of Ljubljana University and a boom in publishing. Winter tourism and skiing became a national obsession, with ski-jumping emerging as the most popular spectator sport.

Austro-Hungarian soldiers at the Soča Front, 1915

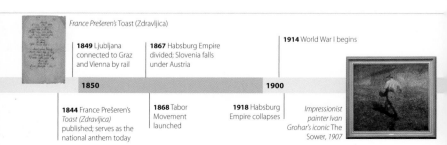

France Prešeren's Toast (Zdravljica)

1849 Ljubljana connected to Graz and Vienna by rail

1867 Habsburg Empire divided; Slovenia falls under Austria

1914 World War I begins

1850

1900

1844 France Prešeren's *Toast (Zdravljica)* published; serves as the national anthem today

1868 Tabor Movement launched

1918 Habsburg Empire collapses

Impressionist painter Ivan Grohar's iconic The Sower, *1907*

Socialist Realist painting in the Slovene Museum of Contemporary History, Ljubljana

World War II, Tito and the Yugoslav Federation

The Kingdom of Yugoslavia came to an end with the German invasion in April 1941 and Slovenia was divided between Germany and Italy. An anti-Fascist partisan movement under the Communists became increasingly influential. Some conservatives collaborated with the occupiers, swelling the ranks of the Quisling-controlled *domobranci* or home guard. Ably led by the half-Slovenian, half-Croatian Josip Broz Tito, the partisan movement became a liberation army, sweeping the occupiers out of Slovenia by May 1945. Over the next few months about 12,000 *domobranci* were massacred by avenging partisans, their bodies dumped in mass graves.

With the war over, Slovenia became a federal republic in Communist Yugoslavia. The fate of Trieste and its hinterland remained undecided until 1954, when it was returned to Italy. Koper, Piran and Portorož were ceded to Slovenia. Federal Yugoslavia was initially allied to the USSR, but Soviet leader Stalin harboured a profound distrust of Tito, and engineered Yugoslavia's expulsion from the Eastern-bloc Cominform

organization in 1948. Tito stayed in power, borrowed money from the West, and built a popular form of Communism. The 1950s saw a rise in living standards and a boom in consumerism. Slovenian goods, such as Gorenje domestic appliances, Cockta soft drinks and Lisca lingerie, became household names and are exported even today. Although Yugoslavia was relatively open to Western culture, freedom had its limits. The intellectual magazine *Revija 57* was closed down in 1958 after publishing articles critical of Socialism (their author Jože Pučnik was jailed), and the journal *Perspektive* faced a similar fate in 1964.

As the most economically advanced republic in the federation, Slovenia frequently felt short-changed by a system where funds were channelled to subsidize projects in the poorer south. In 1969, money for Slovenian road-building was diverted to other republics owing to pressure from Belgrade. Slovenian Communist leader Stane Kavčič was forced out of power in 1972 for defending Slovene interests. Paradoxically, a new constitution in 1974 gave more autonomy to the republics, leaving Slovenia's Communists relatively free to run their own affairs. Yugoslavia's decentralized system worked as long as living standards improved, and the popular Tito remained at the helm. With his death in 1980, and the economic crisis, the federation disintegrated.

The "Slovene Spring"

In Slovenia, the emergence of punk rock in the late 1970s unleashed subcultures that the Communist authorities failed to control. National youth organizations

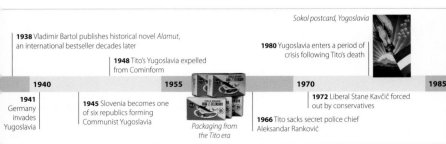

Sokol postcard, Yogoslavia

1938 Vladimir Bartol publishes historical novel *Alamut*, an international bestseller decades later

1948 Tito's Yugoslavia expelled from Cominform

1980 Yugoslavia enters a period of crisis following Tito's death

1940	1955	1970	1985

1941 Germany invades Yugoslavia

1945 Slovenia becomes one of six republics forming Communist Yugoslavia

Packaging from the Tito era

1966 Tito sacks secret police chief Aleksandar Ranković

1972 Liberal Stane Kavčič forced out by conservatives

enthusiastically adopted alternative culture, and the magazine, *Mladina*, became increasingly daring in its criticisms of Communist bureaucracy. The Slovene League of Communists, led by reformist Milan Kučan, relaxed its grip on censorship, allowing these new social phenomena to flourish. In January 1987, the journal *Nova revija* discussed the possibility of independence from Yugoslavia. Slovenia's reformist path was regarded as dangerous by conservative institutions, notably the JLA (Yugoslav People's Army). When a plot to destabilize Slovenia was unearthed by journalists from *Mladina*, the JLA put them on trial in a Ljubljana military court. Beginning in June 1988, the trial provoked huge demonstrations, leading to the creation of a mass civil rights organization. The Slovene League of Communists appeared to sympathize with the demonstrators. The final Congress of the Yugoslav League of Communists was held in 1990. The Slovenian delegation walked out when it realized that their reformist ideas would be rejected by Communists from other republics.

Slovenia's first multiparty elections took place in April 1990, with DEMOS (coalition of non-Communist parties) becoming the leading force in parliament. After the December 1990 referendum, independence was declared on 25 June 1991. The JLA occupied strategic points

Monument to Communist leader Boris Kidrič, Maribor

in the republic, but were outmanoeuvred by Slovenian forces, bringing an end to the so-called Ten-Day War. Slovenian independence was recognized by the European Union nations on 15 January 1992.

Slovenia Today

Slovenia soon established itself as one of the economic and political successes of post-Communist Europe. Parliamentary elections at four-year intervals produced relatively smooth exchanges of power from right-of-centre to left-of-centre coalition governments. For whoever was in power, the main plank of policy throughout the 1990s remained Slovenia's integration into European and global institutions – an ambition achieved in 2004 with the country's admission to both NATO and the EU. Slovenia's adoption of the euro in January 2007 served to confirm the country's extraordinary voyage from a Yugoslav republic to equal partner in a new Europe.

Yugoslav army convoy during the Ten-Day War in Slovenia

1991 Slovenia becomes independent on 25 June

Primož Kozmus celebrates his Olympic gold

2008 Hammer-thrower, Primož Kozmus wins gold at the Beijing Olympics

2012–13 Anti-government protests against reported corruption take place in towns and cities throughout Slovenia

2014 A newly formed centre-left party wins a landslide victory in the parliamentary election

2000

2015

2030

2014 Slovenia wins eight medals at the Sochi Winter Olympics, the largest number it has ever won at a single Olympic games

European Union flag

2004 Slovenia becomes a member of the European Union and NATO

LJUBLJANA AREA BY AREA

Ljubljana at a Glance

Most of Ljubljana's historic sights are located in the Old Town, squeezed between Castle Hill and the Ljubljanica river. However, many of the city's architectural highlights and keynote museums are in the New Town, on the west bank of the river. Both parts of the city are very compact and can easily be explored on foot. Attractions outside the centre, such as Tivoli Park and Metelkova Mesto, are also within walking distance. Suburban sights such as the Žale Cemetery and the Museum of Architecture are accessible by bus.

Winged retable, National Museum of Slovenia

Tivoli Mansion *(see p78)* contains a gallery devoted to contemporary graphic art from around the world.

Orthodox Church of Sts Cyril and Methodius *(see p62)*, built in the Byzantine style in the 1930s, is decorated with colourful modern frescoes executed in the style of medieval Serbian church murals.

SAMOVA ULIC

CELOVŠKA CESTA

CESTA 27 APRILA

NEW TOWN *(see pp60–73)*

AŠKERČEVA C.

Ljubljanica river *(see p51)* flows through the centre of the city, its banks shaded by graceful willow trees. Spanned by attractive pedestrian bridges and lined with outdoor cafés, it is a wonderful place for an evening stroll.

Dragon Bridge *(see p55)* is a much-loved urban landmark, celebrating the beast that, according to local legend, once ruled over the Ljubljana Marshes.

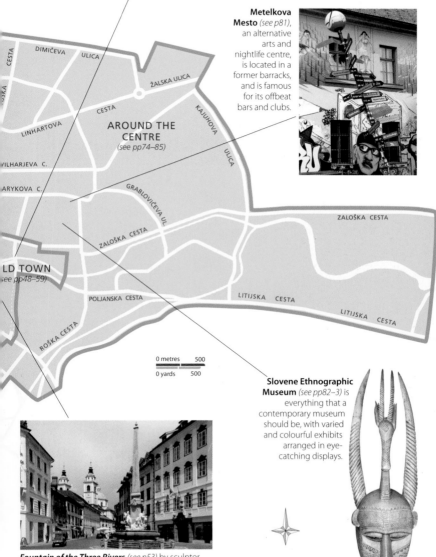

Metelkova Mesto *(see p81)*, an alternative arts and nightlife centre, is located in a former barracks, and is famous for its offbeat bars and clubs.

DIMIČEVA ULICA

CESTA

ŽALSKA ULICA

LINHARTOVA CESTA

AROUND THE CENTRE
(see pp74–85)

KAJUHOVA ULICA

VILHARJEVA C.

ARYKOVA C.

GRABLOVIČEVA UL.

ZALOŠKA CESTA

ZALOŠKA CESTA

LD TOWN
see pp48–59)

POLJANSKA CESTA

LITIJSKA CESTA

LITIJSKA CESTA

ROŠKA CESTA

| 0 metres | 500 |
| 0 yards | 500 |

Slovene Ethnographic Museum *(see pp82–3)* is everything that a contemporary museum should be, with varied and colourful exhibits arranged in eye-catching displays.

Fountain of the Three Rivers *(see p53)* by sculptor Francesco Robba is one of the finest examples of Ljubljana's Baroque heritage. Its replica now stands in the Old Town.

OLD TOWN

Ljubljana is often described as one of the most Mediterranean of Central European cities and it is in the Old Town that this is most apparent. There is a distinct Italian flavour to the Baroque mansions and churches rising above its cobbled streets. The focal point is the Triple Bridge that links Prešernov

trg on the west bank of the Ljubljanica river with the colonnaded Market on the east. South of the Market are the pedestrianized Mestni trg and Stari trg, home to quirky shops and lively restaurants. Looming above the town is Ljubljana Castle, offering unrivalled views of the city.

Sights at a Glance

Historic Buildings, Sites and Streets

④ Fountain of the Three Rivers
⑤ Town Hall
⑧ Bishop's Palace
⑨ Seminary
⑪ *Ljubljana Castle pp56–7*
⑫ Stari trg
⑯ Gruber Palace

Bridges

③ Triple Bridge
⑩ Dragon Bridge

Churches and Cathedrals

② Franciscan Church of the Annunciation
⑦ St Nicholas's Cathedral
⑭ St Florian's Church
⑮ St James's Church

Square

① Prešernov trg

Gallery

⑬ ŠKUC Gallery

Places of Interest

⑥ Market

0 metres		250
0 yards		250

See also Street Finder map 2

For keys to symbols *see back flap*

Street-by-Street: Ljubljana Old Town

Located between the medieval castle and the leafy banks of the Ljubljanica river, Ljubljana's Old Town contains some of the best-preserved Baroque buildings in southeastern Europe. Arcaded 18th-century houses, domed churches, fountain-studded piazzas and narrow cobbled alleys lined with cafés and shops add to the Old Town's elegant character.

❻ ★ Market
Ljubljana's lively outdoor market is known for its fresh herbs and dried mushrooms, sold alongside every kind of local produce.

❿ Dragon Bridge, an example of the Art Nouveau style.

❼ St Nicholas's Cathedral
Created by Giulio Quaglio in 1706, the cathedral's ceiling is a fine example of Baroque illusionist painting, with cherubs, saints and evangelists seemingly ascending through heavenly skies.

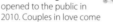

Butchers' Bridge was opened to the public in 2010. Couples in love come here to affix engraved padlocks to the parapet.

Key

— Suggested route

❷ Franciscan Church of the Annunciation is the city's most attractive Baroque church, with an 18th-century altar by Italian sculptor Francesco Robba.

The Prešeren Statue, one of Ljubljana's best-known landmarks, honours Romantic poet and national icon, France Prešeren.

❸ ★ Triple Bridge
Designed for pedestrians by Jože Plečnik in 1929, the three-lane Triple Bridge was part of the renovation of the riverbank area.

For hotels and restaurants in this area see p192 and p200–202

A funicular railway from Krekov trg transports visitors to the castle on the top of the wooded hill. Another option is to take an invigorating walk up the hill.

Ljubljana Castle *(see pp56–7)*

❺ **The Town Hall**, a Renaissance building dating from 1719, has three attractive courtyards.

Locator Map
See Street Finder map 2

NEW TOWN
OLD TOWN
AROUND THE CENTRE

Cobblers' Bridge
Built in 1932, Jože Plečnik's Cobblers' Bridge features several of the architect's decorative trademarks, notably fluted lampstands with bud-shaped bulb holders.

MESTNI TRG

CANKARJEVO NABREŽJE

Cobblers' Bridge

❹ ★ **Fountain of the Three Rivers**
Located on Mestni trg, this replica of Francesco Robba's *Fountain of the Three Rivers* symbolizes the three main rivers of central Slovenia.

0 metres 50
0 yards 50

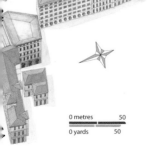

Ljubljanica Riverbank
The east bank of the river is lined with willow trees, orange- and red-roofed town houses and fabulous terrace cafés and restaurants.

❶ Prešernov trg

City Map D2 & D3.

Located between Ljubljana's Old Town and the 19th-century districts on the west bank of the Ljubljanica river, Prešernov trg is, in many ways, the symbolic heart of the city. It is named after France Prešeren, the Romantic poet whose patriotic verses were central to the development of a Slovenian national consciousness. The poet is immortalized by a monument in the centre of the square, with a poetry book in hand, accompanied by a scantily clad muse wielding a sprig of laurel. The unveiling of the statue in 1905 was a major political event, bringing thousands of patriotic Slovenians out on to the street at a time when the city was still ruled by the Habsburg Empire.

Around the square are some of the finest Art Nouveau structures in Ljubljana. The **Centromerkur Building**, on the northeastern corner, was built in 1903 by Austrian architect Friedrich Sigismundt to serve as a department store. Crowning the building is a statue of Mercury, the Roman god of trade. Now occupied by the fashion store Galerija Emporium, the interior retains some stunning Art Nouveau details,

Centromerkur Building, now occupied by the Galerija Emporium

with carved female heads at the bottom of the Y-shaped staircase and some ornate light fittings above.

On the opposite side of the square is the mid-19th-century Hauptman House, renovated in 1904 by the city's leading Art Nouveau architect, Ciril Metod Koch. Edged with green and turquoise tiles, it is an outstanding example of the Viennese-inspired decorative style of the age.

Just behind it, the building at Wolfova No. 4 features a relief of the 19th-century beauty Julija Primic peering from a mock first-floor window. Primic was the object of Prešeren's unrequited love, an obsession that inspired the air of romantic melancholy which characterized much of his writing.

❷ Franciscan Church of the Annunciation

Frančiškanska Cerkev Marijinega Oznanjenja

Prešernov trg. **City Map** D2.
Open 9am–noon & 3–7pm daily.

Dominating the northeast corner of Prešernov trg is the 17th-century Franciscan Church, containing a wealth of Baroque interior detail.

The main attraction is the high altar by Francesco Robba, the Venetian sculptor who spent most of his adult life in Ljubljana and made a huge artistic contribution to the city. Expressive statuettes of St Mary and other saints on either side of the altar showcase Robba's work at its graceful best. The ceiling frescoes were painted by Slovenian artist Matevž Langus in the mid-19th century, and reworked by Slovenian Impressionist Matej Sternen following damage during the 1895 earthquake.

❸ Triple Bridge

Tromostovje

City Map D3.

If the capital city has one immediately recognizable landmark, it is probably the

Pedestrians crossing the Triple Bridge towards the Franciscan Church of the Annunciation

For hotels and restaurants in this area see p192 and p200

Triple Bridge, the three-lane crossing designed in 1929 by the city's most prolific architect, Jože Plečnik *(see p77)*. Faced with the problem of how to widen the city's main crossing point to accommodate increasing traffic levels, Plečnik decided to retain the 19th-century bridge in the middle, adding two angled side bridges for pedestrians. It was an inspired piece of town planning, turning Prešernov trg into the focal point of the city and bringing life to both banks of the river.

The bridge is embellished with the kind of decorations typical of Plečnik, with stone baubles sprouting from the parapets alongside curvy lampstands tipped with buds of milk-coloured glass. The elegant balustrades bring a Venetian sense of style to the whole ensemble.

The replica of the 18th-century *Fountain of the Three Rivers*

The fountain was commissioned in 1743, although it was another eight years before the project reached completion – Robba was in any case constantly busy with Church-commissioned jobs throughout the city. Probable inspiration for the work was Bernini's Fountain of the Four Rivers in Rome's Piazza Navona. What visitors see today is actually a replica – the original fountain was moved to the National Gallery *(see pp64–5)* in 2008, where a modern glass-covered atrium protects it from the elements.

❹ Fountain of the Three Rivers

Vodnjak treh kranjskih rek

Mestni trg. **City Map** D3.

Surrounded by water and rising above the cobblestoned Mestni trg, this tall triangular obelisk is the most celebrated work of Ljubljana-based Venetian sculptor, Francesco Robba. The fountain gets its name from the three pitcher-wielding giants at its base, thought to symbolize the Ljubljanica, Sava and Krka, the three main rivers of the historical duchy Carniola.

Arcaded inner courtyard with a well in the Town Hall

❺ Town Hall

Mestna hiša

Mestni trg 1. **City Map** D3.

Adding an air of distinction to Mestni trg's western side is Ljubljana's 18th-century Town Hall, a Renaissance-influenced structure with an arcaded ground floor and a hexagonal clock tower rising from its pediment. Just inside the entrance is a 17th-century statue of Hercules wielding a club and preparing to batter a wild beast. According to local myth, Hercules visited Ljubljana in the company of Jason and the Argonauts who, having sailed up the Danube and Sava rivers, had to pull their boat overland in order to secure passage to the Adriatic Sea.

Beyond the statue lies a trio of arcaded inner courtyards, which frequently host exhibitions of art or photography. The central courtyard is decorated with a sgraffito frieze featuring horn-blowing cherubs and frolicking unicorns. Slightly hidden in the corner of the courtyard is a fountain overlooked by a statue of Narcissus, attributed to Francesco Robba's workshop.

France Prešeren (1800–49)

The Romantic poet France Prešeren was the first to demonstrate that Slovenian – hitherto considered a peasant language – could serve as the vehicle for great literature. His verse contained a strong patriotic undercurrent, spurring the development of a modern national consciousness. His collection, *Crown of Sonnets* (1834), used the author's own sense of lack of fulfillment as a metaphor for Slovenia's position in the Habsburg Empire. More optimistic is *Zdravljica* (1844), the wine drinking song, the seventh strophe of which later became the text for Slovenia's national anthem. A lifelong drinker himself, Prešeren did not live long enough to enjoy the fame his works ultimately generated.

Prešeren's statue, Prešernov trg

Seafood on sale in Ljubljana's
Market Colonnade

❻ Market

Glavna tržnica

Vodnikov trg. **City Map** D3, E2 & E3.
Market Colonnade: **Open** 7am–4pm
Mon–Thu, 7am–2pm Sat.

The northern end of Ljubljana's
Old Town is largely taken up by
the city's sprawling market.
Apart from being the local
fruit and vegetable market, the
place also has numerous stalls
selling souvenirs, herbs and
speciality foods.

Dominating the market's
northern side is the **Market
Colonnade**, a gently curving
riverside structure that looks like
an elongated Graeco-Roman
temple. It was designed by Jože
Plečnik *(see p77)* in 1942 to
provide shelter for a row of food
stalls. Spiral staircases descend
to the colonnade's lower storey,
home to a fish market filled with
piles of Adriatic octopus, squid
and lobster. The lower storey
also contains a seafood snack
bar and an arcaded terrace
looking out on to the river.

Plečnik initially planned to
build a covered bridge linking
the eastern end of the colonnade to the opposite bank of
Ljubljanica river – a project that
did not take off due to lack of
the funds. The original plan was
partly carried out with the
construction of the Butchers'
Bridge (Mesarski most) in 2010.
Guarding the approaches to the
bridge are the statues of Adam,
Eve and Prometheus by local
sculptor Jakov Brdar (b.1949).
To the east of the colonnade is
the main fruit-and-vegetable
market, where trestle tables fill
the broad expanse of Vodnikov

trg. Presiding over the southern
end of the square is a statue
of Valentin Vodnik, the priest
and poet whose works
helped to shape the modern
Slovenian language.

Immediately east
of Vodnikov trg, at the
corner of Poljanska
cesta and Kapiteljska
ulica, is the so-called Flat
Iron (Peglezen), a four-
storey apartment built
by Jože Plečnik in 1932.
Named after its narrow
wedge shape and flat
roof, the building is a
typical example of
Plečnik's architectural
style – a mix
of Modernist,
Rennaissance and
Classical – with an arcaded
ground floor and geometrical
window frames on the
first floor.

❼ St Nicholas's Cathedral

Stolna Cerkev sv Nikolaja

Dolničarjeva 1. **City Map** D3. **Tel** (01)
234 2690. **Open** 6am–noon & 3–7pm.

Towering above the market
are the twin towers of the
Baroque St Nicholas's Cathedral.
Built on the site of an earlier
church by leading Jesuit
architect Andrea Pozzo in 1707,
this cathedral is dedicated to

St Nicholas, patron saint of
fishermen and sailors. The
relatively plain exterior is
enlivened by the two bronze
doors made to commemorate
Pope John Paul II's visit to
Slovenia in 1996. The west
door depicts scenes
from the history of
Slovenian Christianity –
the top of the door
portrays Pope John
Paul II peering from
a window, while
towards the bottom is
an illustration of the
baptism of the Slovenian
nation. The south door
shows the tall mitred
profiles of six of
Slovenia's 20th-
century bishops
praying at Christ's tomb.

Angel sculpture in
the cathedral

Inside, the cathedral has a
richly decorated sequence of
side chapels as well as a nave
dominated by an Illusionist
ceiling painting of the
Crucifixion by Giulio Quaglio
the Elder (1610–58). The
cathedral is particularly rich
in Baroque sculpture. It has
a Corpus Christi altar (1752)
by the Italian sculptor
Francesco Robba, which is
flanked by statuettes of angels.
Niches in the transept hold
four statues of the bishops
of Roman-era Emona carved
by the 17th-century sculptor
Angelo Putti.

Richly decorated interior of St Nicholas's Cathedral

Frescoes on the ceiling of the Seminary's library

8 Bishop's Palace
Škofijski dvorec

Ciril Metodov trg 4. **City Map** D3.
Tel (01) 234 2600. **Open** Mon–Fri.

Connected to the cathedral by a covered pedestrian bridge is the Bishop's Palace, a distinguished ochre building facing the Ljubljanica river. It was originally built for Bishop Ravbar in 1512. However, its arcaded courtyard, added in the 18th century, gives the building its charm.

The French Emperor Napoleon Bonaparte stayed here after routing Austrian armies in 1797. The palace subsequently served as the official residence of the Governor-General of the French-ruled Illyrian Provinces between 1808 and 1813.

9 Seminary
Semenišče

Dolničarjeva ulica 4. **City Map** D3.
Tel (01) 433 6109.

Immediately northeast of the cathedral is the Seminary, a grand Baroque structure built by the architect Carlo Martinuzzi between 1708 and 1714. The most impressive feature on the exterior is the south portal, an arched doorway flanked by a pair of stone Titans carved by Angelo Putti. The seminary's first-floor library was the first public library in Ljubljana and preserves its Baroque interior.

The ceiling vaults are filled with frescoes by Giulio Quaglio. Books are stored in ornate wooden cases made by local cabinet-maker Josip Wergant. Visits to the library can be arranged in advance through the Ljubljana Tourist Information Centre (see p99).

10 Dragon Bridge
Zmajski most

City Map E2.

Located just beyond the market's eastern boundary, the Dragon Bridge was the first major Art Nouveau project to be built in the city. Designed by the architect Jurij Zaninovič, it was built in 1901 to mark the 60th birthday of Austro-Hungarian Emperor Franz Josef I. The bridge gets its name from the bronze dragons that stand guard over its ends. It is said that the legendary voyagers, Jason and the Argonauts, fought with and killed a dragon in the marshes south of Ljubljana before continuing on their journey towards the Adriatic.

Rising from the bridge's parapet is a line of Art Nouveau lampposts, decorated with griffin motifs and crowned with fruit-like clusters of glass globes. A plaque halfway along the bridge honours Ivan Hribar (1851–1941), the mayor of Ljubljana who oversaw the bridge's construction. The western end of the bridge provides a fine view of Ljubljana's market halls, with the twin towers and dome of the cathedral rising in the distance.

A bronze dragon standing guard on the Dragon Bridge

Valentin Vodnik (1758–1819)

One of the founding fathers of Slovenian literary culture, Valentin Vodnik wrote some of the first poems ever to be published in Slovenian. He also edited the first Slovenian newspaper, *Lublanske novice*. Vodnik was particularly inspired by the Illyrian Provinces, which introduced the local language in schools. His poem *Illyria Revived* (1816) argued that Illyria deserved to be treated as a nation in its own right. The poem became a rallying cry for late 19th-century Slovenian patriots, for whom the notion of Illyria provided a welcome alternative to the harsh realities of Habsburg power.

Statue of Vodnik, Vodnikov trg

⑪ Ljubljana Castle

Ljubljanski Grad

Perched atop a cone-shaped hill, Ljubljana Castle looms above the Old Town. The city's most instantly recognizable landmark originally dates from the 11th century, when the Spannheims adopted Ljubljana as their feudal power base. Following the city's absorption by Austria in 1355, the castle became the property of the Habsburg family, before going on to serve as a barracks, then a refuge for the poor and a prison. The castle is now a popular tourist destination, with many attractions around its irregular courtyard.

Sculpture in the grounds behind the castle

Pentagonal Tower
The 15th-century Pentagonal Tower once guarded the main entrance to the courtyard. Its restored interior now serves as an atmospheric exhibition space for contemporary art.

★ Virtual Museum
A 25-minute 3D animation film on Ljubljana's history, with commentary in various languages, is shown here.

Entrance

Funicular
This state-of-the-art metal-and-glass box zooms up in under a minute to the castle from Krekov trg in the Old Town. It runs during the castle's opening hours.

KEY

① **Wedding hall**

② **Restaurant**

③ **Virtual Museum**

④ **Estate Hall**

⑤ **Casemates**

For hotels and restaurants in this area see p192 and p200

★ Clock tower

The clock tower, built in 1848 to serve as a viewing platform and tourist attraction, provides a wonderful panorama of the city, with the Karavanke range clearly visible to the north.

VISITORS' CHECKLIST

Practical Information
Grajska planota. **City Map** D3.
Tel (01) 306 4230.
Open May–Sep: 9am–11pm daily; Oct–Apr: 10am–9pm daily. 📷 for a fee; Jun–mid-Sep: 10am, 11:30am, 2pm & 4pm; mid-Sep–May: by appt. Funicular: from Krekov trg; every 10 min. ♿ 🖥 🎁
Ⓦ **ljubljanskigrad.si**

Chapel of St George

This 15th-century Gothic chapel's ceiling is decorated with the coats of arms of the noble families of Carniola, accompanied by those of Habsburg emperors Rudolf I and Charles IV. They were painted in 1747 as a romantic expression of nostalgia for the medieval feudal order.

★ Courtyard

During summer evenings, the courtyard is used for music and drama performances. It is also a popular venue for weddings, which are held on Saturdays throughout the year.

Views

The castle parapet offers a bird's-eye view of central Ljubljana's terracotta roofs with the Alps in the background.

Visitors at a charming open-air café on Stari trg

⓬ Stari trg

City Map D4.

The main thoroughfare of the Old Town is Stari trg, a narrow cobbled street overlooked by well-preserved Baroque and Neo-Renaissance houses. Once inhabited by Ljubljana's wealthier merchant families, the street now hosts smart designer clothes boutiques, craft shops and funky restaurants. A lattice of alleyways connects Stari trg to Cankarjevo nabrežje, the café-lined promenade that runs along the riverbank to the west.

The 18th-century Schweiger House (Schweigerjeva hiša), at No. 11, has a portal overlooked by a stone figure of a man holding his finger up to his lips – a witty allusion to the building's original owner, Franz Karl Schweiger von Lerchenfeld; Schweiger in German means "Silent One". A bust mounted on the wall beside the doorway honours one of the house's most famous residents, the poet Lili Novy (1885–1958).

⓭ ŠKUC Gallery

Galerija ŠKUC

Stari trg 21. **City Map** D4.
Tel (01) 251 6540. **Open** 11am–7pm Tue–Sun. **W** skuc.org

Occupying the front half of a corner house at the junction of Stari trg and Gornji trg, ŠKUC Gallery has been Ljubljana's primary venue for contemporary art ever since it first opened its doors in 1978.

Founded as a student cultural centre (Študentski kulturni center, hence the acronym), ŠKUC soon became the focus of radical activity. It has promoted artists from all over "the former" Yugoslavia, released punk-rock records under its own label, supported minority rights groups and organized intellectual discussions. Most of the civil rights activists who shaped the Slovene Spring (*see pp42–3*) of the 1980s were part of ŠKUC at some stage in their lives.

The centre organizes the literature festival, Live Literature (Živa književnost), in June, when international authors give book readings on the street outside the gallery. Let's Meet at ŠKUC (Dobimo se pred Škucem) is a series of outdoor concerts organized in July.

The ŠKUC Gallery still looks like an alternative cultural space, with black doorways and darkened windows eloquently conveying the message that this is not a mainstream art gallery. A full programme of exhibitions presents a great opportunity to see artists from Slovenia as well as from other countries.

⓮ St Florian's Church

Cerkev sv Florjana

Gornji trg. **City Map** E4.

Presiding over the mansard-roofed Baroque houses on the picturesque Gornji trg is the onion-domed St Florian's Church, dedicated to the patron saint of firefighters. A 17th-century structure, damaged by fire in 1774, it was restored by Jože Plečnik (*see p77*) in 1933.

Restored interior of the 17th-century St Florian's Church

Gruber Palace, formerly a school of hydrology and navigation

The church is rarely open to the public, but there are plenty of interesting details on the exterior, such as the faded 18th-century fresco of Our Lady of Mercy, high above the main door. Occupying a niche on the street-facing side of the church is Francesco Robba's (1698–1757) lively sculpture of the Czech martyr St John of Nepomuk. Here, the saint is portrayed being thrown into the Vltava river as cherubs cling to his robes.

⓯ St James's Church

Cerkev sv Jakoba

Gornji trg 18. **City Map** D4. **Tel** (01) 252 1727. ✝ 8am, 9:30am & 5pm Sun, 6:30pm Mon–Sat.

Rising to the south of Stari trg is St James's Church, a church of Gothic origins that received a Baroque makeover when the Jesuits adopted it as their base in 1598. The basilica was damaged in the 1895 earthquake. A second wave of rebuilding resulted in the addition of the Neo-Gothic spire that is the church's focal point today.

The interior remains one of Ljubljana's most outstanding displays of Baroque religious art. There are parallel rows of altars, full of extravagant statuary, including Francesco Robba's high altar (1732), which is flanked by a graceful pair of angels depicted with their hands clasped in prayer.

The octagonal St Francis Xavier Chapel (1709) on the northern side of the church features more angels sculpted by Paolo Groppelli (1677–1751) and female figures by Jacopo Contieri personifying the continents of Europe and Africa – the latter exotically clad in grasses and feathers.

⓰ Gruber Palace

Gruberjeva palača

Zvezdarska 1. **City Map** D4. **Tel** (01) 241 4200. **Open** by appt.

Marking the southern extent of the Old Town is Gruber Palace, a stately yellow building that now houses the State Archives. It originally served as a school of hydrology and navigation, built in the 1770s on the initiative of Jesuit priest and engineer Gabriel Gruber (1740–1805). One of the best-equipped schools of the era, it housed manufacturing workshops, a chemistry laboratory and an astronomical observatory.

A relief just left of the main door shows the school's founder holding a varied collection of scientific instruments. The interior, visits to which can be arranged through Ljubljana's Tourist Information Centre (*see p99*), contains a chapel decorated with paintings by the late-Baroque Austrian artist Kremser Schmidt (1718–1801). There is also a richly stuccoed oval staircase that is overlooked by frescoes of figures symbolizing scientific endeavour.

Gruber's other great contribution to Ljubljana was the construction of the canal that runs south of Castle Hill, diverting seasonal floodwaters away from the city centre.

Sculpture by Francesco Robba in St James's Church

NEW TOWN

Stretching west of the Ljubljanica river is the bustling downtown area of department stores, government ministries and cultural institutions. It was mostly laid out on a grid plan in the 19th century, although the area retains some wonderfully atmospheric Baroque alleyways huddled beside the river. Apart from the best of the city's Art

Nouveau architecture, the New Town contains notable examples of 20th-century Modernism. There are set-piece open spaces – the leafy expanse of Kongresni trg and the courtyards of the Križanke complex – and the pick of museums, including the National Gallery, National Museum of Slovenia and the City Museum.

Sights at a Glance

Buildings and Sights
1. Cooperative Bank
2. Nebotičnik
8. Opera House
9. Slovene Parliament
12. Philharmonic Hall
13. University of Ljubljana
14. National and University Library
16. Križanke

Churches and Cathedrals
4. Orthodox Church of Sts Cyril and Methodius

Museums and Galleries
3. *National Gallery pp64–5*
5. Modern Gallery
6. National Museum of Slovenia
7. Natural History Museum
15. Ljubljana City Museum

Squares
10. Trg Republike
11. Kongresni trg

See also Street Finder maps 1, 2

Colourful façade of the
Cooperative Bank

❶ Cooperative Bank

Zadružna gospodarska banka

Miklošičeva 8. **City Map** D2.

The most vibrantly decorated
building in downtown Ljubljana,
the Cooperative Bank was
designed by Ivan Vurnik (1884–
1971), a Radovljica-born
architect who studied under
Otto Wagner, the *doyen* of
Viennese Art Nouveau. Vurnik
was keen to develop a Slovenian
national style of architecture
by blending traditional folk
motifs with the best in modern
design; this building is his
ideological statement.

Begun in 1921, it represents
a unique mixture of ethnographic detail and Art Nouveau,
with jazzy chevrons and zig-
zags weaving around the oriel
windows on the façade. Rich in
blues, yellows and brick-reds,
the decorative scheme is
inspired by the embroidery of
rural Slovenia. Vurnik, clearly,
was also influenced by folk-art
patterns found throughout
Slavic Europe.

The Cooperative Bank now
houses the Ljubljana Land
Registry Office; visitors can
peek into the extravagantly
decorated lobby during
working hours. Geometrical
patterns frame frescoes painted
by Vurnik's Viennese wife,
Helena Kottler, extolling the
beauty of the Slovenian
landscape and the virtues of
its hard-working peasants.

❷ Nebotičnik

Corner of Štefanova and Slovenska
ulica. **City Map** C2. Kavarna
Nebotičnik: **Open** 8–3am daily.

Adding a dash of Art Deco
elegance to Ljubljana's main
shopping street is Nebotičnik
(Skyscraper), an upmarket
residential block designed
by Vladimir Šubic in 1933.
Although it looks rather
modest in comparison to the
multistorey towers of today,
this 13-storey structure was
the tallest in Yugoslavia when
it was constructed.

In contrast to the building's
stern façade are the round
porthole-style windows on the
ground floor and the arched
window frames just below the
roof. An angelic female figure
sculpted by Lojze Dolinar
(1893–1970) occupies a plinth
on the sixth floor, watching
over the pedestrians on the
pavement below.

Visitors can enter the lobby
from Štefanova ulica to admire
the faux marble walls overlooked by busts of Greek gods.
The spiral staircase is accessible
only to residents. However,
tourists can take the lift up to
Kavarna Nebotičnik that
occupies the top three floors
of the building with its café,
bar and restaurant. The café's
open terrace offers great
views of the city.

Fresco in the Orthodox Church of Sts Cyril
and Methodius

❸ National Gallery

See pp64–5.

❹ Orthodox Church of Sts Cyril and Methodius

*Pravoslavna cerkev sv Cirila
in Metoda*

Prešernova cesta. **City Map** B2.
Tel (01) 252 4002.

Built in 1932 for Ljubljana's
Serbian community, this church
is inspired by the medieval
monastery churches of
southern Serbia, with a cluster
of bulbous cupolas mounted
on a high cross-shaped nave.
Covering every inch of the
spacious interior are frescoes by
contemporary artist Dragomir
Jašović (b.1937). The frescoes
follow centuries-old Serbian
models, with scenes from the
New Testament juxtaposed with
friezes of Serbian saints.

Presiding over the park in
front of the church is a bust
of the Reformation preacher
Primož Trubar, who published
the first books in Slovenian.

Visitors enjoying the view from the terrace café at the Nebotičnik

Art Nouveau Architecture in Ljubljana

Ljubljana experienced a building boom in the early 20th century, when numerous apartment houses and office blocks were built to the north of Prešernov trg. The architecture of these buildings, designed by the Slovenian Art Nouveau architects Ciril Metod Koch, Max Fabiani and Josip Vancaš, was influenced by the Austrian Secessionist style as well as by Slovenian design motifs.

Locator Map
▨ Area Illustrated

⑥ Krisper House
Designed by Max Fabiani, this elegant apartment block looks out on to the leafy Miklošičev park.

④ Čuden House
Built in 1901, this is one of Koch's most ostentatious buildings.

0 metres ——— 100
0 yards ——— 100

⑪ City Saving Bank
This bank bears statues symbolizing Slovenian industry and commerce.

Map labels: TRDINOVA, ULICA, CIGALETOVA ULICA, SLOVENSKA CESTA, TAVČARJEVA, ULICA, ULICA, DALMATINOVA, MIKLOŠIČEV PARK, MIKLOŠIČEVA, CESTA, CESTA, AJDOVŠČINA, SLOVENSKA CESTA, MIKLOŠIČEVA, NAZORJEVA ULICA, ČOPOVA ULICA, TRUBARJEVA CESTA, PREŠERNOV TRG, WOLFOVA ULICA

⑧ Union Hotel
Designed by Josip Vancaš, this statue-encrusted structure was the largest building in Ljubljana when it was built in 1905.

⑩ Hauptman House
This wedge-shaped building is decorated with geometric shapes and floral swirls.

⑨ Centromerkur Building
Now a fashion store, this building is famous for its petal-shaped Art Nouveau canopy.

List of Key Sites

① Trdinova 2
② Trdinova 8
③ Pirc House
④ Čuden House
⑤ Pogačnik House
⑥ Krisper House
⑦ Cooperative Bank
⑧ Union Hotel
⑨ Centromerkur Building
⑩ Hauptman House
⑪ City Saving Bank

❸ National Gallery

Narodna galerija

Slovenia's national art collection occupies an elegant 19th-century building full of stucco ceilings and ornate chandeliers. Erected in 1896 to serve as the Slovene Cultural Centre, the building became home to the National Gallery in 1925. A modern annexe was opened in 2001, with a glass-fronted atrium at the junction of the old and new buildings, holding the collection's pride and joy – Francesco Robba's *Fountain of the Three Rivers*. The collection is particularly rich in Gothic statuary and Baroque religious paintings. Space is also devoted to the Slovenian Impressionists: Rihard Jakopič, Matija Jama, Ivan Grohar and Matej Sternen.

Visitors in one of the brightly lit exhibition areas

★ The Krakovo Madonna
Correctly entitled *The Madonna on Solomon's Throne*, this delicate 13th-century relief from Ljubljana's suburb of Krakovo was the work of an anonymous mason known as the Master of Solčava.

Library

Fountain of the Three Rivers
Robba's 18th-century sculptural masterpiece is surrounded by balconied walkways, providing some wonderful viewpoints. At the base of the fountain are three Tritons pouring water from jugs, symbolizing the three main rivers of Slovenia.

Educational area

The Slovenian Impressionists

In the years before World War I, Rihard Jakopič (1869–1943), Ivan Grohar (1867–1911), Matija Jama (1872–1947) and Matej Sternen (1870–1949) energized the local art scene by painting Slovenian subjects with the kind of style and verve previously associated with French artists such as Renoir and Monet. Initially snubbed by conservative critics, today they are regarded as the high point of the nation's art. All of them were committed landscape painters.

Bridge Over the Dobra by Matija Jama

Gallery Guide

The original 19th-century wing contains the national collection of Slovenian art, from Gothic to the early 20th century. A modern annexe is devoted to European painters. Joining these wings is a modern atrium where temporary exhibitions are held.

Katarina Lukančič
Full of exquisitely rendered detail, this portrait owes a great deal to Flemish painting of the 17th century. It is usually attributed to the Slovenian artist Janez Frančišek Gladič, although some experts believe its quality is far too high to be one of his works.

VISITORS' CHECKLIST

Practical Information
Prešernova 24. **City Map** C2.
Tel (01) 241 5418.
Open 10am–6pm Tue–Sun.
🏛 🎫 ♿ 📷
Ⓦ ng-slo.si

Key to Floorplan

- 🟦 European paintings
- 🟦 Art in Slovenia
- ⬜ Visual collections
- ⬜ Exhibition area
- ⬜ Atrium
- ⬜ Non exhibition area

First floor

Ground floor

★ Red Parasol, **Matej Sternen**
Painted in 1904, this is arguably the best-loved canvas by Sternen (1870–1949), an artist who was particularly known for his female portraits.

★ Solomon's Verdict, **Franc Kavčič**
The Vienna-educated Kavčič (1755–1828) was Slovenia's greatest exponent of Neo-Classicism, painting a series of large-scale mythological or biblical subjects.

The Card Players, **Almanach**
Almanach was a 17th-century Flemish painter who stopped off in Ljubljana during the later stages of his career. *The Card Players* was painted for Mark Anton, owner of Polhov Gradec Castle.

The entrance to the Modern Gallery, home to fascinating art exhibitions

❺ Modern Gallery
Moderna galerija

Tomšičeva 14. **City Map** B2.
Tel (01) 241 6800. **Open** 10am–6pm
Tue–Sun. 🅿 ♿ 📷 🅦 mg-lj.si

Housed in a low grey building designed in 1947 by Edvard Ravnikar, a disciple of the Swiss-French architect Le Corbusier, the Modern Gallery comprises the national collection of post-World War II art.

Despite the imposition of Communist ideology in the late 1940s, Slovene art was remarkably free and varied from the mid-1950s onwards. Ample evidence of this is provided by the surreal figurative paintings of Gabriel Stupica (1913–90) and the more abstract work

of Janez Bernik (b.1933). More perplexing is the work of the 60s art collective OHO, whose ambiguous conceptual performances (most famously, dressing up in a huge dark gown to resemble Slovenia's highest mountain, Triglav) are documented in a series of black-and-white photographs. Representing the turbulent changes of 1980s are works by IRWIN, a group of artists who mixed avant-garde art and extreme political symbolism to produce some ironic statements on national identity.

Standing on the lawn of the gallery are several notable sculptures, including Drago Tršar's abstract *Manifestants* (1959) and France Rotar's *Dissected Sphere* (1975).

❻ National Museum of Slovenia
Narodni muzej Slovenije

Prešernova cesta 20. **City Map** B2.
Tel (01) 241 4400. **Open** 10am–6pm
Fri–Wed, 10am–8pm Thu (Jun–Sep:
10am–8pm Sat). 🅿 📷 🅦 nms.si

Occupying one wing of an imposing Neo-Renaissance pile dating from the 1880s, the main branch of the National Museum of Slovenia concentrates on the country's archaeological

Statue of an aristocrat

heritage. The collection of applied art is on display in a separate branch of the museum on Metelkova ulica *(see p81)*.

The ground floor of the museum contains an extensive collection of expressively carved funerary monuments from the Roman settlement of Emona, together with a gilded bronze statue of a young male aristocrat. Ancient Egypt is represented by a 6th-century BC coffin of the priest Isahta, decorated with brightly painted hieroglyphics. First-floor galleries contain locally excavated pottery, decorated with geometric designs, from the 3rd millennium BC. The most valued item on display is the 6th-century BC Vače situla, a 30-cm- (12-inch-) high bronze bucket that once served as a ritual drinking vessel. On the outer surface of the situla are reliefs depicting a parade of horsemen, a drinking party and a row of antelope-like animals being stalked by a big cat.

Dominating the park in front of the museum is a monument dedicated to Janez Vajkard Valvasor *(see pp94–5)*, the 17th-century antiquarian and publisher who pioneered the documenting of history in Slovenia.

Schoolchildren on an educational visit to the National Museum of Slovenia

For hotels and restaurants in this area see p192 and pp200–201

❼ Natural History Museum

Prirodoslovni muzej

Prešernova cesta 20. **City Map** B2.
Tel (01) 241 0940. **Open** 10am–6pm
Fri–Wed, 10am–8pm Thu. 🖼 🖼
ⓦ pms-lj.si

Located in the same building as the National Museum of Slovenia, the Natural History Museum offers informative insight into the flora, fauna and geology of Slovenia.

The most memorable of the museum's exhibits is an almost complete skeleton of a mammoth found near Kamnik. The museum also has an audiovisual display devoted to *Proteus anguinus* or the human fish *(see p155)*, a salamander-like denizen of Slovenia's karst caves.

❽ Opera House

Operna

Cankarjeva cesta 11. **City Map** C2.
Tel (01) 241 5959; (01) 241 5960.
ⓦ opera.si

The home of Slovenia's national opera and ballet companies was built in 1892 by Czech architects Jan Vladimir Hrasky and Anton Hruby. Ljubljana's cultural centre has elements of Neo-Classical, Neo-Renaissance and Neo-Baroque styles, all apparent on the building's semicircular façade.

Sculptor Alojz Gangl (1859–1935) was responsible for much of the exterior decoration, which features statues of griffins, cherubs and scantily clad nymphs on the pediment and in niches on either side of the main entrance. Above the pediment is the sculpture of an androgynous figure wielding a torch – a symbol of artistic inspiration.

The building's opulently decorated auditorium was reopened in 2011 after extensive renovation. Completed at the same time was the annexe at the back of the building, constructed to provide extra rehearsal rooms and office space.

Sculptures adorning the Slovene Parliament's façade

❾ Slovene Parliament

Parlament Slovenije

Šubičeva 4. **City Map** C3.
Tel (01) 478 9400.

A Modernist block of concrete and glass designed by the architect Vinko Glanz in 1960, the political heart of Slovenia resembles a typical office building. However, the Slovene and European Union flags near the entrance hint at its importance.

The sculpted figures on the building's façade comprise one of former Communist Europe's more artistic statements. The work of 20th-century sculptors Zdenko Kalin and Karel Putrih, the ensemble offers a utopian vision of Socialism – workers, peasants, scientists and engineers striving together to create a new and beautiful society.

Cankar Hall, with the monument to Ivan Cankar in front

❿ Trg Republike

City Map C3.

Stretching south of the Parliament building, Trg Republike (formerly Trg Revolucije) was developed in the 1960s to provide a modern focal point to the capital's New Town. With the Maximarket department store on the eastern side, and two large office blocks, originally owned by Ljubljanska banka and the Iskra telecommunications company, to the south, the whole unit was intended as a powerful expression of socialist progress. Today, a major part of the square serves as a car park.

Located behind the two office blocks is **Cankar Hall** (Cankarjev dom), a prestigious cultural centre. Opened in 1982, it was designed by Slovenia's leading postwar architect Edvard Ravnikar and named after Slovenia's greatest novelist and playwright, Ivan Cankar *(see p89)*. Covered with slabs of Carrara marble, the building contains a concert hall with seating for 1,500 people, three smaller multipurpose halls and an exhibition gallery.

Outside the main entrance is the cube-shaped monument to Ivan Cankar by the Slovenian sculptor Slavko Tihec (1928–93). At first glance it looks rather like a rusty box, although an image of Cankar's face, formed by the dark fissures covering the monument's surface, is visible.

Street-by-Street: Ljubljana University District

The University District contains many examples of Ljubljana's finest 19th-century architecture, much of it laid out around the leafy Kongresni trg. The area resonates with history, its buildings occupied by many of Slovenia's most important cultural and educational institutions. This part of the city is closely associated with 20th-century architect Jože Plečnik, who designed the National and University Library and renovated the courtyards of the Križanke monastery.

Sculpture near the Philharmonic Hall

Drama Theatre

⓮ ★ National and University Library
The most famous of Jože Plečnik's many buildings in Ljubljana, this library features a rough-and-smooth façade of stone and brick. Its bay windows are in the shape of open books.

⓰ ★ Križanke
Renaissance arcades and Post-Modern lamp fittings mark the former monastery of Križanke as one of Jože Plečnik's foremost restoration projects. The court-yards now host major outdoor concerts.

The Illyrian Monument

VEGOVA ULICA

TURJAŠKA UL

GOSPOSKA ULI

Key

— Suggested route

ZOISOVA CESTA

Academy of Arts and Sciences
The Academy is located in the Lontovž or "Landhaus", home to the provincial assembly during the Habsburg era. Presiding over a courtyard on the eastern side of the building is a Baroque statue of Neptune.

Ljubljana City Museum

Zois House, home of Baron Žiga Zois (1747–1819), was a meeting point for Slovenian intellectuals.

For hotels and restaurants in this area see p192 and pp200–201

Café Zvezda
Occupying the eastern corner of Kongresni trg *(see p72)* is Kavarna Zvezda, long famous for its delicious cakes, pastries and ice cream.

Locator Map
See Street Finder maps 1, 2

Café Zvezda

KONGRESNI TRG

NOVI TRG

LJUBLJANICA

⑬ University of Ljubljana
This building has witnessed many historical events, with Tito speaking from the balcony in May 1945 and political reformers addressing large crowds in June 1988.

⑫ Philharmonic Hall
The Philharmonic Hall is home to the nation's leading orchestra, which descended from the Academia Filharmonicorum, a cultural society founded in 1701.

★ Illyrian Monument
This stately obelisk recalls Ljubljana's role as the capital of the French-run Illyrian Provinces from 1809 to 1813. Reliefs of Napoleon Bonaparte and female heads adorn it.

| 0 metres | | 50 |
| 0 yards | | 50 |

⓫ Kongresni trg

City Map C3.

The gently sloping rectangle of grass and trees known as Kongresni trg, or Congress Square, takes its name from the Congress of the Holy Alliance – Russia, Austria and Prussia – held in Ljubljana in 1821. Hosted by Emperor Francis I of Austria and attended by dignitaries from all over Europe, most notably Tsar Alexander I of Russia, the Congress aimed to bring stability to the pan-European political system agreed upon at the Congress of Vienna in 1815. With four months of negotiations accompanied by an endless round of dinners, firework displays and masked balls, it was the biggest party in Ljubljana's history.

The event involved a major overhaul of the city's infrastructure; the square was levelled and expanded to host the daily military parades, roads were repaved and street lighting was installed. The square also played an important role in the Slovene Spring (see pp42–3) – mass demonstrations in support of the Ljubljana Four were held here in June 1988.

The most appealing of the buildings surrounding the square is the Baroque Ursuline Church at the western end. Most of the other buildings on the square, including the pink-hued Neo-Classical palace (Kazina) on the northern side, are from the 19th century.

Sculpture of well-known Ljubljana mayor Ivan Hribar, on Breg

Originally a club for Ljubljana's wealthier citizens, the Kazina was briefly the seat of the Slovenian parliament in the years following World War II.

⓬ Philharmonic Hall

Filharmonija

Kongresni trg 10. **City Map** D3. **Tel** (01) 241 0800. **W** filharmonija.si

Sitting on the southeastern corner of Kongresni trg is the Philharmonic Hall, Ljubljana's main venue for classical music, built in 1891 on the site of a former German-language theatre. The inscription "1701" on the façade refers to the date of the foundation of Academia Filharmonicorum, Ljubljana's first musical society. The academy's members performed only at state occasions and society funerals, and it was not until the formation of the Philharmonic Society in 1794

that Ljubljana gained a regularly performing orchestra. During his brief tenure as conductor at Ljubljana's Provincial Theatre, Gustav Mahler, then 21 years old, was invited by the society to play piano at their concerts in 1882.

Ljubljana did not have a full symphony orchestra in the years following World War I until 1947, when the Slovene Philharmonic was refounded and this building was adopted as its permanent home.

⓭ University of Ljubljana

Univerza v Ljubljani

Kongresni trg 12. **City Map** C3. **Tel** (01) 241 8500. **W** uni-lj.si

The most prominent building on the southern side of Kongresni trg is the Neo-Renaissance palace that serves as the main headquarters of the University of Ljubljana. Built in 1902 to provide the Duchy of Carniola with a prestigious venue for meetings and receptions, the palace is adorned with ornate corner towers and spires.

Arranged in a semicircle in front of the entrance are sculptures and busts of noteworthy academic figures, including that of Ivan Hribar (1851–1941), the long-serving mayor of Ljubljana who was instrumental in getting the university off the ground. Mooted by leading Slovenian politicians in the 1890s, the university did not come into being until 1919. It is now one of the biggest universities in Central Europe, with over 65,000 students.

⓮ National and University Library

Narodna in univerzitetna knjižnica

Turjaška 1. **City Map** C4. **Tel** (01) 200 1110. **Open** 8am–8pm Mon–Fri, 9am–2pm Sat. 🎫 book in advance.

Located off the west bank of the Ljubljanica river, the National and University Library is considered the masterpiece of architect Jože Plečnik

Façade of the Philharmonic Hall

Aerial view of the National and University Library building

(see p77). Completed in 1940, the building is characteristic of Plečnik's work, combining the straight lines of modern architecture with organic surfaces and inspired decorative details. The exterior features a patchwork of different hues, mixing grey hunks of Slovenian granite with terracotta-coloured brickwork. Inside, a dark stairway of polished black limestone leads to the brightly lit, first-floor reading rooms, symbolizing the transition from ignorance to knowledge. The doorknobs, window fittings and wooden beamed ceilings were all designed by Plečnik himself, fusing Art Deco with folk-influenced motifs to create a highly personalized style. For a glimpse of the reading rooms, furnished with ornate desk lamps and chandeliers, visitors are free to enter the lobby during opening hours.

⑮ Ljubljana City Museum
Mestni muzej Ljubljana

Gosposka ulica 15. **City Map** C4.
Tel (01) 241 2500. **Open** 10am–6pm Tue–Sun, 10am–9pm Thu. 🅿 ♿ ▣
🅿 ⓦ **mestnimuzej.si**

Occupying the 17th-century Auersperg Palace, at the eastern end of Trg francoske revolucije, this museum is one of the principal venues for large-scale themed exhibitions in Ljubljana. The museum was given a bold contemporary facelift between 2000 and 2004. A curved glass atrium was added, along with a spiral walkway that links the building's basement to the upper floors. Archaeological finds, such as bits of Roman road and medieval brickwork, unearthed during renovation, are on display in the basement.

The museum's permanent collection features a variety of artifacts illustrating the daily life of the city dwellers in the past. Exhibits include painted targets used by archers in the 19th century as well as a Fičko (Fiat 750), the car that became a symbol of Slovenia's burgeoning consumer society in the 1960s. Art on display includes an 18th-century bust of Emperor Charles VI by Francesco Robba as well as 15th-century statues of Adam and Eve that once stood in niches on the façade of the Town Hall (see p53).

Painted archery target

⑯ Križanke

Trg francoske revolucije. **City Map** C4.
🎫 Ljubljana Festival (Jul & Aug).

South of the National and University Library lies Križanke, a former monastery complex that now serves as a concert venue. It is also where orchestral events are held during the Ljubljana Festival as well as major rock, jazz and world music concerts from spring through to autumn. Classical music concerts are held in the indoor Knight's Hall throughout the year. Križanke dates from the 13th century, when Duke Ulrich III of Spannheim invited the Teutonic Knights to Ljubljana to develop schools and hospitals for the poor. The complex of ceremonial halls and interlocking courtyards dates from the 16th and 18th centuries. The monastery fell into disrepair after the Communists moved the monks out in 1945; Plečnik was given the task of restoring it as a cultural centre.

The main courtyard is usually open only to concertgoers, although visitors are free to explore the entrance courtyard (Malo dvorišče), where a bust of Plečnik adorns a balustrade. The courtyard is lined by arcades on three sides, with bold sgraffito decorations conveying an air of Renaissance gaiety. The occasional outdoor chamber concerts held in the Peklensko dvorišče, an intimate quadrangular courtyard, are worth buying tickets for.

Exhibition room in the Ljubljana City Museum

Manicured gardens in Tivoli Park

Sights at a Glance

Historic Buildings, Streets and Neighbourhoods

2 Krakovo
4 Plečnik House
5 Tobacco Factory
7 Tivoli Mansion
15 Metelkova Mesto
19 Sokol Hall
21 Kodeljevo Castle

Churches and Cathedrals

3 St John's Church
12 St Bartholomew's Church
14 Church of St Francis of Assisi

Museums and Galleries

8 Slovene Museum of
   Contemporary History
11 Brewery Museum
13 Railway Museum
16 Slovene National Museum
   (Metelkova)
17 Museum of Contemporary Art
   (+MSUM)
18 *Slovene Ethnographic Museum
   pp82–3*
22 Museum of Architecture
   and Design

Parks and Sanctuaries

6 Tivoli Park
10 Zoological Gardens
20 Botanical Garden

Sites of Interest

1 Roman Wall
9 Rožnik Hill
23 Žale Cemetery

AROUND THE CENTRE

Arranged in an arc around the centre, Ljubljana's suburbs are surprisingly rich in attractions. Many of the sights of interest lie within easy strolling distance of the Old and New Towns – in particular the neighbourhoods of Krakovo and Trnovo, which are characterized by vegetable gardens and willow-lined waterways. Equally refreshing are the open spaces of Tivoli Park, where a tangle of footpaths and cycle tracks leads past flowerbeds and open meadows. Within the park are the Tivoli Mansion, home to superb seasonal art exhibitions, and the Slovene Museum of Contemporary History, with displays devoted to Slovenian

independence. West of Tivoli Park is Rožnik Hill, where woodland paths and a polyphony of birdsong provide a taste of the Slovenian countryside. The main destination north of the centre is the former military barracks, Metelkova Mesto, home to bohemian bars, clubs and artists' workshops, and a museum quarter with an outstanding ethnographic collection and a contemporary art museum. The work of prolific architect Jože Plečnik looms large in suburban Ljubljana. The Church of St Francis of Assisi in Šiška, Žale Cemetery and the Museum of Architecture and Design in Fužine Castle are all important places to visit while on a tour of Plečnik's works.

0 metres   500
0 yards   500

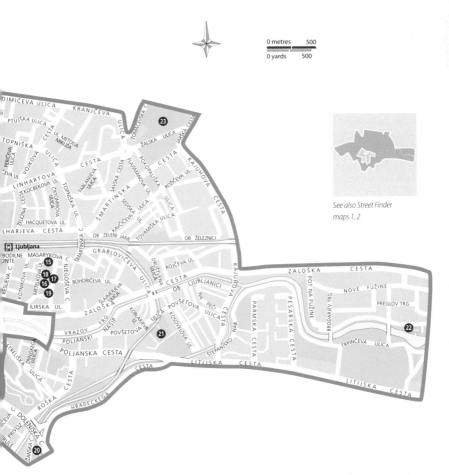

See also Street Finder
maps 1, 2

❶ Roman Wall
Rimski zid

Mirje. **City Map** B4.

The long straight street of Mirje marks the southern end of the original Roman settlement of Emona (modern-day Ljubljana), founded between AD 14 and 25 as a legionary base and subsequently a major mercantile city. Parallel to the street, a 300-m- (985-ft-) long stretch of the Roman Wall that bordered the settlement has been partially rebuilt, providing an evocative indication of what Emona's boundaries once looked like. The architect Jože Plečnik *(see p77)* was responsible for the reconstruction. He added various decorative details of his own – notably the brick pyramid rising above an arched gateway halfway along the wall.

Behind the house at No. 4 Mirje is the **Jakopič Garden**, where the remains of a 1st-century Roman house can be seen. Consisting of four separate apartments grouped around an entrance hall, the dwelling was warmed by a heating system under the floor. The building was abandoned some time in the 5th century.

The garden gets its name from the Impressionist painter Rihard Jakopič (1869–1943), who had a studio in the adjacent house. The garden can be visited by appointment through the Ljubljana City Museum *(see p73)*.

The 19th-century, twin-towered St John's Church, Trnovo

❷ Krakovo

City Map C4–5.

Despite its location on the fringes of central Ljubljana, the suburb of Krakovo is famous for having preserved its medieval street plan and rustic appearance. Narrow streets such as Krakovska, Kladezna and Rečna feature rows of houses standing with their backs to the road in typical village style, many featuring three windows on the street-facing gable – a surviving relic of medieval edicts that specified how many and what kind of windows each house could have.

Detail on the altar, St John's Church

Krakovo originally served as the quarter for boatmen and fishermen, although, from the mid-19th century, locals increasingly turned towards vegetable growing and market trading. Krakovo's vegetable plots are still a major feature of the suburb, providing a refreshingly bucolic contrast to the relatively dense urbanization on show elsewhere in the city.

❸ St John's Church
Cerkev sv Janeza Krstnika

Kolezijska 1. **City Map** C5. **Tel** (01) 283 5060. 🕇 7:30am & 6:30pm Mon–Sat, 8am, 9:15am, 11am & 6:30pm Sun.

With its Neo-Romanesque twin towers soaring above the willow-lined Gradaščica stream, St John's Church is one of the most inspiring sights in southern Ljubljana. According to local legend, it was here that the Romantic poet France Prešeren *(see p53)* first set eyes on Julija Primic, the woman who was the unattainable object of his desire and provided the inspiration for many of his love poems.

Renovation of the church's interior in the 1950s was entrusted to architect Jože Plečnik, who added several characteristic design details such as the small brass lamps that hang from the ceiling and the pillars.

Gateway in the Roman Wall leading to a park

For hotels and restaurants in this area see p192 and pp201–2

Desk in the workshop at Plečnik House

In front of the church is the Trnovo Bridge (Trnovski most), a Plečnik-designed single-arch bridge with pyramid-shaped obelisks protruding from the parapet. Standing between the obelisks is the sculptor Nikolaj Pirnat's (1903–48) statue of St John the Baptist, with his face turned towards the church.

❹ Plečnik House
Plečnikova hiša

Karunova 4. **City Map** C5. **Tel** (01) 280 1600. **Open** 10am–6pm Tue–Sun, 10am–3pm Fri, 9am–3pm Sat. 🚫 📷 🌐 aml.si

The architecture of Jože Plečnik is visible at every step in Ljubljana, and a visit to his former home provides an ideal introduction to his life and work.

After studying in Vienna and enjoying early success in Prague, Plečnik returned to Ljubljana in 1922 and set about transforming this property into a home and studio. The two traditional-style houses that came with the plot accommodated Plečnik's housemaid and gardener. Behind these, he built a modern two-storey house for himself and his brother.

Hourly guided tours of the house begin with the light-filled entrance lobby, decorated with some of the stubby Classical columns left over from Plečnik's

building projects. Also on the ground floor is Plečnik's study, a circular room whose curving windows admit light whatever the time of day. Roosting on a corner of Plečnik's desk, a sleek black trophy in the shape of an eagle, made for the Orel or Eagle gymnastics society, demonstrates Plečnik's artistry as a designer. Elsewhere are plans, models and photographs of his major works. Most famous among his unfinished projects is the Slovene Acropolis, a monumental parliament building in the form of a huge cone, originally intended for Ljubljana's Castle Hill. A more down-to-earth aspect of his taste is revealed by the rustic wood-panelled meeting room, filled with folksy ornaments brought from Czechoslovakia.

Looking out on to the rectangular vegetable garden is the sunny conservatory, accommodating a handful of palm and fig trees.

❺ Tobacco Factory
Tobačna tovarna

Tobačna. **City Map** A3–4. **Tel** (01) 241 2500. **Open** 11am–5pm Tue–Fri. 🌐 mgml.si

Founded in 1871, Ljubljana's Tobacco Factory was a major regional cigarette manufacturer until 2004, when production at this site ceased. Although Imperial Tobacco still has an administrative office here, plans are afoot to turn the rest of the complex into a residential and business quarter.

One restored building houses the Tobačna 001 Cultural Centre, home to a gallery of contemporary art as well as the **Tobacco Museum**. The museum covers the history of smoking, as well as that of cigarette production in the capital. Sepia pictures show life on the factory floor, with its mainly female work-force, known as the cigar ladies.

Exhibit at the Tobacco Museum, Tobacco Factory

Jože Plečnik (1872–1957)

Bust of Plečnik, Trnovo

Few men have left such a lasting imprint on their home city as Jože Plečnik, the Vienna-educated architect whose work can be seen throughout Ljubljana. Initially an exponent of the Art Nouveau movement, Plečnik developed a uniquely eclectic style, blending Graeco-Roman models with Egyptian motifs and Slovenian folk art. His development of a Slovenian national style won him prestigious commissions, notably Ljubljana's Market, the National and University Library and the Žale Cemetery. A master of innovative forms and inspired decoration, he is considered to be one of the greatest architects of the 20th century.

Tree-lined pedestrian path leading up to Tivoli Mansion

❻ Tivoli Park
Tark Tivoli

City Map B2. Indoor Swimming Pool:
Tel (01) 430 6668. **Open** 6am–2pm
Mon, 6am–2pm & 6pm–10pm Tue–Fri,
10am–8pm Sat & Sun.

Stretching to the west of the
city centre is Tivoli Park, a leafy
expanse much loved by strollers,
joggers and dog-walkers.
Named after the Jardins de
Tivoli in Paris, it was first laid out
during the period of Napoleonic
rule in the early 19th century.
    Today, it offers an appealing
mix of order and wilderness,
with well-tended lawns and
trimmed shrubs alternating
with wildflower meadows and
thickets of trees. The park's
main avenue, Jakopičevo
sprehajališče, is lined with
display stands where outdoor
exhibitions of art and photography are held.
    The northern end of the park
is dominated by the Tivoli Hall
(Hala Tivoli), Ljubljana's main
venue for basketball, ice hockey
and big rock and pop concerts.
Designed by architect Marjan
Božič (b.1932), this grey-brown
rectangular building was a
widely admired example of
architectural Modernism when
it first opened in 1965.
    The northern end of the park
also contains a popular **Indoor
Swimming Pool** (Kopalisce
Tivoli), tennis courts and a
playground for children.

❼ Tivoli Mansion
Tivolski grad

Pod turnom 3. **City Map** A2. **Tel** (01)
241 3800. **Open** 11am–6pm Wed–
Sun. 🅿 🖥 ♿ Biennial of Graphic
Arts (Jun–Sep: every odd-numbered
year). 🅦 **mglc-lj.si**

Built in the 18th century as a
villa for the local Jesuit hier-
archy, Tivoli Mansion stands
at the top of a stone staircase
guarded by sculptures of fierce-
looking dogs. The mansion
subsequently served as the
summer residence of the
Ljubljana archbishops before
it was presented in 1852 to the
86-year-old hero of Habsburg
military campaigns, Field
Marshal Josef Radetzky.
Radetzky was a much-loved

Fountain surrounded by flowers, one of
several in Tivoli Park

symbol of Austrian patriotism,
a status immortalized by
Johann Strauss the Elder's
famous tune *Radetzkymarsch*.
    The mansion now houses
the International Graphic Arts
Centre (Mednarodni grafični
likovni center), which organizes
the prestigious Ljubljana
Biennial of Graphic Arts, the
world's longest-running
graphic-arts exposition. The
centre also holds high-quality
exhibitions of posters, prints
and drawings.

❽ Slovene Museum of Contemporary History
Muzej novejše zgodovine Slovenije

Celovška cesta 23. **City Map** A1.
Tel (01) 300 9610. **Open** 10am–6pm
Tue–Sun. 🅿 ♿ 🅦 **muzej-nz.si**

Located behind Tivoli Hall is a
stately pink-coloured mansion
that was built in 1752 for
Count Leopold Karl Lamberg.
The building was adapted
to house the Museum of
the Revolution in 1952 and
became the Slovene Museum
of Contemporary History
following the end of the
Communist regime in 1991.
    Parked in front of the building
is an ex-Yugoslav army (JLA)
tank commandeered by the
Slovenian territorial defence
forces during the Ten-Day War
of June/July 1991.

For hotels and restaurants in this area see p192 and pp201–2

Inside, the museum tells the story of 20th-century Slovenia using film footage and sound recordings to bring each period to life. The 30-minute film with English subtitles, documenting the impact of World War I on Slovenia, is well worth a watch; visitors can ask the curator if they wish to see it. There is also a re-creation of World War I trenches and a display of World War II uniforms and weaponry.

Other exhibits reveal the good and bad sides of Tito's Yugoslavia – a collection of posters and consumer products pays tribute to social progress under Communism, while a side room commemorates the anti-Communist activists who were imprisoned during the same period.

❾ Rožnik Hill

Rising above the western end of Tivoli Park are a series of small wooded hills grouped around the 390-m- (1,285-ft-) high Rožnik Hill, a popular destination for weekend walkers. The main route to the hill begins just south of the Slovene Museum of Contemporary History, looping around the 430-m- (1,410-ft-) high peak of Šišenski hrib before following an undulating trail to Rožnik.

Occupying the ridge just below the summit is the Gostilna Rožnik inn, where novelist and playwright Ivan Cankar (see p89) lived from 1910 to 1917. The innkeeper's wife, Štefanija Franzotova, was a childhood friend of Cankar's, and offered the writer free use of an attic room in the hope that his presence at the inn would bring in added custom. The impoverished Cankar's appetite for free food and drink soon took its toll on his friendship with the innkeeper's family, and the writer was eventually persuaded to move out. Occupying the former barn opposite the inn, the **Ivan Cankar Memorial Room** (Spominska soba Ivana Cankarja) preserves his writing desk and other possessions.

Just uphill from the inn is the 18th-century **Church of the Visitation** (Cerkev Marijinega obiskanja), a rose-coloured structure that contains a painting of the *Visitation* by Jurij Šubic (1855–90). The church is rarely open outside Sunday mass times. The meadow below the church is the scene of an all-night bonfire party on 30 April, an annual celebration of spring that involves much drinking and feasting.

Ivan Cankar Memorial Room
Rožnik. **Tel** (01) 241 2506.
Open Apr–Oct: 11am–6pm Sat & Sun.
Ⓦ **mgml.si**

🏠 **Church of the Visitation**
Rožnik. ✝ May–Sep: 10:30am Sun.

Yellow squirrel monkey at the Zoological Gardens

❿ Zoological Gardens
Zivalski vrt

Večna pot 70. **Tel** (01) 244 2188.
🚌 May–Sep: 23. **Open** May–Oct: 9am–7pm; Nov–Apr: 9am–4pm.
🅿 ♿ 🖥 🏠 Ⓦ **zoo.si**

Spread across the densely wooded southern slopes of Rožnik Hill is Ljubljana's zoo, which houses a wide variety of creatures from around the world. Near the entrance is a selection of animals such as horses, goats and geese that one might find on the average Slovenian farm. A re-created thatch-roofed farm cottage displays the kind of insects and rodents that traditionally live in proximity to humans. Further on is a varied collection of more exotic animals such as giraffes, Siberian tigers, Persian leopards and an energetic family of gibbons that can be seen leaping from branch to branch in their enclosure. The zoo extends quite a long way up the hillside, with wooded paths leading to large enclosures housing wild cats, wolves and bears.

The Zoological Gardens made international news in May 1969, when the bears Piki and Miki broke out of their enclosure and had to be tracked by hunters through Ljubljana's western suburbs.

Bust of Ivan Cankar

Rose-coloured Church of the Visitation, Rožnik Hill

Locomotives on display in the Railway Museum

⓫ Brewery Museum
Pivovarski muzej

Pivovarniška 2. **Tel** (01) 471 7330.
Open 8am–1pm 1st Tue of the
month. 🅿 🚻 🌐 pivo-union.si

Dominating the horizon just
north of Tivoli Park is the tall
grey façade of the Union
Brewery (Pivovarna
Union), Slovenia's
second-largest beer
producer. A small
museum in an old
malting house
depicts the history
of the brewery along
with a display of
brewing equipment
through the ages.
Of particular interest
are the horse- and
hand-drawn carts
once used to deliver the brew
around the city. Visitors can
also visit the factory floor and
sample a selection of the
company's products.

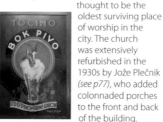
Old poster, Brewery Museum

The brewery was founded
by Kočevje-born Germans
Ivan and Peter Kosler in
1864; the latter used the
wealth he amassed from
beer brewing to purchase the
Lamberg Mansion in Tivoli
Park, which is today the
Slovene Museum of
Contemporary History
(see pp78–9). Popular legend
maintains that Kosler had
beer delivered from the
brewery to his palatial home
via an underground pipe,
enabling him to test the
quality of the brew whenever
he wanted to.

⓬ St Bartholomew's Church
Cerkev sv Jerneja

Celovška cesta.

A grey-brown edifice that
looks more like a village church,
St Bartholomew's dates from
around the 1370s and is
thought to be the
oldest surviving place
of worship in the
city. The church
was extensively
refurbished in the
1930s by Jože Plečnik
(see p77), who added
colonnaded porches
to the front and back
of the building.
Standing at the
bottom of the
staircase beside the
church is another example of
Plečnik's architectural style – a
lampstand made up of bubble-
like forms mounted one on top
of the other.

Display of brewing equipment at the Brewery Museum

⓭ Railway Museum
Železniški muzej

Parmova 35. **Tel** (01) 291 2641.
Open 10am–6pm Tue–Sun. 🅿 🚻
🌐 slo-zeleznice.si

The history of railways in
Slovenia began with the
Südbahn, the line southwest
from Vienna that reached
Maribor in 1844 and Ljubljana in
1849. Many of the locomotives
that plied this route are on
display in the Railway Museum's
main exhibition space – a
crescent-shaped engine shed
packed with vintage rolling
stock. The oldest locomotive on
show is the sleek SB 718, built in
Vienna by Scottish engineer
John Haswell in 1861 and in use
in Yugoslavia until 70 years later.
More elegant still is the SB 17c,
an express locomotive built in
1896, which rattled along at a
speed of 80 kmph (50 mph).
Particularly delightful are the
squat locomotives with funnel
chimneys; these were once
used on Slovenia's numerous
narrow-gauge railways.

A hall across the road from
the shed displays antiquated
signalling equipment. There
is also a re-created station-
master's office from the 1920s.
A room full of railway uniforms
reveals the different styles
adopted by the various states to
have ruled over the region, from
the Ruritanian finery of the
Habsburg era to the black
overalls and red-star insignia
adopted during the early years
of Communist rule.

⓮ Church of St Francis of Assisi
Cerkev sv Frančiška Asiškega

Černetova ulica 20. **Tel** (01) 583 7270.
🚌 1, 3, 5 (to Šiška). ✝ 7am, 8am &
7pm daily.

Located in the suburb of Šiška
and begun in 1924, the Church
of St Francis of Assisi was one
of the first major projects by
Jože Plečnik in Ljubljana
and contains many of the
distinctive elements associated
with his style.

As you approach it from the
east, the church looks like a

Pyramid-shaped high altar, Church of St Francis of Assisi

Classical temple, with a façade supported by four columns. Adorning the pediment is a statue of St Francis, with his head tilted to one side as if sermonizing. The most bizarre part of the structure is the hollow belfry, with two tiers of colonnades topped by the greenish cone of a spire.

The main entrance to the church is on the southern side, where a small courtyard is illuminated by lamps that resemble large eggs. The interior features a host of equally inventive touches; the central chandelier is made up of small dangling lanterns and the tall main altar is shaped like a pyramid.

⓵ Metelkova Mesto

Corner of Masarykova cesta and Metelkova ulica. **City Map** F1.
ⓦ **metelkovamesto.org**

Visitors looking for a glimpse into contemporary Ljubljana will enjoy spending time in Metelkova Mesto, the city's alternative social centre that occupies one half of a large area of old army barracks to the east of Ljubljana Railway Station. Built by the Habsburgs and subsequently used by the Yugoslav People's Army (JLA), the abandoned barracks were encroached upon by a varied

group of musicians and artists in the early 1990s. The city authorities initially wanted them evicted, but ultimately let them stay, allowing Metelkova to develop into one of the most vibrant alternative communities in Central Europe. Metelkova's buildings, covered in colourful murals and splashes of mosaic, house a number of bars, clubs, artists' workshops and NGOs, driving home the nonconformist message.

In many ways Metelkova is the natural successor to the post-punk alternative culture of the 1980s, from which Slovenia's civil rights movement was born. Providing a link to the past is **Hostel Celica**, which occupies a former military prison at No. 8. It was here that the Ljubljana Four were incarcerated in 1988 *(see p43)* sparking demonstrations that ultimately led to Slovenia's independence. The rooms in the former cells have been redesigned by contemporary artists.

Otherwise, Metelkova Mesto is a night-time attraction – its large central courtyard is usually filled with revellers attracted by its bars and live music venues *(see pp98–9)*.

Hostel Celica
Metelkova 8. **Tel** (01) 230 9700.
📷 2pm daily. 🅿
ⓦ **hostelcelica.com**

Colourful façade of a building in Metelkova Mesto

⓰ Slovene National Museum (Metelkova)

Narodni muzej Slovenije (Metelkova)

Maistrova 1. **City Map** F1.
Tel (01) 230 7030. **Open** 10am–6pm Tue–Sun. 🎫 📷 🅵 📷 ⓦ nms.si

The grand-looking trio of Habsburg-era barrack buildings, at the southern end of Metelkova ulica, form a museum complex known as the Museum Quarter, comprising the Ethnographic Museum *(see pp82–3)* and the National Museum (Metelkova).

Occupying the eastern and southern side of the complex's central plaza is the Metelkova branch of the National Museum of Slovenia *(see p66)*. It displays over 2,500 objects, including costumes, toys and applied art showing a rich diversity of styles from the 14th century to the present day. The notable furniture collection includes ornate medieval storage chests and opulent Baroque wardrobes as well as the mass-produced plywood furniture eagerly purchased by Slovenian households in the 1960s. Temporary historical exhibitions take place on the ground floor of the building.

⓱ Museum of Contemporary Art (+MSUM)

Muzej Sodobne Umetnosti Metelkova

Maistrova 3. **City Map** F1.
Tel (01) 241 6834. **Open** 10am–6pm Tue–Sun. 📷 🅵 ⓦ mg-lj.si

Adjacent to the Slovene National Museum, on Maistrova ulica, is the Museum of Contemporary Art (+MSUM). Its permanent collection focuses on contemporary works by Eastern European avant-garde artists and includes exhibits from its sister institution, Modern Gallery *(see p66)*. It also hosts temporary exhibitions and houses Slovenia's largest research library for modern and contemporary art.

⑱ Slovene Ethnographic Museum
Slovenski etnografski muzej

Opened in stages between 2007 and 2009, the Slovene Ethnographic Museum is one of the most imaginative of its kind in Europe, exhibiting artifacts from Slovenia and around the globe in a series of visually captivating displays. The collection is brought to life with the help of documentary films, sound recordings and a computer lounge allowing visitors to access audiovisual content. The setting is itself impressive, occupying a 19th-century barracks to which a futuristic glass-and-steel façade has been added. The museum is particularly suited to younger visitors, with interactive toys on the top floor, an ethnoalphabet display and a merry-go-round and see-saw on the lawn outside the café.

The permanent exhibition on the second floor

Folk costumes

Objects of Life, Objects of Desire
This room on the third floor sheds light on the industrious and creative side of human society, with traditional trades such as shoe-making and clock-making displayed alongside wonderful examples of folk costume, painting and wood sculpture.

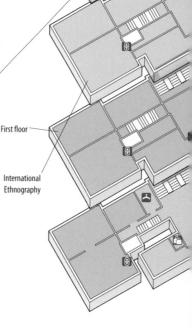

First floor

International Ethnography

★ Čupa
This dugout canoe, carved out of a log, dominates the Water and Earth section, which is devoted to local agriculture and trade. It was used for fishing by Slovenians living on the Adriatic coast north of Trieste (now in Italy).

Workshops
Artisans in the museum's ground-floor workshops are on hand to demonstrate traditional pottery and weaving techniques. Visitors can buy textiles, including contemporary accessories such as ponchos, bags and scarves with folk motifs.

Key to Floorplan
- ☐ Slovene life and culture
- ☐ I, We and Others
- ☐ Temporary exhibition space
- ☐ Non-exhibition space

Painted Furniture
Children's cradles and chests are among the most popular pieces of painted furniture on display on the third floor.

Third floor

Second floor

★ **Painted Beehive Panels**
These hand-painted panels are a typically Slovenian form of popular art. As well as scenes of daily life, they frequently portray parades of animals dressed in human clothes.

West African Ritual Masks
Brought back to Slovenia by Anton Petkovšek, who toured Africa as a trade representative, these masks shed light on the role of private collectors in shaping the Slovenian public's vision of the wider world. Nearby are Javanese puppets collected by Slovenian diplomat Aleš Bebler.

Ground floor

Workshop space

★ **Folk Costumes**
The display includes costumes from all regions of Slovenia and the fine clothes worn by 19th-century town-dwellers. There is also a fascinating collection of bonnets, important symbols of regional and national identity.

Gallery Guide
The ground floor is devoted to craft workshops, café and a shop. The permanent collection begins on the second floor with a display, "I, We and Others", which looks at ethnography globally. The third floor showcases Slovene life and culture through the ages.

For keys to symbols *see back flap*

Visitors taking a stroll through the lush Botanical Garden

🄳 Sokol Hall
Sokolski dom

Tabor 13. **City Map** F2. **Tel** (01) 232 2528. **W** sportnodrustvo-tabor.si

This sports hall was one of the most unconventional buildings to emerge from the Slovenian Modernist Movement of the 1920s. It was designed for the Sokol (Falcon) Sports Club by Ivan Vurnik, architect of the Cooperative Bank *(see p62)*. The building features rows of Graeco-Egyptian columns, each decorated with zig-zags, chevrons and other geometric shapes inspired by Slavic folk art.

Originally founded in Prague in 1862, the Sokol Movement sought to encourage solidarity among the Slavs of the Habsburg Empire by promoting physical exercise, especially gymnastics. Like its Czech counterpart, the Slovenian branch of the Sokol used sport as a means to nurture national values among the youth by organizing gymnastic displays that were rousingly patriotic as well as spectacular to watch. Now the property of the Tabor Sports Association (Športno društvo Tabor), the hall retains its social importance for the locals, offering sporting and fitness programmes for all ages.

🄴 Botanical Garden
Botanični vrt

Ižanska cesta 15. **Tel** (01) 427 1280. **Open** Apr–Jun, Sep & Oct: 7am–7pm daily; Jul & Aug: 7am–8pm daily; Nov–Mar: 7am–5pm daily. **W** botanicni-vrt.si

Located to the southeast of the Old Town, Ljubljana's small Botanical Garden was founded in 1810 during French rule. The linden tree planted by French governor Marshal Marmont still presides over a compact park featuring an array of beech, pine and chestnut trees, while paths weave their way through shrubs and flowers indigenous to central Europe. A palm house at the southern end of the garden has displays of more exotic flora.

🄵 Kodeljevo Castle
Grad Kodeljevo

Koblarjeva ulica 34. Grad Kodeljevo restaurant and pizzeria: **Tel** (01) 544 3067. **Open** 11am–10pm daily.

Built by the Thurn family in the early 17th century, Kodeljevo Castle is one of Ljubljana's best-preserved Renaissance residences. It gets its name from the Codelli family, who bought it in 1700 and added the Baroque chapel to the building's western wing. Lavishly decorated with frescoes by France Jelovšek (1700–64), the chapel is rarely open to the public. A plaque on the castle wall honours its most famous resident, Baron Anton Codelli von Fahrenfeld (1875–1954), the first man to drive an auto-mobile – a Benz Comfortable acquired in 1898 – on the streets of Ljubljana.

Several of the castle's atmospheric rooms are occupied by the **Grad Kodeljevo restaurant and pizzeria**.

Façade of the early 20th-century Sokol Hall

For hotels and restaurants in this area see p192 and pp201–2

㉒ Museum of Architecture and Design

Muzej za arhitekturo in oblikovanje

Pot na Fužine 2. **Tel** (01) 548 4270. 🚌 20. **Open** 10am–6pm Tue–Sun. 🅿️ 📷 ♿ 🏪 Biennial of Industrial Design (Oct–Nov: every even-numbered year). **W** **mao.si**

Occupying an attractive riverside site on the city's eastern outskirts, this museum makes for a rewarding excursion, not least because of its setting in **Fužine Castle** (Grad Fužine). The castle was originally built in the mid-16th century by the Kisls, a family of merchants attracted by the iron foundries around the Ljubljanica river. Restored in the 1990s, it is a fine example of a Renaissance chateau, with cylindrical corner towers and an arcaded central courtyard.

As well as hosting the Biennial of Industrial Design, the museum is also the permanent home of the Plečnik Exhibition, a collection of materials including plans, models and furniture first shown at Paris's Centre Pompidou in 1986. Visitors can enjoy scale models of Plečnik's most famous buildings as well as maquettes of projects that were never built. The most famous of these designs is the Slovenian Acropolis, a magnificent parliament house topped by a huge conical spire that sadly never left the drawing board *(see p77)*.

Candles and offerings at a grave in the Žale Cemetery

㉓ Žale Cemetery

Med hmeljniki 2. **Tel** (01) 420 1700. 🚌 2. **Open** Apr–Sep: 7am–9pm daily; Oct–Mar: 7am–7pm daily. **W** **zale.si**

On the city's northeastern outskirts, Žale Cemetery is another of the iconic sights associated with architect Jože Plečnik. The cemetery itself has been Ljubljana's main burial ground since 1906, but it was in 1937 that Plečnik – then at the height of his career – was given carte blanche to redesign the entrance and provide facilities for mourners. The graveyard is entered via an archway flanked by two-tiered colonnades, intended by

Sculpture at Žale Cemetery

Plečnik to mark the transition from the world of the living to that of the dead.

Immediately beyond the gateway lies the All Saints' Gardens (Vrt vseh svetih) with a cluster of Plečnik-designed chapels, executed in radically differing styles to express humanity's religious and cultural diversity. Both the central prayer room *(molilnica)* and the nearby Chapel of St John (kapela sv Janeza) follow Classical models with triangular pediments held up by Doric and Ionic columns, flanked by amphora-like urns.

In total contrast are the Chapel of St Agathius (kapela sv Ahaca), an ivy-covered cone inspired by Etruscan grave mounds, and the octagonal Chapel of St Peter (kapela sv Petra), which recalls the Moorish styles of southern Spain.

To the north of the chapel lies the graveyard proper, a grid of plots edged by trimmed hedges and shrubs.

To the east is the Ossuary of Victims of World War I, an impressive rotunda designed by Plečnik's student, Edvard Ravnikar, in 1939. It commemorates the Slovenians who served in the ranks of the Austro-Hungarian army; the remains of Russian and Serbian POWs are also housed within. The entrance to the ossuary is via a stepped bridge watched over by Lojze Dolinar's (1893–1970) statue of a soldier.

Running between the central part of the cemetery and the newer plots to the north is the Path of Remembrance and Comradeship (Pot spominov in tovarištva), a 33-km- (21-mile-) long walking and cycling route. This path follows the barbed wire fence that was built around Ljubljana by Fascist Italian occupiers in 1942. Visitors who want to explore the route can pick up maps from the Ljubljana Tourist Information Centre *(see p99)*.

Fužine Castle, home to the Museum of Architecture and Design

FURTHER AFIELD

The area of low hills and farmland that lies beyond Ljubljana's suburbs holds a lot of potential for day trips. Immediately south of the city lie the flatlands of the Ljubljana Marshes (Ljubljansko barje), crisscrossed with tracks that provide the perfect terrain for cyclists. Enthusiastic hikers can tackle the Šmarna Gora hill, located just north of the capital, or venture into the forest-shrouded Iški Gorge that lies to the south. Historical attractions include the Slovene Technical Museum at Bistra Castle and the Cistercian monastery at Stična to the south, and the splendours of 17th-century Bogenšperk Castle to the east. To the northwest, huddled beneath its Baroque castle, well-preserved Škofja Loka offers the perfect taste of small-town Slovenia.

Sights at a Glance

Historic Buildings
❸ Polhov Gradec Castle
❺ Bistra Castle
❾ Turjak Castle
❿ Stična Monastery
⓬ *Bogenšperk Castle pp94–5*

Towns and Villages
❹ Vrhnika
❻ *Škofja Loka pp90–91*

Sites of Interest
❶ Šmarna Gora
❷ Lake Zbilje
❼ Ljubljana Marshes
❽ Iški Gorge
⓫ Arboretum Volčji Potok

Key

▪ Central Ljubljana
▬ Motorway
▬ Major road
═ Minor road
— Railway

0 kilometres 5

0 miles 5

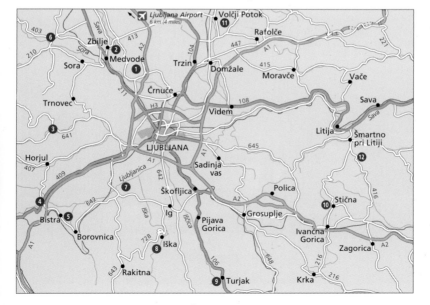

❶ Šmarna Gora

Road map B3. 6 km (4 miles) N of
Ljubljana. 🚌 from Ljubljana.
Ⓦ smarnagora.com

Rising above Ljubljana's
northern suburbs, the smooth-
topped Šmarna Gora is a
popular destination for
Ljubljana dwellers seeking to
stretch their legs. The hill has
two peaks: the 676-m- (2,218-ft-)
high Grmada lies to the west
and the 669-m- (2,195-ft-) high
Šmarna Gora lies to the east.
Most people head straight for
the latter, where the fortified
Church of the Holy Mother
crowns the summit, and
expansive views of the city
open up to the south. Also at
the summit is the miraculous
Bell of St Anthony. According
to legend, Ottoman raiders
were ordered to capture Šmarna
Gora before noon. The bell
tolled half an hour early,
confusing the attackers and
sending them into retreat. It is
said that the wishes of those
who ring the bell come true.

The hill is particularly busy on
fine Sundays, when it seems as
if the entire city is swarming up
and down its slopes. Numerous
paths lead up the hill, although
the most popular is the ascent
that begins in the suburb of
Tacen. A steeper approach
heads up the eastern side of the
hill from the village of Šmartno.
Both suburbs are accessible by
bus from central Ljubljana.

Hiker walking up one of the several trails
on Šmarna Gora

❷ Lake Zbilje
Zbiljsko jezero

Road map B3. 20 km (13 miles) NW
of Ljubljana.

A reservoir fed by the Sava river,
Lake Zbilje came into being
with the construction of a dam
at Medvode in 1953. It soon
became a popular location for
summertime swimming and
boating, with the village of
Zbilje at the lake's northern
end offering a number of
recreational facilities.

Stretching south of the
village is a grassy lakeside area
featuring cafés, a children's
play park and boat-rental
facilities. Although busiest in
summer, it is a popular place for
walks throughout the year, with

abundant swans, ducks
and other waterfowl adding
to the charm.

❸ Polhov Gradec Castle
Polhograjska graščina

Road map B3. 22 km (14 miles) W
of Ljubljana; Polhov Gradec 61.
Tel (01) 364 5694. 🚌 from Ljubljana.
Open 10am–5pm Tue–Fri & Sun.
📷 Ⓦ grad-polhovgradec.si

Nestling among wooded hills,
the village of Polhov Gradec
grew around its castle, a
medieval stronghold that
was rebuilt as an aristocratic
residence during the Baroque
period. During the late 16th
century, the castle was owned
by Jurij Kisl, grandson of Vid
Kisl, founder of Fužine
Castle – now the Museum
of Architecture and Design
(see p85) – in Ljubljana. Jurij Kisl
was a statesman, intellectual
and soldier who distinguished
himself in campaigns against
the Ottoman Turks.

The castle now houses the
Slovene Museum of Post and
Telecommunications, which has
colourful and entertaining
displays. There are also
specimens of Morse code
machines, telephones through
the ages and postal uniforms.
Visitors can also admire the
castle's richly stuccoed chapel
before taking a stroll in the
19th-century ornamental park.

Picturesque Lake Zbilje against the backdrop of Zbilje and the Alps

For hotels and restaurants in this area see p192 and p202

The octagonal St Leonard's Church dating back to the 18th century, Vrhnika

❹ Vrhnika

Road map B3. 32 km (20 miles) SW of Ljubljana. 🚗 18,000. 🚌 from Ljubljana. 🛈 Jelovškova 1; (01) 755 1054. 🌐 **zavod-cankar.si**

Spread between low hills, Vrhnika is a pleasant market town that was originally the Roman town Nauportum in the 1st century AD. Nothing from that period has survived. However, there is a pleasant ensemble of historic buildings near the central Cankarjev trg, starting with the octagonal St Leonard's Church facing the broad mansard roof of the former Court House.

The most visited spot in town is the **Ivan Cankar Memorial House**, just west of the centre in the Na klancu district. It was here that the famous Slovenian writer Ivan Cankar was born in 1876. The house itself is not original, having been built on the site of the earlier Cankar family cottage, which burned down in 1880. The interior contains photographs and manuscripts, alongside the kind of furniture that a 19th-century artisan's family would have owned.

🏛 **Ivan Cankar Memorial House**
Na klancu 1. **Tel** (01) 755 1054.
Open Apr–Oct: 9am–1pm Tue–Fri, 2–6pm Sat & Sun. 📷

❺ Bistra Castle
Grad Bistra

Road map B3. 36 km (22 miles) SW of Ljubljana.

Set against a hillside some 3 km (1 mile) east of Vrhnika, Bistra Castle began life as a Carthusian monastery founded by Ulrich III of Spannheim in 1260. Later an aristocratic residence, Bistra was an important centre for saw-milling throughout its history, and several reconstructed water-powered workshops lie alongside the stream that runs through the heart of the estate. The castle now provides a rather grand home to the **Slovene Technical Museum** (Tehniški muzej Slovenije), one of the country's most varied collections.

A pavilion near the entrance to the castle houses vintage trams and automobiles, including several official cars that were once used by Yugoslav president Josip Broz Tito. Elsewhere, there are exhaustive displays of agricultural, forestry and fishing equipment, alongside early examples of steam power and electricity generation. Carrying on with the technological theme is a room devoted to Nikola Tesla (1856–1943), the prolific Yugoslav-born inventor who spent most of his career in the USA, developing alternating current, electric light systems and radio waves in the process.

🏛 **Slovene Technical Museum**
Bistra 6. **Tel** (01) 750 6670.
Open Mar–Jun & Sep–Nov: 8am–4pm Tue–Fri, 9am–5pm Sat; Jul & Aug: 10am–6pm Tue–Fri, 9am–5pm Sat.
📷 🎥 🌐 **tms.si**

Model of an old petrol station in the Slovene Technical Museum

Ivan Cankar (1876–1918)

Few writers have shaped the modern Slovenian psyche in the way that Ivan Cankar has. The writer's vast output of poetry, novels and plays occupies a dominant position in Slovenian culture. His works rarely offered a flattering portrayal of Slovenian society, frequently focusing on ineffectual dreamers, corrupt managers and cruel officials. Cankar always supported the downtrodden, conveying a new sense of sympathy for the aspirations of the rural and urban poor. His most famous short story is *Hlapec Jernej* (Jernej the Bailiff), in which an ageing servant is deprived of his rights – a metaphor for Slovenia under Austrian domination. Cankar was a supporter of the Yugoslav ideal but insisted on the uniqueness of Slovenian language and culture.

Ivan Cankar

6 Škofja Loka

Located at the confluence of two branches of the Sora river and backed by wooded ridges, Škofja Loka (Bishop's Meadow) is one of the most attractively situated towns in Slovenia. It gets its name from the bishops of Freising, who were granted ownership of the town by King Otto II of Germany in AD 973. A major trade and craft centre throughout the Middle Ages, the town was hit by an earthquake in 1511 and rebuilt in a uniform, early Baroque style. More recently, Škofja Loka became famous for its Passion Play, written by a Capuchin friar in 1721 and revived in 1999. Involving hundreds of costumed locals, the play is enacted every six years at Easter.

Detail on the ceiling of St James's Church

Mestni trg

Central Škofja Loka consists of a warren of streets woven tightly around the oblong Mestni trg, the medieval market square. Dominating the square's northern end is the 16th-century Homan House (Homanova hiša), whose lively façade features jutting oriel windows, squiggly sgraffito patterns and a larger-than-life painting of St Christopher. Occupying the building's ground floor is the Café Homan, long the centre of the town's social life and once the favoured sketching spot of Impressionist painter Ivan Grohar (1867–1911).

Midway along the square is the former Town Hall (Mestna hiša), its façade enlivened by the fragmented remains of 17th-century frescoes. They are unexpectedly exotic in content, showing friendly-looking sphinxes squatting on pillars. Diagonally opposite the Town Hall is the Plague Column, topped by a serene statue of the Virgin and Child. The column was erected in 1751 to ensure divine protection from disease and natural disasters.

St James's Church

Cankarjev trg 13.
Built in 1471, St James's Church (Cerkev sv Jakoba) has preserved much of its late-Gothic appearance. Of note is the delicate stone relief above the main entrance showing Judas grasping a bag of money,

Dancers at the medieval festival in the Old Town centre

watched expectantly by Herod's soldiers. After the earthquake in the early 16th century, the church's belfry was remodelled, when it acquired a characteristically bulbous Baroque spire.

Inside, the ceiling is a masterpiece of Gothic vaulting, with brightly coloured floral designs filling the spaces between the stone ribs. Hovering above the pews is a forest of brass chandeliers and lanterns, added by 20th-century architect Jože Plečnik (see p77). Behind the church stands a sturdy 16th-century schoolhouse, with a plaque honouring its founder Michael Papler, lord of Škofja Loka Castle (Grad Škofja Loka).

Mihelič Gallery

Spodnji trg 1. **Tel** (04) 517 0400.
Open by appt only. for a fee.
loski-muzej.si

Dominating Spodnji trg is a 15th-century granary, a severe-looking stone building with tiny rectangular windows. This was once one of the most important buildings in town, housing the food supply as well as the citizens' tax records. Today, the granary's timber-beamed upper storeys accommodate the Mihelič Gallery (Galerija Mihelič), devoted to artist France Mihelič (1907–98), who was born in Škofja Loka.

Mihelič is primarily known for his distinctively surreal graphic works, in which human forms were made to resemble twig-like creatures and distorted insects. Among his most striking works are the series of lithographs depicting the Kurenti, masked men who lead the Kurentovanje revels in Ptuj.

Castle Museum

Grajska pot 13. **Tel** (04) 517 0400.
Open Apr–Sep: 10am–6pm Tue–Sun; Nov–Mar: 10am–5pm Tue–Sun.
loski-muzej.si

Squatting on a hillock directly above the town centre, Škofja Loka's Baroque castle served as the seasonal residence for the bishops of Freising and was the seat of their administration when the prelates were away.

The so-called "black kitchen" in the 16th-century Nace's House

Easily reached via a winding pathway from Mestni trg, the building now houses the extensive and varied collections of the Town Museum (Mestni muzej).

Highlights of the museum include the brightly decorated pottery used in Loka households through the ages, as well as painted wooden furniture and original wares from the lace- and hat-making workshops that once figured prominently in the local economy. The corridors are filled with canvases by local painters, including several works by Ivan Grohar.

Displayed in the castle's octagonal chapel are four 17th-century altars from the Church of St Lucy in Dražgoše in northwestern Slovenia. Each altar is encrusted with gilded statuettes of saints and gambolling cherubs.

🏛 Nace's House
Puštal 74. **Tel** (04) 176 9425.
Open by appt. 🏠 🍴 for a fee.
🌐 nacetovahisa.com

Southeast of the centre, on the opposite bank of the Poljanska Sora, spreads the suburb of Puštal, a pleasant neighbourhood of one- or two-storey houses surrounded by gardens and orchards. The oldest of the surviving dwellings in this part of town is the 16th-century Nace's House (Nacetova hiša), a beautifully preserved, largely timber building whose spindly wooden balconies are sheltered under a steep overhanging roof.

Named after its early 19th-century owner Ignac "Nace" Homan, the house served as an inn until 1907 – it was here that farm workers would return to from the fields, have a drink and change into their town clothes before venturing homewards. The interior is packed with traditional furnishings and original features. One of them is the archaic "black kitchen" so-called because it did not have a standard chimney – smoke from the fire escaped upwards through the rafters, drying the household's grain and curing sausages as it went. A traditional timber granary and a hay barn can be seen in the garden.

Škofja Loka Town Centre

① Mestni trg
② St James's Church
③ Mihelič Gallery
④ Castle Museum

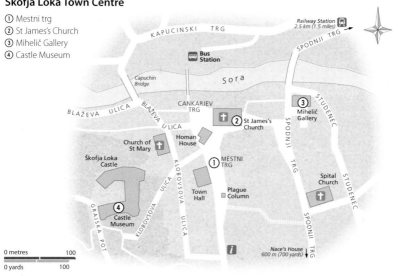

❼ Ljubljana Marshes
Ljubljansko barje

Road map B3. 10 km (6 miles) S of Ljubljana. **W** ljubljanskobarje.si

Stretching beyond Ljubljana's southern suburbs, the grassy plain known as the Ljubljana Marshes began life as a shallow lake formed at the end of the last Ice Age. It was an important centre of Neolithic culture in the 4th millennium BC, when locals lived in wood-pile dwellings above the lake's surface and used log-carved canoes to commute. With time the lake dried out, leaving a soggy area of peat bog. From the 18th century onwards, the digging of drainage ditches rendered the area suitable for agriculture, and in 1830, the marsh was sold off as plots, largely to soldiers for whom the land purchase offered exemption from further military service. The bogs were over-harvested for peat and only survive in isolated pockets nowadays. However, they remain an important breeding ground for birds, with herons, curlews and corncrakes among the regular nesters. The best way to explore the marshes is by bike, thanks to a network of trails that run alongside the drainage channels.

The area's one prominent architectural attraction is the **Church of St Michael** (Cerkev sv Mihaela) in the village of Črna vas. Built between 1925 and 1939 by architect Jože Plečnik *(see p77)*, the structure utilizes local wood as well as a mixture of grey limestone and red brick – a technique also employed in the National and University Library *(see pp72–3)* in Ljubljana. The ivy-covered bell tower, perforated with arches of various sizes, is one of Plečnik's most arresting creations. The church features a nave raised above ground level to guard it against seasonal flooding, and is entered via an unusual arched stairway. Inside, wooden pews and timber ceiling beams contrast with the warm sheen of a high altar constructed with burnished copper sheets.

Bell tower of the Church of St Michael, Ljubljana Marshes

❽ Iški Gorge
Iški Vintgar

Road map C3. 25 km (16 miles) S of Ljubljana. **W** iski-vintgar.si

Flowing into the Ljubljana Marshes from the south, the Iška river cuts through the dolomite rock of the Bloke Plateau to form the Iški Gorge, a V-shaped valley with steep, densely wooded sides.

The most interesting stretches of the gorge lie just beyond the Gostišče Iški Vintgar, a guesthouse accessible via the paved road from the marshes. From the guesthouse, a footpath leads along the bank of the river, passing a sequence of cataracts and pools. The going gets more difficult as the gorge narrows, and visitors should be prepared to get their feet wet to be able to enjoy the waterfalls and rock formations of the gorge's upper stretches.

For those who want to explore the hilly terrain above the gorge, a path ascends west from the Gostišče Iški Vintgar towards the Orlek ridge, before descending into an isolated dell, site of the Krvavice Partisan Hospital during World War II – a few wooden huts remain. More ambitious hikers can carry on uphill to the 1,107-m- (3,632-ft-) high summit of Krim hill, which offers wonderful views back across the marshes towards Ljubljana.

❾ Turjak Castle
Grad Turjak

Road map C4. 25 km (16 miles) SE of Ljubljana. **Tel** (01) 788 1006. **Open** May–Oct: noon–7pm Sat & Sun.

An important stronghold in the Middle Ages, Turjak Castle got its present form in the 16th century, when the castle's characteristic barrel-shaped bastions and arcaded inner courtyard were built. The masters of the castle were the Auerspergs, who turned it into a key stronghold in Austria's defences against Ottoman incursions. The famous Andreas Auersperg led the Carniolan forces during the 1593 battle

Wooden water mill at the Iški Gorge

Permanent exhibition at Turjak Castle

⓫ Arboretum Volčji Potok

Road map C3. 22 km (14 miles) NE of Ljubljana; Volčji potok 3. **Tel** (01) 831 2345. **Open** Mar & Oct: 8am–5pm; Apr–Aug: 8am–7pm; Sep: 8am–6pm; Nov: 8am–3:30pm daily. 🅿 🗹 🖵 🗺 🆆 **arboretum-vp.si**

Just north of the Domžale exit on the Ljubljana–Maribor motorway lies the Arboretum Volčji Potok, once Ljubljana University's botanical study centre and now the most popular horticultural attraction in the country.

Formerly a landscaped park belonging to the Souvan estate, the arboretum features 3,000 species of trees and shrubs, neat ornamental gardens and numerous floral displays. Seasonal attractions include tulips in April, a wide range of blossoms in May, roses from June onwards and an explosion of autumn colours in October.

An autumn pumpkin festival celebrates one of Slovenia's best-loved vegetables. Facilities for children include an attraction-packed play park, a maze and a tractor-pulled train dressed up to look like a vintage steam locomotive.

Sculpture, Stična

The arboretum's shop is a great place to buy seeds. There is an 18-hole golf course situated right next to the arboretum.

of Sisak, when a combined Croatian-Slovenian force crushed an advancing Ottoman army. Andreas is credited with the capture of a bridge crucial to the struggle, causing the enemy to flee.

Several rooms in the castle can be visited. These include the Renaissance Knights Hall and the castle chapel, decorated with 15th-century frescoes. Temporary exhibitions of arts and crafts are held in one of the towers. Below the castle are the ruins of almshouses built by the owners for their ageing servants.

❿ Stična Monastery

Samostan Stična

Road map C3. 35 km (22 miles) SE of Ljubljana. **Tel** (01) 787 7100. **Open** 8am–noon & 2–5pm Tue–Sat, 2–5pm Sun. 🅿 🗹 🆆 **sticna.eu**

Set among meadow-carpeted hills just north of the main road from Ljubljana to Novo Mesto is Stična Monastery. It was founded in 1136 by Patriarch Peregrine I of Aquileia, who was keen to provide the Cistercian order with a base from which to spread their teachings. The monastery was one of the richest in Slovenia and became an important centre of education and manuscript production. Heavily fortified in the 15th and 16th centuries in order to withstand Ottoman raids, Stična has retained its sturdy outer appearance to this day.

Emperor Joseph II's decision to dissolve the big monasteries in 1781 led to the abandonment of Stična and the sale of its treasures. It was refounded in 1898 by Cistercian monks from Bavaria.

The 12th-century monastery church retains several original Romanesque features, although repeated rebuildings during the Baroque era bequeathed a bulbous belfry and an altar-filled interior. The monastery's administrative buildings now house the Slovene Religious Museum, crammed with reliquaries, candelabras and religious paintings. Highlights include 15th-century fresco fragments painted by Master Janez of Ljubljana for one of the monastery chapels.

Flowers blooming in the Arboretum Volčji Potok

⑫ Bogenšperk Castle

Grad Bogenšperk

The Renaissance castle of Bogenšperk was built for the Wagen family in the early 16th century. Its place in Slovene history is due to Janez Valvasor, the antiquarian and author who bought the castle in 1672 and turned it into his printing workshop. Here, he produced the copper-plate engravings subsequently published as part of his magnum opus, *The Glory of the Duchy of Carniola*. Printing debts forced Valvasor to sell his books and artifacts, but his castle survives as a popular tourist attraction.

Flowering plants adorning the stark courtyard walls

Entrance

★ Folk Costumes
Clothes worn by Slovenians in the 17th century are re-created in this display of costumes from all over the country.

KEY

① Ticket office

② Hunting room

Janez Vajkard Valvasor's Work

A traveller, historian and collector, Valvasor is primarily remembered for the four-volume work, *The Glory of the Duchy of Carniola* (*Die Ehre des Herzogtums Crain*), published in Nuremberg in 1689. It was the first fully researched description of central and western Slovenia, containing comments on history and human geography.

The Glory of the Duchy of Carniola, a 3,500-page illustrated work, remains valuable for researchers. Valvasor spent 15 years preparing the book and was ruined by the cost of its publication, forcing him to sell the castle in 1692.

Valvasor sold his library to the Bishop of Zagreb, and died in poverty in Krško in 1693.

Former Library
The largest room in the castle, Valvasor's former library is nowadays mainly used as an atmospheric venue for wedding ceremonies.

VISITORS' CHECKLIST

Practical Information
Road map C3. 41 km (26 miles)
E of Ljubljana. 🚌 🚗
Tel (01) 898 7664.
Open Apr–Oct: 10am–5pm Tue–
Sat, 10am–6pm Sun; Mar & Nov:
10am–5pm Sat & Sun.
W bogensperk.si

★ **Re-created Study**
Period furnishings shed light on Valvasor's day-to-day working life. Also on display is an original copy of *The Glory of the Duchy of Carniola.*

★ **Copper-engraving Workshop**
This display of 17th-century paper-making and printing machines reveals just how labour-intensive book production was.

Death was a popular subject for Baroque illustrators, focusing minds on the transience of earthly life.

Printing was complex and expensive in the 17th century. Valvasor was a leader in the production of beautiful books and many people came to Bogenšperk Castle especially to study his technique.

Accurately drawn townscapes were an important element of Valvasor's book on Carniola, which aimed to be a visually appealing complete guide to the nation's riches as well as a scholarly text.

SHOPPING IN LJUBLJANA

Central Ljubljana is a treasure-trove of characterful shops, with the boutiques of the Old Town offering everything from kooky arts and crafts to haute couture. There are also plenty of souvenir outlets, with lace, embroidery, handmade chocolates and Slovene wines featuring among the most popular wares. Visitors to the capital city also have the option of browsing the market stalls – the fresh fruit, vegetable and fish stalls in Ljubljana's Market are an attraction in their own right, while the weekly bric-a-brac market on the riverbank is also a social event. In December, the Advent market in the Old Town generates plenty in the way of Christmas gift ideas alongside a festive atmosphere.

Daily morning fruit and vegetable market, Vodnikov trg

Opening Hours

Shops in Ljubljana are usually open from 9 or 10am until 7 or 8pm from Monday to Friday and from 9 or 10am until 1 or 2pm on Saturday. Be aware that almost all shops in the city centre – supermarkets and newspaper kiosks included – are closed on Sunday. The best places to shop for basic provisions on Sundays are the shopping centres on the eastern outskirts of Ljubljana or petrol stations throughout the city.

Department Stores and Shopping Centres

Central Ljubljana's main department store is **Nama**, offering five storeys of clothes, accessories, household goods and toys. A range of upmarket international fashion brands is sold at **Galerija Emporium**, which occupies the Centromerkur building *(see p63)* on Prešernov trg. Otherwise, the best places for general shopping, ranging from clothes to homeware, are the large mall-style complexes on the outskirts of the city. The biggest of these are **BTC City**, 4 km (3 miles) east of the centre, and **Citypark** right next to it. The BTC complex also boasts a multiplex cinema, an aquapark and other leisure facilities.

Markets

Ljubljana's colourful Market *(see p54)*, at the northern end of the Old Town, offers a wide variety of fresh fruit and vegetables, featuring local seasonal produce. Indigenous vegetables include asparagus in spring and mushrooms in autumn. The Market's riverside colonnade is the place for fresh seafood from the Adriatic. There are also specialist stalls selling honey, olive oil and dried herbs.

The antiques and bric-a-brac market on the riverside on Breg every Sunday morning is full of potential discoveries. It is also an occasion for the locals to enjoy coffee and conversation in the nearby cafés after browsing the stalls.

Food and Drink

Many Slovenian specialities such as honey, olive oil and pumpkin oil can be picked up in the Market, although you will find a better choice of delicacies in specialist stores spread throughout the centre. **Kraševka** is the place to seek out goods from the Karst region, including home-cured *pršut* (ham), teran red wine, and olive oil. Handmade chocolates are on offer at **Čokoladnica Cukrček** – who count *Prešernove kroglice* (chestnut paste and chocolate balls) among their specialities – and **Čokoladni atelje**, known for their chocolate-coated figs, plums and pralines. Souvenir bags of Piran sea salt crystals *(see p137)* can be bought from **Piranske soline**. The **Maximarket**, located in the subterranean shopping mall on Trg Republike *(see p67)*, has an extensive delicatessen selection and a good choice of Slovenian wines. A selection of Slovenian wines can be found in any large supermarket, although

Antiques on display at the riverfront market

Contemporary gifts on display at the Ika shop

if you need specialist advice on what to buy, head for **Vino Boutique** or **Vinoteka Dvor**, both in the city centre on the western side of the river. **Vinoteka Movia**, in the Old Town, sells quality wines from the Movia estates in Goriška Brda *(see p149)*.

Crafts and Souvenirs

A wide range of folksy textiles, ceramics and crafts can be found in the boutiques of Ljubljana's Old Town. **Galerija**

Rogaška sells a range of cut glass and crystalware from the famous glassworks in Rogaška, while traditional hand-woven lace from Idrija *(see p150)* can be bought at **Galerija Idrijske čipke** store nearby. **Etnogalerija Skrina** has a broad selection of authentic crafts, including embroidered blouses, glass paintings and painted beehive panels *(see p115)*. For more contemporary gifts and souvenirs, head for **Ika**, which sells affordable fashion accessories and goods made by young Slovene designers.

Music

The best place to buy CDs by contemporary Slovenian artists is **Big Bang** in the BTC shopping centre. The centrally located **Dallas Mute Shop** is particularly good for rock, pop, jazz and world music. Ljubljana is also a good place to browse for second-hand recordings. The former Yugoslavia was home to a huge music industry, releasing albums by local and international artists, and collectors will find a lot of them in specialist stores such

as **Vom Second Hand** near Prešernov trg and **Spin Vinyl** in the Old Town.

Books

Ljubljana's biggest bookshop, **Mladinska knjiga Konzorcij**, offers a wide choice of books about Slovenia in various languages, alongside a selection of English-language fiction. The small and welcoming **Knjigarna Behemot**, tucked away on a stepped alleyway, is a gold mine of English-language books, with plenty of literary fiction and a wealth of titles on the culture and history of Slovenia and its surroundings.

Racks of albums for sale at the Spin Vinyl record shop

DIRECTORY

Department Stores and Shopping Centres

BTC City
Šmartinska 152.
Tel (01) 585 2222.

Citypark
Šmartinska 152g.
Tel (01) 587 3050.

Galerija Emporium
Prešernov trg 5A.
City Map D2.
Tel (01) 5884 4800.

Nama
Tomšičeva 2.
City Map C2.
Tel (01) 425 8300.

Food and Drink

Čokoladni atelje
Trg republike 1.
City Map C3.
Tel (01) 425 3141.

Čokoladnica Cukrček
Mestni trg 11.
City Map D3.
Tel (01) 421 0453.

Kraševka
Ciril-Metodov trg 10.
City Map D3.
Tel (01) 232 1445.

Maximarket
Trg republike 1.
City Map C3.
Tel (01) 476 6800.

Piranske soline
Mestni trg 19.
City Map D3.
Tel (01) 425 0190.

Vino Boutique
Slovenska cesta 38.
City Map C2.
Tel (01) 425 2680.

Vinoteka Dvor
Dvorni trg 1. **City Map** D3.
Tel (01) 251 3644.

Vinoteka Movia
Mestni trg 4.
City Map D3.
Tel (051) 304 590.

Crafts and Souvenirs

Etnogalerija Skrina
Breg 8. **City Map** D4.
Tel (01).425 5161.

Galerija Idrijske čipke
Mestni trg 17.
City Map D3.
Tel (01) 425 0051.

Galerija Rogaška
Mestni trg 22.
City Map D3.
Tel (01) 241 2701.

Ika
Ciril-Metodov trg 13.
City Map D3.
Tel (01) 232 1743.

Music

Big Bang
BTC. **Tel** (01) 309 3768.

Dallas Mute Shop
Rimska 14. **City Map** C4.
Tel (01) 252 4591.

Spin Vinyl
Gallusovo nabrežje 13.
City Map D4.
Tel (01) 251 1018.

Vom Second Hand
Čopova ulica 14. **City Map** C2. **Tel** (01) 252 7921.

Books

Knjigarna Behemot
Židovska steza 3.
Tel (01) 251 1392.

Mladinska knjiga Konzorcij
Slovenska cesta 29. **City Map** C2. **Tel** (01) 241 4761.

ENTERTAINMENT IN LJUBLJANA

Ljubljana may not be one of the biggest European capitals but it is extraordinarily vibrant for its size. Local classical music, dance and theatre companies are of the highest quality, and the city's year-round repertoire of cultural festivals attracts a steady stream of international names. The city's vibrant bar culture provides a wealth of nightlife opportunities, especially in the summer, when the café-lined banks of the Ljubljanica river take on a Mediterranean joie de vivre. The city also has a history of pop, rock and alternative music, a heritage that manifests itself in an impressive range of concert venues and clubs.

Visitors watching artists perform on Prešernov trg

Practical Information and Tickets

The Ljubljana Tourist Office website features a list of the major cultural events. The best way to find out about the events being organized in the city is to consult the websites of the venues that host them.

Tickets for many events can be bought through **Eventim**, which has outlets in the **Ljubljana Tourist Information Centre** and in the international travel company **Kompas**'s offices. The Eventim website also offers tickets on sale and is a handy, if limited, guide to upcoming attractions.

Cultural Centres

Playing a crucial role in Ljubljana's cultural life are the multipurpose cultural centres that host a wide range of events from classical music to theatre, cinema, jazz and rock. The main venue for cultural events is Cankar Hall (*see p67*) in the city centre, a large, partly underground complex comprising concert halls, congress facilities and an art gallery. Less formal venues include **KUD France Prešeren**, just south of the centre in Trnovo; **Stara Elektrarna**, an atmospheric former power plant near the train station; and **Španski borci** in the western suburb of Moste – all of which host a mix of jazz, theatre and children's events.

Opera and Classical Music

Ljubljana's most prestigious venues for classical art forms are the 19th-century **Slovene**

Bass player of the Marc Duret Trio band during a gig, Ljubljana

National Theatre Opera and Ballet, where opera and ballet performances are staged; and the Philharmonic Hall (*see p72*), home to the national symphony orchestra. Križanke (*see p73*), with outdoor and indoor stages, is a great venue for classical music. Local and international recitals also take place in Cankar Hall.

Rock and Jazz

The capital regularly plays host to major international rock acts, with performances in the **Arena Stožice** or the slightly smaller Tivoli Hall (*see p78*). The best venue for medium-sized acts is **Kino Šiška**, a restored cinema with great sound. The other major location for live music is the Metelkova Mesto Alternative Cultural Centre, with clubs such as **Menza pri koritu**, **Gala Hala** and **Channel Zero** all grouped around a central courtyard. Outdoor jazz, rock and world music gigs also take place in Križanke through the summer. **Jazz Club Gajo**, founded by drummer Drago Gajo, hosts regular concerts and jam sessions.

Theatre

Theatre is of a very high standard in Ljubljana, with several European directors of renown working in the city's theatres. Performances are in Slovenian, unless visiting companies are in the city. However, most productions feature a level of movement

Kinodvor theatre, a venue for art films

and stagecraft that will hold the audience's interest. The Slovene National Theatre Drama (Slovensko narodno gledališče), also known as **Drama**, and the **Ljubljana City Theatre** (Mestno gledališče ljubljansko) concentrate on the classics and on contemporary local and international drama. Slightly more edgy is the **Youth Theatre** (Mladinsko gledališče), founded in 1955 specifically for young people. Nowadays, it stages experimental drama for all ages. Established in 1970,

Gledališče Glej, the oldest independent performing arts venue in Ljubljana, has a line-up of experimental, but accessible, productions.

Cinema

Films are screened in their original language with Slovenian subtitles. Hollywood movies are shown in multiplexes, the biggest of which is **Kolosej**, 4 km (3 miles) east of the centre. The best place for watching new international movies is

Kinodvor, which also shows art films and has a daytime café and bookshop. On certain summer evenings, outdoor screenings take place on the adjacent courtyard. **Kinoteka** is the place to watch cinema classics.

Nightlife

Ljubljana's vibrant nightlife focuses on the cafés and bars along the Ljubljanica river, a majority of which remain open until the early hours. The areas around Prešerenov trg and Cankarjevo nabrežje are very lively in spring and summer. The **Kavarna Nebotičnik** bar, on the top floors of the Art Deco skyscraper (see p62), offers superb views of the city.

The clubbing scene, with venues such as **Top Six Klub Cvetličarna**, **K4**, **Cirkus** and **Orto Bar**, offers a mix of live music and DJ-driven sounds. K4 hosts a gay night usually on Sundays.

DIRECTORY

Practical Information and Tickets

Eventim
w eventim.si

Kompas
Pražakova 4.
Tel (01) 200 6333.
w kompas.si

Ljubljana Tourist Information Centre
Adamič-Lundovo nabrežje 2. **City Map** D3.
Tel (01) 306 1215.
w visitljubljana.si

Cultural Centres

KUD France Prešeren
Karunova 14.
Tel (01) 283 2288.
w kud.si

Španski borci
Zaloška 61.
Tel (01) 620 8790.
w spanskiborci.si

Stara Elektrarna
Slomškova 18.
City Map E1.
Tel (051) 269 906.
w bunker.si

Opera and Classical Music

Slovene National Theatre Opera and Ballet
Zupančičeva 1. **City Map** C2. **Tel** (01) 241 5900.
w opera.si
w balet.si

Rock and Jazz

Arena Stožice
Vojkova 90.
Tel (01) 430 6660.

Channel Zero
Metelkova 4. **City Map** F1.
w ch0.org

Gala Hala
Masarykova 24. **City Map** F1. w galahala.com

Jazz Club Gajo
Beethevnova 8.
City Map C2.
w jazzclubgajo.com

Kino Šiška
w kinosiska.si

Menza pri koritu
Metelkova. **City Map** F1.
w menzaprikoritu.org

Theatre

Drama
Erjavčeva 1. **City Map** B3.
Tel (01) 252 1462.
w drama.si

Gledališče Glej
Gregorčičeva 3.
City Map B3.
Tel (01) 421 9240.
w glej.si

Ljubljana City Theatre
Čopova 14.
City Map C2.
Tel (01) 251 0852.
w mgl.si

Youth Theatre
Vilharjeva 11.
Tel (01) 300 4900.
w mladinsko.com

Cinema

Kinodvor
Kolodvorska 13.
City Map E1.
w kinodvor.org

Kinoteka
Miklošičeva 38.
City Map D2.
w kinoteka.si

Kolosej
Šmartinska 152.
w kolosej.si

Nightlife

Cirkus
Trg mladinskih delovnih brigad 7. **City Map** B4.
Tel (051) 631 631.

Cvetličarna
Kranjčeva 20.
w cvetlicarna.info

K4
Kersnikova 4.
City Map C1.
Tel (01) 438 0261.
w klubk4.org

Kavarna Nebotičnik
Štefanova 1.
City Map C2.
Tel (040) 233 078.
w neboticnik.si

Top Six Klub
Tomšičeva 2. **City Map** B2.
Tel (040) 66 8844.
w topsixclub.si

Orto Bar
Grablovičeva 1.
Tel (01) 232 1674.
w orto-bar.com

LJUBLJANA STREET FINDER

The map on the right shows the areas of the capital city, Ljubljana, which are covered by the Street Finder maps on the following pages. All map references given for sights, entertainment venues and shops described in this section of the guide refer to the Street Finder maps. Map references are also provided for Ljubljana hotels *(see p192)* and restaurants *(see pp200–202)* as well as for useful addresses in the *Travellers' Needs* and the *Survival Guide* sections at the back of the book. The main sights in the city's Old Town, the New Town and some in the Around the Centre areas can be found on pages 102–3. The letter and the number that follows in the map reference indicate the map's grid for the entry. There is also an index of street names opposite for quick reference. The symbols used to represent sights and useful information on the Street Finder maps are listed in the key given below.

Visitors enjoying an open-air music performance at Prešernov trg

Key to Street Finder

Major sight	Hospital		
Other sight	Police station		
Other building	Church		
Railway station	Railway line		
Bus station	Pedestrian street		
Funicular			
Visitor information			

Scale of Maps 1–2

0 metres	200
0 yards	200

Street Finder Index

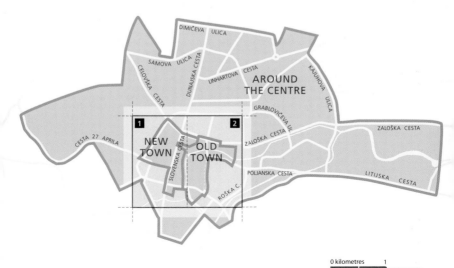

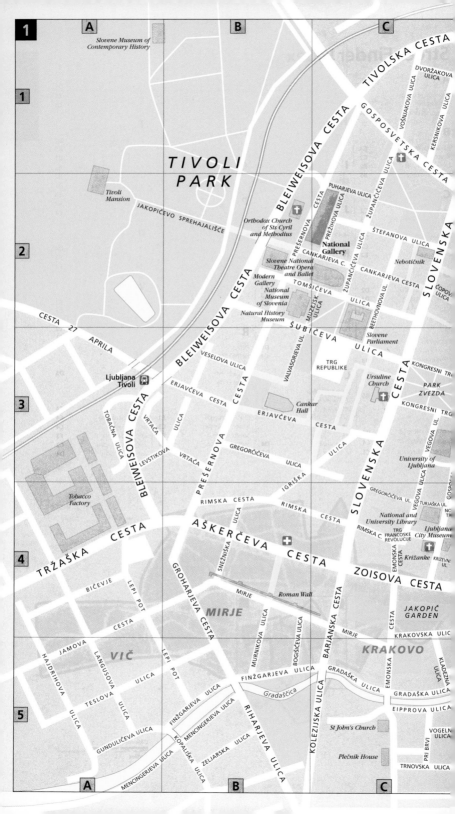

SLOVENIA REGION BY REGION

Slovenia at a Glance

The landscape in Slovenia frequently changes within the space of a short car ride. Much of the country comprises mountains cloaked in dark green forest, especially in the north with its dramatic alpine terrain. From the grey peaks of Triglav National Park to the turquoise waters of the Soča river, the scenery is exhilarating. The topography of central and eastern Slovenia is more gentle, with green hills merging with the Pannonian plain. In the west, the limestone caves give way to a narrow strip of coast.

Bled *(see pp112–13)* offers picturesque lakeside scenery with an island church and a breathtaking mountain backdrop.

Kranjska Gora *(see p120)*, a leading ski resort, makes the perfect base from which to explore Triglav National Park.

Goriška Brda *(see p149)*, a region of rolling hills close to the Italian border, is famous for its vineyards.

Kranjska Gora

Bovec

Bled

Tržič

THE ALPS
(see pp108–129)

Kranj

Kamnik

Tolmin

Škofja Loka

Idrija

Ljubljana

Nova Gorica

LJUBLJANA
(see pp46–103)

Ajdovščina

COASTAL SLOVENIA AND THE KARST
(see pp130–159)

Cerknica

Ribni

Ilirska Bistrica

Piran

Koper

Piran *(see pp134–5)* is a former salt-trading town and fishing port with numerous fine examples of Venetian architecture.

◀ Idyllic view of Lake Bled against the backdrop of snowcapped mountains

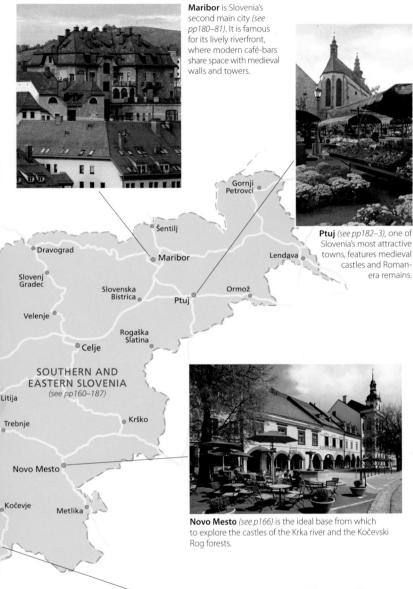

Maribor is Slovenia's second main city *(see pp180–81)*. It is famous for its lively riverfront, where modern café-bars share space with medieval walls and towers.

Ptuj *(see pp182–3)*, one of Slovenia's most attractive towns, features medieval castles and Roman-era remains.

Gornji
Petrovci

Šentilj

Dravograd

Maribor

Lendava

Slovenj
Gradec

Slovenska
Bistrica

Ormož

Ptuj

Velenje

Rogaška
Slatina

Celje

**SOUTHERN AND
EASTERN SLOVENIA**
(see pp160–187)

Litija

Trebnje

Krško

Novo Mesto

Kočevje

Metlika

Novo Mesto *(see p166)* is the ideal base from which to explore the castles of the Krka river and the Kočevski Rog forests.

0 kilometres   25

0 miles   25

Kolpa Valley *(see p165)*, marking the border between Slovenia and Croatia, offers unspoiled countryside, historic castles and churches as well as opportunities for cycling, fishing and whitewater rafting.

THE ALPS

Spectacular alpine scenery coupled with a rich history make northwest Slovenia the most acclaimed and visited region in the country. The focus for walkers, skiers and adrenaline sports enthusiasts alike is the picturesque Triglav National Park, whose mountains form the heart of the area. Soaring above all is Mount Triglav, so iconic that it features on the national flag.

Excavations around Most na Soči reveal that a rich Bronze and Iron Age culture, which traded with ancient Greece and Italy, flourished in the upper Soča Valley. The Romans settled in the valley in the 1st century AD and established a military base at what is now Kranj. That site was developed in the 7th century by early Slavic tribes, who also established an island settlement at Lake Bled.

The 12th century brought a period of cultural vitality to this protectorate of Frankish aristocracies. Churches were built throughout the region and towns such as Radovljica, Kamnik and Kranj developed. The latter two emerged as important trade and religious centres in the Middle Ages and both served as capitals of Carniola until the Habsburgs won control of the area in the late 13th century. Until the 20th century, farming was the region's mainstay, with dairy herds being taken to high alpine meadows in summer and returned to the lowlands in September. Apiculture reached its zenith through Carnolian honeybee breeding in the 17th century. Logging was another minor industry.

Tourism began in the late 19th century. Lake Bled morphed from a health retreat to a fashionable resort frequented by Viennese high society. Austro-Hungarian and Slovenian hikers began to explore the area.

The greatest upheaval in the region's history came during World War I, when the Soča Valley saw horrific fighting between Italian and Austro-Hungarian forces. Farming returned to the area and was joined by tourism in the 1990s. Today, Soča Valley, Kranjska Gora and Lake Bled are trademark destinations.

Visitors hiking in the Julian Alps, Triglav National Park

◀ Soča river, making its way through Triglav National Park

Exploring the Alps

Triglav National Park, with its crown of limestone mountains rising above picturesque glaciated lakes at Bled and Bohinj, is the poster-destination of the Alps. Bohinj, due to its good resort facilities and fairy-tale setting, makes an excellent base for day trips to the medieval cores of Radovljica and Kranj. To the north, the country's leading ski resort, Kranjska Gora, doubles as a gateway to the beautiful Soča Valley, which is littered with reminders of the three-year conflict between Austro-Hungary and Italy during World War I, a bloody and futile story best explained by a museum in Kobarid. The spectacular Kamniško-Savinjske Alps, the meadows of Velika Planina and the stupendous Logarska dolina Valley lie to the east.

Boats waiting to take visitors to Bled Island

Getting Around

The easiest way to visit the Alps is by car. Traffic is only heavy around Lake Bled in high season. The roads are open year round except the one over Vršič Pass, which may close due to snow from November to April. Buses connect most destinations, although services to villages are infrequent. Rail links connect to Ljubljana with some of the destinations; a car train also runs from Bohinjska Bistrica, 6 km (4 miles) east of Lake Bohinj.

Museum of Triglav National Park, Trenta

For hotels and restaurants in this region see pp193–4 and pp202–3

Brilliant blue waters at Most na Soči

Sights at a Glance

Villages, Towns and Cities
① Bled
④ Radovljica
⑤ Tržič
⑦ Kranjska Gora
⑨ Trenta
⑪ Bovec
⑫ Kobarid
⑬ Tolmin
⑮ Kanal
⑯ Kranj
⑱ Kamnik
⑲ Velika Planina
⑳ Kamniška Bistrica

Tour
㉑ A Tour of the Kamniško-
Savinjske Alps pp126–7

National Park
⑥ Triglav National Park pp116–17

Areas of Natural Beauty
② Vintgar Gorge
③ Pokljuka Gorge
⑧ Vršič Pass

Resort
⑰ Krvavec

Historical Sites
⑩ Kluže Fortress
⑭ Most na Soči

Key
▭▭▭ Motorway
▬▬▬ Main road
═══ Minor road
▬▭▬ Railway
:::: Road tunnel
:::: Railway tunnel
▬▬▬ International border
△ Peak

For keys to symbols *see back flap*

❶ Bled

With its placid lake, fairy-tale island church, clifftop castle and girdle of grey mountains, Bled has become a visual trademark for the Slovenian tourist industry. Although it emerged as a popular spa resort in the mid-19th century, Bled's key attractions today consist of boat trips to the island church and excursions into the alpine surroundings. Offering plenty of hotels, Bled also makes a good base for exploring nearby places of interest such as the enchanting Triglav National Park *(see pp116–17)* and Lake Bohinj *(see pp118–19)*. In winter, buses connect Bled with the skiing and snowboarding centre at Mount Vogel, near Lake Bohinj.

The Church of the Assumption on scenic Bled Island

🌿 Lake Bled

Just over 2 km (1 mile) long, 2 km (1 mile) wide and 30 m (98 ft) deep, Lake Bled (Blejsko jezero) fills a hollow gouged out by retreating glaciers towards the end of the last Ice Age. With wooded hills surrounding the lake and alpine peaks in the distance, it is nothing less than truly entrancing. The best way to enjoy the landscape is to walk along the asphalt path which leads right around the lake, a circuit that takes about an hour to complete. The most stunning views are from the western end, with the church spire on Bled Island (Blejski otok) set against the stupendous backdrop of the snowcapped Karavanke Alps.

On the lake's southern shore, visitors can stop by Vila Bled. The estate was occupied by Yugoslav president Josip Broz Tito (1890–1980) in 1947 and has now been converted into an upmarket hotel.

🏰 Bled Castle

Grajska cesta 25. **Tel** (04) 572 9782.
Open Nov–Mar: 8am–6pm daily; Apr–Oct: 8am–8pm daily. 🎧 🚫 🖥 🎁
w blejski-grad.si

Dramatically located on a sheer cliff overlooking the lake's eastern end, Bled Castle (Blejski grad) began as the 11th-century stronghold of the Bishops of Brixen, who ruled over the area until 1803. Rebuilt by various owners over the years, the castle now houses an absorbing

Bled Castle, perched on a cliff above the town

museum and a restaurant. The former features an audiovisual display, detailing both the history of the castle and the development of tourism in the region. Replicas of historical costumes recall the Slavs who first settled in the area in the 6th century, while a natural-history section exhibits the 5th-century skeleton of an elk. The frescoed Gothic chapel, wine cellar and herb gallery are also worth a visit.

Outside, the castle terrace commands an outstanding view, with the lake directly below and the Karavanke mountain range looming in the distance.

Bled Island

Open Nov–Mar: 9am–4pm daily; Apr & Oct: 9am–6pm daily; May–Sep: 9am–7pm daily. 🚤 🖥
w blejskiotok.si

Perched atop the hummock-shaped Bled Island, the Church of the Assumption (Cerkev Marijinega vnebovzetja) occupies a site that has been sacred for centuries.

The island initially served pagan Slavs as a shrine, inspiring a famous episode in France Prešeren's epic poem *Baptism on the Savica (Krst pri Savici)*, in which the Slovenian prince, Črtomir, falls in love with the beautiful Bogomila, daughter of the island shrine's guardian.

After the region's conversion to Christianity, the island became a focus of Catholic pilgrimage. It has been associated with the cult of the Virgin Mary since the early Middle Ages, when a wooden chapel stood on the site of the current church. Pilgrimages boomed

Traditional canopied rowing boats on
Lake Bled

the front door of the church.
Inside are the fragmentary
remains of some 15th-century
frescoes illustrating the lives of
the Virgin Mary and Jesus Christ.

Hanging from a small tower
above the nave is the 15th-
century Wishing Bell, presented
to the church by a pilgrim
whose prayers had been
answered. It is believed that all
those who ring the bell to
honour the Blessed Virgin will
have their wishes granted.

VISITORS' CHECKLIST

Practical Information
Road map B2. 53 km (34 miles)
NW of Ljubljana.  5,500.
ℹ️ Ljubljanska cesta 27;
(04) 578 9205.
🎭 Bled Days (Jul), Ascension
(Aug 15), Birth of the Virgin (Sep 8).
W **bled.si**

Transport
✈️ Lesce-Bled. 🚃 Bled Jezero.
🚌

during the Baroque era, when
the church was expanded and
redecorated. Today, the island
remains a popular place for
pilgrimages on the Marian feast
days, notably the Ascension and
the Birth of the Virgin. These are
traditionally all-night affairs with
participants arriving late in the
evening and celebrating mass
at 4am. The island can be
reached either by motor launch
or by traditional canopied
rowing boat (*pletna*). Visitors
disembark at the bottom of a
99-step staircase that leads to

Arnold Rikli (1823–1906)

Bled owes its success as a resort to the physician Arnold Rikli.
An advocate of the benefits of sunshine, fresh air and clean
water, the Swiss "sun doctor" founded
the Institute of Natural Healing by
Lake Bled in 1855. The first visitors
sought cures for rheumatism,
migraines, insomnia, poor blood
circulation and obesity. But as word
of the spectacular scenery spread,
they were joined by tourists. Yugoslav
King Aleksander I (r.1929–34)
nominated Bled as his summer
residence in 1921, as did Tito, who
entertained world statesmen at Vila
Bled. Relics of bygone Bled include
the late 19th-century Grand Hotel
Toplice and the small spa park
beneath the castle.

Painting of Dr Arnold Rikli on display
at a college in Bled

Bled Town Centre

① Lake Bled
② Bled Castle
③ Bled Island

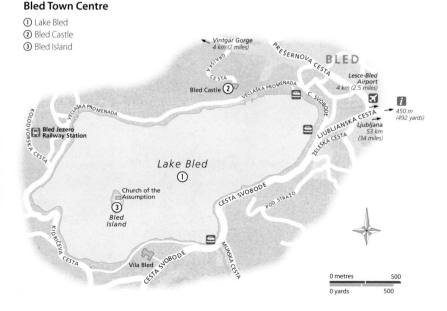

Vintgar Gorge
4 km (2 miles)

GRAJSKA CESTA

PREŠERNOVA CESTA

BLED

Bled Castle ②

VELAŠKA PROMENADA

C. SVOBODE

Lesce-Bled
Airport
4 km (2.5 miles)

ℹ️

450 m
(492 yards)

LJUBLJANSKA CESTA

ŽELEŠKA CESTA

Ljubljana
53 km
(34 miles)

VELAŠKA PROMENADA

KOLODVORSKA CESTA

🚃 Bled Jezero
Railway Station

Lake Bled
①

Church of the
Assumption

③
**Bled
Island**

CESTA SVOBODE

POD STRAŽO

KIDRIČEVA CESTA

Vila Bled

CESTA SVOBODE

MLINSKA CESTA

| 0 metres | | 500 |
| 0 yards | | 500 |

For keys to symbols *see back flap*

Hikers on a wooden walkway over the river at Vintgar Gorge

❷ Vintgar Gorge

Soteska Vintgar

Road map B2. 4 km (2 miles) NW of Bled. **Tel** (031) 344 053. 🚌 May–Sep: tourist shuttle from Bled. **Open** late Apr–Oct: 8am–7pm daily. 🚶 📱

Located just north of Bled, Vintgar Gorge is a 2-km- (1-mile-) long ravine carved by the rushing waters of the Radovna river. It was discovered by chance in February 1891 during a period of unusually low water level in the river. The local mayor and a cartographer friend were amazed at the beauty of this usually impassable ravine and established a committee to construct wooden walkways to cater to the increasing number of visitors to Bled. The gorge became a major tourist attraction as soon as it opened in August 1893.

Visiting the gorge remains an exhilarating experience as the trail winds along sheer cliffs, passing gurgling rapids and whirlpools, crisscrossing the river on bridges. The walkway culminates at the 16-m- (52-ft-) high Šum waterfall, which marks the northern end of the gorge. The cascade is at its most impressive during spring, when its thundering torrent throws up clouds of spray and even steam on very cold days. From here, Bled is within easy walking distance via a pretty footpath up Hom hill that leads to the village of Zasip and the

15th-century Church of St Catherine (Cerkev sv Katarine) from where there are good views over the area.

❸ Pokljuka Gorge

Pokljuška soteska

Road map B2. 7 km (4 miles) W of Bled. 🚌 from Bled.

Not as popular as the Vintgar gorge, the 2-km- (1-mile-) long Pokljuka gorge, which spears into the national park west of Bled, is a destination for more isolated walking in pristine scenery. Although the gorge has some walkways, most of the route is along a permanently dry, rough river bed, so walking boots are advisable.

Other sights in the gorge include the Pokljuka Cave (Pokljuška luknja), with a fallen roof that lets light into the cave;

Façade of the late-Gothic-style Šivec House, Radovljica

and tiny circular fields formed in the limestone depressions, known locally as *vrtci*, meaning little gardens. The prettiest formation is just beyond the ravine's narrowest part.

It is easiest to access the gorge from Krnica village, situated below the picturesque centre of the ravine, where the walls rise 40 m (130 ft) high. By bus, the ravine can be accessed along a short woodland path from Krnica. A car park is sign-posted above the village at the entrance of the ravine. Maps of the area are sold at the Bled information centre.

❹ Radovljica

Road map B2. 5 km (3 miles) SE of Bled. 🏛 18,000. 🚊 from Ljubljana and Kranj. 🚌 from Bled and Kranj. 🛈 Linhartov trg 9; (04) 531 5112. 🎵 Classical music (mid-Aug). 🌐 radolca.si

The pretty core of Radovljica is one of the Gorenjska region's best-preserved old towns, defensively perched 75 m (246 ft) above the Sava river valley. Cocooned from traffic, Linhartov trg is boxed in by painted Gothic and Renaissance burgher mansions that testify to medieval prosperity. The mansion at No. 23 has a fresco of St Florian dousing a fire in the 18th-century town, while No. 24, the late-Gothic Malijeva House (Malijeva hiša), retains a penalty bench used to chain criminals. The museum and gallery **Šivec House** (Šivečeva hiša) is late Gothic with Renaissance living quarters.

The square's architectural highlight is the large Thurn Mansion. Built as a ducal castle, then renovated into a palace and given a decorative Baroque façade, it houses the fascinating **Museum of Apiculture** (Čebelarski muzej). Displays of quirky carved bee-hives show, for example, a Turk in bloomers with a treasure casket. A marvellous collection of painted beehive panels helps bring to life this Slovenian folk tradition. A municipal museum on the first floor documents the life of Slovenian dramatist Anton Tomaž Linhart (1756–95).

Off the square is the late-Gothic Church of St Peter (Cerkev sv Petra). It has a Baroque high altar with a statuary by the architect of St Nicholas's Cathedral, Ljubljana, Angelo Pozzo. The choir stalls have a carved boss depicting Pozzo in a hat and blue tunic.

Environs
Located about 10 km (6 miles) south of Radovljica, Kropa is a blacksmiths' village which, in its 18th-century heyday, had 50 forge waterwheels. The **Iron Forging Museum** (Kovaški muzej) displays wares, and a smithy opposite sells decorative ironwork. The village of Brezje, 8 km (5 miles) southeast of Radovljica, annually hosts about 300,000 pilgrims at the nation's most revered shrine – a miracle-working Madonna and Child painting in the Basilica of the Virgin (Marija Pomagaj).

🏛 Šivec House
Linhartov trg 22. **Tel** (04) 532 0523. **Open** Jun & Sep: 10am–noon & 5–7pm Tue–Sun; Jul & Aug: 10am–noon & 6–8pm Tue–Sun; Oct–May: 10am–noon & 4–6pm Tue–Sun.
🏛 **W** muzeji-radovljica.si

🏛 Museum of Apiculture
Linhartov trg 1. **Tel** (04) 532 0520. **Open** Jan & Feb: 8am–3pm Tue–Fri; Mar, Apr, Nov & Dec: 8am–3pm Tue, Thu & Fri, 10am–noon & 3–5pm Wed, Sat & Sun; May–Oct: 10am–6pm Tue–Fri. **W** muzeji-radovljica.si

🏛 Iron Forging Museum
Kropa 10. **Tel** (04) 533 7200. **Open** Jan & Feb: 8am–3pm Tue–Fri; Mar, Apr, Nov & Dec: 10am–noon & 3–5pm Wed, Sat & Sun, 8am–3pm Tue, Thu & Fri; May–Oct: 10am–6pm Tue–Fri.
🏛 **W** muzeji-radovljica.si

Model at the Tržič Museum, dedicated to shoe-making

🟠 Tržič

Road map B2. 23 km (14 miles) E of Bled. 🚊 15,000. 🚌 from Kranj & Radovljica. **ℹ** Trg svobode 18; (04) 597 1536. **W** trzic.si

Lying just below the foothills on the Austrian border, the riverside town of Tržič was synonymous with the artisan handicrafts of wheel- and shoe-making. Both withered in the face of industrial mass production leaving the town a sleepy one-street place – only carriage-sized portals on the high street, Trg svobode, hint at the booming 18th and 19th centuries.

The modest **Tržič Museum** (Tržiški muzej), located in a former tannery at the upper end of the town, illustrates shoe-making as well as the leatherwork trade that fed it.

Around 3 km (2 miles) north lies the Dovžan Gorge (Dovžanova soteska). This narrow ravine is a protected natural monument due to the abundance of Palaeozoic fossils found here, which were laid down when the area was covered by a warm shallow sea. Carved out by the rushing Tržiska Bistrica river, the gorge begins just beyond a road tunnel.

🏛 Tržič Museum
Muzejska ulica 11. **Open** 9am–3pm Mon, Tue, Thu & Fri, 9am–5pm Wed. 🏛

Painted Beehive Panels

No folk tradition is more Slovenian than that of painting beehive panels. During the mid-1600s, hives were created as shelf-like units allowing bee-keepers to harvest individual honeycombs without damaging the entire hive. Panels were – and still are – coloured to guide bees home but the practice of painting on to their front panels emerged in the mid-1700s and reached its zenith during the 19th century. Religious motifs and battle scenes are popular themes, but the jokes and satirical images appeal the most: a hunter carried on a stretcher by his quarry, for example, or the gossip whose tongue is sharpened by the devil.

Painted beehive panels in the Museum of Apiculture, Radovljica

⑥ Triglav National Park

Triglavski narodni park

Established in 1961, Slovenia's only national park is centred on the country's highest mountain, the 2,864-m- (9,396-ft-) high Triglav. Starkly beautiful outcrops of bare limestone characterize the higher altitudes of the park, while its lower reaches encompass forests of spruce and beech, which are home to a fantastic range of flora and fauna. An outstanding network of picturesque trails, valleys, deep-blue lakes and peaks makes Triglav National Park one of the most visited places in the country.

Alpinum Juliana
Located on the southern approaches of the Vršič Pass, this lush botanical garden showcases the diverse flora of the Slovenian Alps. About 600 botanical species can be found here.

ITALY

PLANICA VALLEY

TAMAR VALLEY

Vršič

Strmec

Log pod Mangartom

MLINARICA GORGE

Trenta

Kršovec

ZADN VALL

Zgornja Bavšica

206

TRENTA VALLEY

Soča

Soča

Great Lake

Pristava Lepena

Black L

Komar 1,520 m (4,987 ft)

△ Krn 2,182 m (7,159 ft)

LOWER BOHINJ MOUNT

Kranjsk Go

Soča Trail
This 20-km- (12-mile-) long trail runs along the Soča river as it carves its way through the pine-fringed Trenta Valley to the tiny hamlet of Kršovec.

| 0 kilometres | 5 |
| 0 miles | 5 |

Valley of the Triglav Lakes
One of the park's most captivating sights, this sequence of seven glacial lakes is surrounded by boulders and spruce trees.

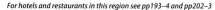

Vrata Valley
A classic glacial valley on the northern side of Triglav, Vrata Valley is overlooked by towering limestone rock formations.

VISITORS' CHECKLIST

Practical Information
Road map A2.
26 km (16 miles) W of Bled.
i Bled: Ljubljanska cesta 27, (04) 578 0200; Trenta: Na Logu, (05) 3889 330; Zgornja Radovna: Pocar Farm, Zgornja Radovna 25, (04) 5780 200. 🎫 🖼 at Lake Bohinj, Bled and Kranjska Gora, just outside the park.
W tnp.si

Transport
🚌 from Bled.

Gozd
Martuljek

VRATA VALLEY

Zgornja
Radovna

RADOVNA VALLEY

Radovna

②

KOT VALLEY

KRMA VALLEY

Debela Peč
△ *2,014 m*
(6,608 ft)

Triglav
2,864 m
(9,396 ft)

Bled
6 km (4 miles)

Vec
n
ft)

POKLJUKA PLATEAU

**Rudno
polje**

③

VOJE VALLEY

Gorjuše

Pršivec
1,761 m
(5,778 ft)

Studor

Ukanc

*Lake
Bohinj*

904

**Stara
Fužina**

④

Ribčev Laz

Vogel
1,922 m (6,306 ft)

Triglav
Slovenia's highest peak, Triglav is a national symbol; its three-peaked silhouette appears on the national flag.

Key

△	Peak
═══	Minor road
‒ ‒	Walking trail
‒ ‒	Cycle route
▪ ▪	Park boundary
▬ ▪	International border

KEY

① **Vršič Pass**, a spectacular mountain road cutting through the heart of the park, features an exhilarating sequence of hairpin bends.

② **The Radovna cycle route** leads visitors through verdant farmland dotted with traditional villages.

③ **The Goreljek Peat-Bog Nature Trail** passes through unspoiled wetlands, rich in cranberries, bilberries and the insect-devouring sundew plant.

④ **Lake Bohinj** (*see pp118–19*) is the largest body of water in Slovenia.

Pokljuka Plateau
This unspoiled area of pine forests and pastures is criss-crossed by nature trails. The highlight is the Pokljuka Gorge, which burrows through the plateau's northern flanks.

Triglav National Park: Lake Bohinj

Tucked into the southeastern corner of Triglav National Park, Lake Bohinj (Bohinjsko jezero) is a beautiful expanse of water with high mountains on almost all sides and surrounded by some of Slovenia's best-preserved rustic villages. Fed by clear mountain streams, it is ideal for swimming and kayaking and an excellent base from which to explore the region's hiking trails. In winter, Vogel, to the south of the lake, is a popular spot for skiing and snowboarding, while the frozen lake provides a great opportunity for ice skating.

Visitors canoeing near Ribčev Laz, at the eastern end of Lake Bohinj

Slap Savica

A popular walking trail west from Ukanc leads to Slap Savica, a pair of waterfalls surrounded by high cliffs. Their waters feed the Sava river, which flows southeast to meet the Danube at Belgrade in Serbia.

Slap Savica
1.5 km (1 mile)

Savica

UKANC

Vogel
1.5 km (1 mile)

Ukanc

The small village of Ukanc, at the lake's western end, has pebbly beaches and is surrounded by Komna Plateau and Pršivec peak.

Vogel

At an altitude of 1,922 m (6,306 ft), the Vogel resort is a paradise for skiers in winter and hikers in summer. The cable car from the shores of Lake Bohinj ascends to a plateau that offers breathtaking views of the snow-clad Triglav massif to the north.

Key

═══ Minor road

▬ Trail

Stara Fužina
With charming alpine farmhouses, Stara Fužina is one of the best-preserved traditional villages in western Slovenia. The 13th-century St Paul's Church on the outskirts of the village is also worth a visit.

VISITORS' CHECKLIST

Practical Information
Road map A2. 29 km (18 miles) SW of Bled. **i** Ribčev Laz 48; (04) 572 3370. **▲** Zlatorog camp site; (04) 572 3482. *Vogel Cable Car:* **Open** 8am–6pm daily. **⚠** Note: cable car runs every 30 minutes from May to mid-Oct and hourly at other times. *Church of St John:* **Open** Jul & Aug: 10am–noon & 4–7pm daily. **W** bohinj.si

Transport
🚆 from Lesce-Bled.
🚌 from Bled and Ljubljana.

Lake Bohinj

STARA FUŽINA

904

③

Church of
St John

P **i**
**RIBČEV
LAZ**

Kozolec
The meadows around Stara Fužina are dotted with canopied hay-drying racks or *kozolec*, a common feature of Slovenian farms.

0 metres   500
0 yards   500

KEY

① **The cable car to Vogel** begins from the southern shores of Bohinj.

② **A World War I cemetery** holds the graves of about 300 Austro-Hungarian soldiers buried between 1915 and 1917.

③ **The Church of the Holy Spirit** (Cerkev sv Duha) has a fine bell tower and contains a number of notable 15th- and 16th-century frescoes.

Ribčev Laz
The main settlement at the eastern end of Lake Bohinj, Ribčev Laz is famous for its dainty parish Church of St John (Cerkev sv Janeza), which has some late-Gothic frescoes.

For keys to symbols *see back flap*

Façade of the traditional Liznjek House, Kranjska Gora

a smoke-stained "black kitchen". Traditional furnishings such as painted trousseau chests and a grandfather clock in the living quarters date back to the 1800s, as does the religious iconography in a tiny bedroom. The former stables have displays on local author Josip Vandot (1884–1944), a popular children's writer who penned tales about an inquisitive shepherd boy called Kekec.

Liznjek House
Borovška cesta 63. **Tel** (04) 588 1999.
Open May–Oct: 10am–6pm Tue–Sat, 10am–5pm Sun; Dec–Apr: 10am–4pm Tue–Fri, 10am–5pm Sat & Sun.
gornjesavskimuzej.si

❼ Kranjska Gora

Road map A2. 39 km (24 miles) NW of Bled. 5,500. from Bled & Ljubljana. Tičarjeva ulica 2; (04) 580 9440. **kranjska-gora.si**

Beautifully located in the Sava Dolinka Valley beneath jagged alpine peaks, Kranjska Gora is the northern gateway to the Soča Valley. This former dairy village was a key supply base for the Soča Front (see p123) during World War I.

Since the 1930s it has been Slovenia's premier winter sports playground. In early March, the village hosts the Vitranc Cup in slalom and giant slalom for the ski World Cup. The World Ski-Flying Championship is held at Planica, the world's highest ski-jumping hill, 3 km (2 miles) to the west. In summer, Kranjska Gora is a popular base for hiking in Triglav National Park (see pp116–17). Starting at Mojstrana, 13 km (8 miles) east of Kranjska Gora, the Triglavska Bistrica walking trail runs up the ruggedly beautiful Vrata Valley before reaching the forbidding north face of Mount Triglav.

The Church of the Assumption (Cerkev Device Marije Vnebovzete) on the town's main square dates from Kranjska Gora's earliest days in the 14th century. A Roman-esque bell tower survives from the original building but the church has been rebuilt in Gothic style and features fine roof vaulting.

Beyond the church is **Liznjek House** (Liznjekova domačija), which provides a glimpse into the past of this traditional alpine village. This shingle-roofed residence of a wealthy landowner was built in 1781. It has a brick ground floor and

❽ Vršič Pass

Road map A2. 51 km (32 miles) NW of Bled. late Jun–Aug: from Kranjska Gora & Bovec. Tičarjeva ulica 2, Kranjska Gora; (04) 5889 440.

The drive over this 1,611-m- (5,285-ft-) high mountain saddle, with its crisp clear air and close-up views of corkscrew peaks, is arguably the most spectacular in Slovenia. The route's 50 hairpin bends are negotiable in most vehicles between May and October – snowfall can close the pass at other times, so it is best to check conditions in Kranjska Gora or Bovec (see p122) before attempting a crossing. The road is unsuitable at all times if towing a trailer or caravan.

Breathtaking view of snow-covered Alps from Vršič Pass

Originally a shepherds' track, the road south of Kranjska Gora was created to supply ammunition and food to Austro-Hungarian troops on the Soča Front during World War I. Russian prisoners of war who were put to the task of building the road suffered hard labour, starvation, frostbite and sunstroke. The 13,000 POWs also faced avalanches – one ripped through a work camp in March 1916 and claimed around 300 lives. A tiny Russian chapel (Ruska kapela) at bend 8 serves as a memorial to the victims. An Austro-Hungarian military graveyard lies beneath a hikers' hostel-restaurant before bend 22. This remote spot affords good views of Prisank mountain.

Sheltered from chilly north winds, the route downhill is less spectacular but provides occasional sweeping views down the broad valley. At bend 48 is a monument to Dr Julius Kugy (1858–1944), a botanist who promoted the beauty of these mountains while hunting for new alpine species. Off the hairpin bend below, a dirt-track leads to a car park from where begins the 2-km (1-mile) walk to the source of the Soča river, a karst spring that gushes out from a cleft and down a rockface to begin its 136-km- (85-mile-) long journey to the Adriatic Sea.

❾ Trenta

Road map A2. 64 km (40 miles) W of Bled. 🚐 115. 🚌 late Jun–Sep: from Kranjska Gora & Bovec. 🛈 Trenta 31; (05) 388 9330. 🆆 trenta-soca.si

On the banks of the Soča river is Trenta – home to shepherds and lumberjacks. Its villagers led the first hikers into the Julian Alps in the late 1800s. A votive plaque at the northern entrance to the village commemorates an injured woodcutter's lucky rescue by a walker in 1891. Just uphill from this, Slovenia's only alpine botanical garden, the **Alpinum Juliana** (Alpski botanični vrt Juliana), spills down the hillside. The 600-plus alpine and karst species found here represent the diversity of

Monument to botanist Julius Kugy, Vršič Pass

the nation's alpine flora. There are plants from the Julian and Friuli Alps, the Karst region and pre-alpine meadows as well as from the Kamnik-Savinja Alps. The best time to visit the garden is in May and early June, when the flowers are in bloom.

Downhill, in the heart of the village, **Trenta Lodge** (Dom Trenta) contains an excellent information centre for Triglav National Park. It also houses a local museum on geology and fauna, with displays on shepherd and mountaineering traditions, including a re-creation of a shepherd's dwelling.

🌼 Alpinum Juliana
Trenta. **Tel** (05) 388 9306. **Open** May–Sep: 8:30am–6:30pm daily. 🅿

🏛 Trenta Lodge
Na Logu vi Trenti. **Tel** (05) 388 9330. **Open** Apr–Oct: 10am–6pm daily; Dec–26 Apr: 10am–2pm daily. 🅿 ♿ 🆆 trenta-soca.si

❿ Kluže Fortress
Trdnjava Kluže

Road map A2. Trg golobarskih žrtev 8, Bovec; 84 km (52 miles) W of Bled. **Tel** (05) 388 6758. **Open** May, Jun, Sep & Oct: 9am–5pm Sun–Fri, 9am–6pm Sat; Jul & Aug: 9am–8pm daily. 🎭 🎭 Music and Theatre Festival Kluže (late Jul). 🆆 **kluze.net**

Impressively located between the Koritnica Gorge and Mount Rombon, Kluže Fortress is the last of a number of strongholds that once guarded the valley. It is believed that the Romans originally had a fort here, which was supplanted by a wooden fortress. Today's massively fortified bastion was built to serve as a command post during the Soča Front campaign (*see p123*). The fortress withstood Italian shelling, protected by its sheltered location and 2-m- (7-ft-) high reinforced walls.

Inside the fortress are displays on its history and on the Soča Front. The courtyard serves as the venue for mock battles organized by the Slovene Cultural and Historical Foundation in July and August. The gorge of the Koritnica river forms a 70-m- (230-ft-) deep natural moat around the fortress; the bridge across it affords breathtaking views of the Alps and the gorge.

A path off the main road leads to Fort Hermann, the twin fortress that was nearly obliterated during the Soča Front campaign.

Kluže Fortress against the backdrop of Mount Rombon

⓫ Bovec

Road map A2. 84 km (52 miles) W of Bled. 🚶 1,700. 🚌 from Tolmin & Ljubljana; from Kranjska Gora (late Jun–Aug). 🚆 Jul & Aug: 7am–5pm daily; Sep–Jun: 8am–4pm daily. 🛈 Golobarskih žrtev 8; (05) 384 1919. 🌐 **bovec.si**

Once a dairy centre, Bovec has transformed into a premier adrenaline sports destination in Slovenia mainly because of its spectacular setting between high alpine peaks and the china-blue Soča river.

Between April and October, several agencies organize whitewater rafting, kayaking and canyoning trips. There are signposted trails for mountain biking and a dedicated bike park; a brochure available in the tourist office outlines the routes. In winter the focus is on Kanin which at 2,300 m (7,546 ft) is the highest skiing destination in Slovenia. It can be reached by a cable car that also provides access to high-altitude walking paths in summer as well as a stunning view that stretches to the Adriatic Sea.

More astounding scenery lies 6 km (4 miles) south at the Boka waterfall (Slap Boka) near Žaga, which plummets 106 m (348 ft) from a cliff.

⓬ Kobarid

Road map A2. 91 km (57 miles) SW of Bled. 🚶 1,500. 🚌 from Bovec, Nova Gorica & Ljubljana. 🛈 Trg svobode 16, (05) 380 0490; Gregorčičeva 8, (05) 389 0167. 🌐 **dolina-soce.com**

Italian influence can be seen in Kobarid's shuttered houses, dusty pastel paintwork and fine restaurants. Italy occupied this town between the world wars and during the battle for the Soča Front, until the final blitzkrieg in Europe broke the stalemate between Italy and Austro-Hungary.

The excellent **Kobarid Museum** (Kobariški muzej), a block north of the central square, provides detailed information on the war. Other war reminders can be seen along the **Kobarid Historical Walk**

Boka waterfall plummeting down a cliff

(Kobariška zgodovinska pot), whose 5-km (3-mile) circuit starts from Trg svobode.

🏛 Kobarid Museum
Gregorčičeva 10. 🛈 (05) 389 0000. **Open** Apr–Sep: 9am–6pm Mon–Fri, 9am–7pm Sat & Sun; Oct–Mar: 10am–5pm Mon–Fri, 10am–6pm Sat & Sun. 🚹 🌐 **kobariski-muzej.si**

🚶 Kobarid Historical Walk
Gregorčičeva 8. 🛈 (05) 389 0167. **Open** by appt only. 🚹 🎫 🌐 **potmiru.si**

⓭ Tolmin

Road map A3. 75 km (47 miles) SW of Bled. 🚶 3,800. 🚌 from Bovec, Nova Gorica & Ljubljana. 🛈 Petra Skalarja 4; (05) 380 0480. 🎪 Metalcamp (mid-Jul), Reggae Riversplash (mid-Jul). 🌐 **dolina-soce.com**

This area's administrative centre, Tolmin warrants a visit for its absorbing archaeological collection in the **Tolmin Museum**. Displayed on the first floor are grave finds, jewellery and pottery that attest to the presence of sophisticated prehistoric cultures. Some items were imported, such as an exquisite Attic cup that has become the trademark of the museum.

Painted Attic cup, Tolmin Museum

Environs
Located nearby are the Tolmin Gorge (Tolminska korita) and Dante's Cave (Zadlaška jama).

🏛 Tolmin Museum
Mestni trg 4. **Tel** (05) 381 1360. 🚹 🌐 **tol-muzej.si**

⓮ Most na Soči

Road map A3. 70 km (44 miles) SW of Bled. 🚶 240. 🚆 from Bohinjska Bistrica & Nova Gorica. 🚌 from Tolmin & Idrija.

One of the most advanced prehistoric settlements in Slovenia developed on this peninsula created by the confluence of the Soča and Idrija rivers. Over 7,000 grave sites from the Bronze and Iron Age have been excavated, ranking it among Europe's most important settlements. The Romans were here too, and an archaeological trail visits the remains of a Roman villa among its 21 sites. Other sites on this cultural treasure hunt include a re-created Bronze Age Hallstatt dwelling in the local school (accessed through the Tolmin Museum) and the Church of St Lucy (Cerkev sv Lucije).

⓯ Kanal

Road map A3. 95 km (59 miles) SW of Bled. 🚶 1,500. 🚆 from Nova Gorica. 🚌 from Most na Soči. 🛈 Pionirska 2; (05) 398 1213. 🏊 High Diving World Cup (early Jul). 🌐 **tic-kanal.si**

There is an iconic single-span bridge that crosses into this small town, from which competitors in the High Diving World Cup plunge 23 m (56 ft) into the Soča river below. On the opposite side of the bridge, an archway beside the church is a post-World War I rebuild of the 16th-century original. Through this is the Kontrada courtyard, the oldest part of the town, which began as a castle in 1140 and developed into a square village protected by walls and two gatehouse towers. The tower on the north side survives and houses the **Galerija Rika Debenjaka**, showcasing the work of Kanal-born 20th-century artist Riko Debenjak.

🏛 Galerija Rika Debenjaka
Pionirska ulica bb. **Tel** (05) 163 6930. **Open** 10am–noon Tue, 5–7pm Fri. 🚹

The Soča Front

In January 1915, in a bid to weaken Austro-Hungary with a war on two fronts, the Allies lured Italy into World War I with the promise of territorial gains. Italy poured 50 per cent of its forces over the border into the Soča Valley in Austro-Hungarian Slovenia. So, the Soča Front (Isonzo in Italian), a 90-km (56-mile) frontline extending from Mount Rombon near Bovec to the Adriatic, came into being and witnessed some very brutal fighting. The casualties in the 12 offensives during the 30-month war are estimated to have been around 1.2 million. After rapid Italian gains, the front stagnated into a war of attrition between two entrenched armies.

The 12th Offensive

On 24 October 1917 the 12th Offensive began. A lightning-fast action routed the Italians near Bovec. The next day the 14th Austro-German army (formed when Austro-Hungarian Emperor Karl I sought help from Germany's Wilhelm II) seized Kobarid, and by 28 October the Italians had been chased back to the Friulian plain, a chaotic retreat described by author Ernest Hemingway, who served on the front, in A Farewell to Arms. The "miracle of Kobarid" was one of the most decisive actions in World War I.

Kobarid Museum displays maps and relief models showing the positions of the troops as well as weapons and other memorabilia.

Machine gun posts have been restored to their former positions and can be visited near Bovec and Kobarid.

Key

- ■ Austro-German army
- ■ Italian army
- --- Battlefront
- -- International border
- △ Peak

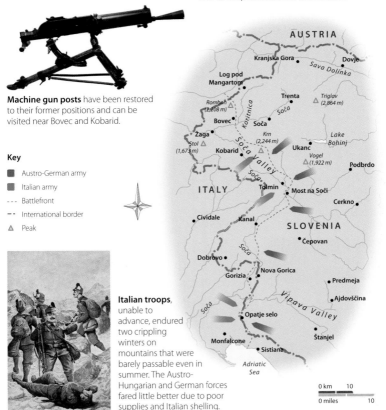

Italian troops, unable to advance, endured two crippling winters on mountains that were barely passable even in summer. The Austro-Hungarian and German forces fared little better due to poor supplies and Italian shelling.

⓰ Kranj

Road map B3. 27 km (17 miles) SE of Bled. 🚍 53,000. 🚆 from Ljubljana. 🚌 from Ljubljana, Bled, Kamnik & Škofja Loka. ℹ️ Glavni trg 2; (04) 238 0450. 🅦 **tourism-kranj.si**

The country's fourth-largest settlement and an industrial centre, Kranj has an appealing Old Town spread along a promontory, the site of early Celtic and Roman settlements.

Kranj is known for its links with France Prešeren (see p53), the most celebrated of Slovenia's poets. The modest residence in which he spent the last three years of his life, **Prešeren House** (Prešernova hiša), contains his personal effects as well as a display dedicated to his muse Julija Primic, the unrequited love of his life.

The heart of the Old Town is Glavni trg. Located on this square is the former city hall, which houses the **Gorenjska Museum** (Gorenjski muzej), with displays on regional archaeology and charming exhibits of folk culture. The museum has a ceremonial Renaissance hall as well as sculptures by the Modernist sculptor Lojze Dolinar (1893–1970), a student of the Croatian sculptor Ivan Meštrovič (1883–1962). Also on the square is the grandest hall church in Slovenia, the Church of St Cantianus and Disciples (Cerkev sv Kancijana in tovarišev). The Star of Beautiful Angels, a fresco depicting angels, dating from the 15th century, adorns the ceiling of the nave. The church

Exterior of the chapel at Little Castle, Kamnik

was built over the country's largest Slavic graveyard. Visits to the ossuary can be arranged through the Gorjenska Museum.

Off the square is the Church of the Holy Rosary (Roženvenska cerkev) and next to it, a ceremonial staircase by Jože Plečnik (see p77).

🏛 **Prešeren House**
Prešernova ulica 7. **Tel** (051) 615 388. **Open** 10am–6pm Tue–Sun. 🖼

🏛 **Gorenjska Museum**
Tomšičeva 42. **Tel** (01) 201 3950. **Open** 10am–6pm Tue–Sun. 🖼 🅦 **gorenjski-muzej.si**

⓱ Krvavec

Road map C2. 59 km (37 miles) SE of Bled. 🚠 winter: 8am–5pm daily; summer: 7am–5pm Mon–Fri, 8am–6pm Sat & Sun. ℹ️ Grad 76; (04) 252 5911. 🚫 🖼 🅦 **rtc-krvavec.si**

Its proximity to Ljubljana and Kranj ensures that this ski destination, located on the 1,853-m- (6,079-ft-) high Krvavec mountain, is one of the busiest in Slovenia. Access to the mountain summit, marked by a tall radio antenna, is by cable car from a small ski resort at Gospinca at an altitude of

1,480 m (4,856 ft). It can be reached on a narrow twisting road, or, during snowfall, by a cable car north of Cerklje. From Gospinca, marked trails ascend to the summit; the blue, 3-km- (2-mile-) long Path of History (Poti zgodovine) takes visitors past a modern chapel and the excavated site of a 10th-century settlement. The mountain is also popular in summer due to the good walking and mountain-biking opportunities it affords.

⓲ Kamnik

Road map C3. 52 km (32 miles) SE of Bled. 🚍 26,600. 🚆 from Ljubljana. 🚌 from Ljubljana & Kranj. ℹ️ Glavni trg 2; (01) 831 8250. 🛒 Tue & Sat. 🎭 Medieval Days (2nd weekend of Jun), Kamfest (mid-Aug), National Costumes Festival (2nd weekend of Sep). 🅦 **kamnik-tourism.si**

This pleasing old-fashioned town was a regional capital in the Middle Ages. The Franciscan Monastery (Frančiškanski samostan) off Glavni trg, the town's main square, has a library that houses a rare copy of the Bible (1584) by the Slovenian translator Jurij Dalmatin (1547–89); visits can be arranged through the

The simple interior of a room in Prešeren House, Kranj

tourist office. The attached Baroque Church of St James (Cerkev sv Jakoba) houses the **Chapel of the Holy Sepulchre** (Kapela Božjega groba), which was created in 1952 by Jože Plečnik and is full of motifs of Resurrection.

Perched atop the rocky hillock at the end of Glavni trg is the so-called **Little Castle** (Mali grad). All that remains of this fortification, first documented in 1202, is a two-storey chapel. Its portal bears a Romanesque carving of angels and a crucifix, but the architecture within is Gothic and adorned with restored Baroque frescoes. Another reason to visit the chapel is the panorama it affords over Kamnik, up to the Kamniško-Savinjske Alps.

Šutna, the town's main street and Kamnik's former medieval thoroughfare, ends beneath the **Intermunicipal Kamnik Museum** (Medobčinski muzej Kamnik). The museum has displays of archaeological finds, memorabilia of the 19th-century bour-geoisie and bentwood furniture from a local factory. Outside the museum is a lapidarium with specimens of traditional granaries from the Tuhinj Valley.

Altar at the Chapel of the Holy Sepulchre

Environs
Volčji Potok Arboretum, 4 km (2 miles) south of Kamnik, and en route to Radomlje, is Slovenia's finest botanical park. Its 88 ha (218 acres) are beautifully and creatively landscaped in a number of gardening styles.

🔒 Little Castle
Glavni trg. **Open** mid-Jun–mid-Sep: 9am–noon & 2–7pm daily. 🌐

🏛 Intermunicipal Kamnik Museum
Muzejska pot 3. **Tel** (01) 831 7662. **Closed** Mon. 🌐
W muzej-kamnik-on.net

🌳 Volčji Potok Arboretum
Volčji Potok 3. **Tel** (01) 831 2345. **Open** summer only. **Closed** during snowfall. 🌐 📷
W arboretum-vp.si

The lush green forest and the Kamniška Bistrica river

⑲ Velika Planina

Road map C2. 76 km (47 miles) E of Bled. 🚌 from Kamnik. 🚠 open daily. ℹ Kamniška Bistrica 2; (01) 832 7258. 📷 💻 🌐 ⚠ **W** velikaplanina.si

The world's fourth-longest unsupported cable car, which starts midway up the Kamniška Bistrica Valley, provides access to the 1,666-m- (5,466-ft-) high Velika Planina. This mountain plateau is the best destination from which to get a sense of the Kamniško-Savinjske Alps.

Velika Planina is a popular destination for skiing in winter and walking in summer. During summer the local herdsmen migrate to their picturesque settlements to graze cattle on the plateau's lush alpine meadows. Most of the unique, shingle-roofed wooden huts were rebuilt

after they were destroyed during World War II – the Germans suspected that this area was a base for resistance fighters. **Preskar's Hut** (Preskarjev stan), which survived the onslaught, has been preserved as a museum. It is located about an hour's walk south of the upper cable car terminal, near the Church of Our Lady of the Snows (Kapela Marije Snežne).

🏠 Preskar's Hut
Kamniška Bistrica 2. **Open** Jul & Aug: 10am–4pm Sat & Sun. 🌐

⑳ Kamniška Bistrica

Road map C2. 65 km (40 miles) E of Bled. 🚌 from Kamnik. ℹ Glavni trg 2; (01) 831 8250. 📷 🌐

Around 4 km (2 miles) north of the lower cable car station to Velika Planina, the Kamniška Bistrica river valley terminates in a stupendous amphitheatre of Alps that are over 2,000 m (6,561 ft) high. Serious hikers can ascend from the car park at the terminal through pine woods and climb up to the saddles that lie between the jagged summits. A short walk takes visitors to the Orglice waterfall (slap Orglice), which falls 30 m (98 ft) from a cleft. A similar walk leads to a woodland hunting lodge, known as Plečnik's Mansion (Plečnikov dvorec), built in 1932 for the Yugoslav King Aleksander I by Jože Plečnik.

Shingle-roofed herdsmen's huts, Velika Planina

㉑ A Tour of the Kamniško-Savinjske Alps

As the road twists uphill east of Kamnik, the farming villages and agricultural landscapes of the Dreta Valley give way to alpine settlements in the valley on the northern side of the Kamniško-Savinjske Alps. Off its upper reaches are two of the most beautiful alpine valleys in Slovenia – Robanov kot and Logarska dolina – each enclosed by a jagged wall of peaks. Logarska dolina literally means Loggers' Valley, referring to the timber industry, which, along with farming, was the main livelihood of the people of the valley. Today, tourism is the area's largest industry.

⑧ Rinka waterfall
A footpath from the car park at the head of the valley leads to this 80-m- (262-ft-) high waterfall.

⑦ Logarska dolina
Lush meadows, speckled by wildflowers and clear rivers, backdropped by a wall of the Alps at its head, make this U-shaped valley one of the most picturesque.

AUSTRIA

Solčava

428

Savinja

KAMNIŠKO-SAVINJSKE ALPS

Ojstrica
2,350 m

Key

▬▬ Tour route
══ Other road
△ Peak
▬·▬ International border

⑥ Robanov kot
Accessed only via footpaths, this alpine valley, with steep wooded slopes framing the 2,350-m- (7,710-ft-) high Ojstrica mountain, is popular with walkers who seek unspoiled nature.

⑤ Snow cave
Visitors carry carbide lamps to view the ancient limestone features and ice formations, preserved year long because of very low temperatures, inside this cave in Raduha mountain. Access to the cave is via a forest road.

① Gornji Grad
The main attractions in this small town are the Cathedral of Sts Hermagor and Fortunat, and the summer residence of the Ljubljana bishops. The latter houses an ethnographic museum displaying old religious books.

② Radmirje
This is a pretty agricultural village known for its traditional *kozolci* haystacks and the Church of St Francis Xavier. Its treasury contains a golden chalice donated by the 18th-century Habsburg Empress Maria-Teresa and mantles gifted by Polish and French royalty.

Tips for Drivers

Starting point: Gornji Grad.
Length: 40 km (25 miles).
Duration: 2 hours; allow half a day each to walk around Robanov kot and Logarska dolina.
Driving conditions: the roads are narrow and winding but well signposted.
Stopping-off points: there are restaurants and cafés in the towns, and a tourist office in Luče ob Savinji.
Visitor information: Logarska dolina 9; (03) 838 9004;
Ⓦ **logarska-dolina.si**

③ Ljubno ob Savinji
Until as late as the 1950s, Ljubno ob Savinji, located at the confluence of the Ljubnica and Savinja rivers, maintained a tradition of *flosarji* (rafters) who navigated felled logs to markets as far afield as Hungary. A small museum documents the tradition's history, with displays on how the rafters lived while afloat.

④ Luče ob Savinji
A small town in the upper Savinja Valley, Luče ob Savinji is where most of the local administrative infrastructure, including a bank, supermarkets, cafés and an outstanding inn, is located.

Snow-covered peaks of Mount Triglav ▶

COASTAL SLOVENIA AND THE KARST

Slovenia is often described as a transitional zone between Mediterranean and alpine Europe. This is most apparent in southwestern Slovenia, where the craggy ridges and highland meadows of the limestone plateau, known as the Karst, descend suddenly to meet a lush coastal strip rich in olive groves, palms as well as a number of important historic towns.

Western Slovenia has long been the meeting point of Slav and Italian cultures. The region's inclusion in Slovenia was largely the result of the partisan struggles of World War II and memories of the Communist-led liberation movement are still cherished. War memorials are an important feature of regional towns and many streets and squares are still named after partisan heroes. Many Italian speakers left the coastal towns when they were awarded to Slovenia after World War II, but Italian is the official language and street signs are bilingual.

The region's arid sunny climate produces some of Slovenia's best-known wines, including the famous crisp white wines from the Goriška Brda and Vipava regions, and the sharp red teran from the coast. The spectacular mix of cultural influences is evident in the food as well, with menus fusing seafood from the Adriatic with truffles, mushrooms and home-cured ham, *pršut*, from the inland towns and villages.

Slovenia's short Adriatic coastline is packed with variety. Historic ports such as Koper and Piran, which were ruled by Venice for five centuries, still bear that city's architectural imprint. Nearby, Portorož is Slovenia's prime beach resort, offering boisterous nightlife in summer and soothing spa tourism the whole year round. Inland, the Karst region is riddled with gorges and caverns, of which the renowned show-caves at Postojna and Škocjan are the most visited. A dramatically situated castle at Predjama, mercury mines at Idrija and the white horses of Lipica add to the broad palette of attractions.

Terraced vineyards in the Goriška Brda winemaking region

◀ Predjama Castle, carved into a cave, northwest of Postojna

Exploring Coastal Slovenia and the Karst

Ranging from limestone plateaus to vine-covered slopes and from hilltop villages to coastal towns, southwestern Slovenia offers a diverse landscape to its many visitors. Koper, a bustling city with a well-preserved medieval Old Town at its heart, is the main centre of the region. All of the coast's attractions, especially the evocative, peninsular towns of Izola and Piran, are within easy reach of the city. Just inland are some of Slovenia's most compelling day-trip attractions such as Štanjel, Lipica and the Škocjan and Postojna caves. Equally perfect for touring are the country roads of the Vipava Valley and the Goriška Brda hills, both important wine-producing regions. Roads in the Goriška Brda and northern Karst regions are particularly scenic, winding their way around hills or following meandering rivers.

Sights at a Glance

Villages, Towns and Cities

1. Piran pp134–5
2. Portorož
4. Sečovlje
5. Izola
6. Ankaran
7. Koper pp138–9
8. Hrastovlje
9. Lokev
10. Lipica
11. Sežana
13. Vipava
14. Ajdovščina
15. Vipavski Križ
16. Štanjel
17. Nova Gorica
19. Idrija
20. Cerkno
32. Ilirska Bistrica

Castles

22. Predjama Castle pp152–3
30. Snežnik Castle

Tour

18. A Tour of the Goriška Brda Region p149

Parks

25. Pivka Park of Military History
27. Rakov Škocjan Regional Park

Areas of Natural Beauty

3. Cape Seča
12. Škocjan Caves pp142–3
23. Postojna Caves pp154–5
24. Pivka Cave
26. Planina Cave
28. Lake Cerknica
29. Križna Cave
31. Snežnik Plateau
33. Reka river valley

Sites of Interest

21. Franja Partisan Hospital

Holy Trinity Chuch in Hrastovlje

Statue of Tartini in Tartinijev trg, Piran

Key

≡≡ Motorway

≡≡ Dual carriageway

— Main road

≡ Minor road

⟋ Railway

:::: Road tunnel

■■ International border

△ Peak

Getting Around

Despite its hilly topography, southwestern Slovenia is easy to get around, and most of its settlements are a 30- to 60-minute drive from each other. Regular buses and trains run from Ljubljana to the region's main centres. It is also possible to get to Karst destinations such as Štanjel and Lipica on public transport, although visitors keen to explore caves at Škocjan, Vilenica, Pivka and elsewhere will either need their own transport or have to join a tour. The main two-lane highways from Ljubljana to Koper and from Ljubljana to Nova Gorica ensure easy progress for drivers at all times of year, although single-lane roads, especially on the coast, tend to get clogged with traffic in summer.

For keys to symbols *see back flap*

❶ Piran

A delightful warren of pastel-coloured houses squeezed on to a small peninsula, Piran represents coastal Slovenia at its most charming. It has largely preserved its medieval street plan, with narrow alleys emerging into unexpected squares. A walled town with a grand cathedral, Piran grew weathly on the salt produced at Sečovlje *(see pp136–7)* and shipped to Venice. Piran became part of Slovenia in 1954 and a majority of the Italian-speaking population left town, to be replaced by Slovenians from the interior. Long an important port, the town retains a few fishing boats and some excellent seafood restaurants.

Tartinijev trg with St George's Cathedral in the background

🏛 Tartinijev trg

Piran is centred around the oval-shaped Tartinijev trg, which occupies the former inner harbour *(mandrač)*. The harbour was filled in at the end of the 19th century to free the town of the stench of stagnant water, and the resulting space was named after local-born violinist and composer, Giuseppe Tartini (1692–1770). The square's focal point is the 19th-century statue by Venetian artist Antonio dal Zotto portraying the composer with a violin bow, as if addressing an audience of students.

On the western side of the square is the Neo-Renaissance Town Hall (Občinska palača), built in 1879. The building's four Corinthian columns are decorated with cherubs holding garlands. Jutting out on to the square's northern side is the wine-red 14th-century

Venetian House (Benečanka hiša), boasting delicate Gothic windows and a balustraded, L-shaped balcony with stone-carved human and animal heads.

Nearby, the Neo-Classical St Peter's Church (Cerkev sv Petra) contains a 14th-century crucifix that shows Jesus nailed to an unusual fork-shaped cross thought to symbolize the Tree of Life.

🏛 Tartini House

Kajuhova 12. **Tel** (05) 663 3570.
Open Jun–Aug: daily; Sep–May: Tue–Sun. 🖼

Tucked away in a small plaza north of Tartinijev trg, Tartini House (Tartinijeva hiša) has a modest collection of the composer's heirlooms, including one of his violins. Also on display are Tartini's death mask, old musical scores, letters and artworks that were inspired by Tartini's music.

🏛 Piran Art Gallery

Tartinijev trg 3. **Tel** (05) 671 2080.
Herman Pečarič Gallery: Cankarjevo nabrežje. **Open** Jun–Aug: 5–10pm Tue–Sat, 8–10pm Sun; Sep–May: 11am–5pm Tue–Sat, 11am–1pm Sun.
W obalne-galerije.si

Located just off the square, the Piran Art Gallery (Obalne galerije Piran), with a regular programme of exhibitions by local and international artists, is one of the best places to see contemporary art in south-western Slovenia.

A branch of the gallery is located a short distance south of Tartinijev trg in the **Herman Pečarič Gallery**, housed in a beautifully restored late 19th-century house. The gallery's schedule of contemporary exhibitions is augmented by a display of paintings and graphics bequeathed to the town by local artist Herman Pečarič (1908–81), best known for his Istrian landscapes and seascapes.

🏛 St George's Cathedral

Adamičeva ulica. **Tel** (05) 673 3440.
Open 10am–5pm Wed–Mon. 🖼 📷

Narrow streets climb uphill from Tartinijev trg towards St George's Cathedral (Stolna cerkev sv Jurija), a single-nave structure begun in 1641. It has splendid side altars that feature several depictions of St George by Venetian Baroque painters. The church can be accessed via a passageway from the small Parish Museum (Župnijski muzej) in the baptistry. The museum displays the church silverware, including an

Interior of the 17th-century St George's Cathedral

18th-century statuette of St George studded with semi-precious stones.

Topped by a statue of the Archangel Michael, the church's freestanding campanile is a faithful copy of that in St Mark's Cathedral in Venice.

🏠 Town Wall
Adamičeva ulica. **Open** daily. 🎫
A steep walk uphill from the cathedral is a 200-m- (660-ft-) long stretch of the Town Wall, built in 1470. Visitors can scale the gate tower and walk along a stretch of the parapet, which offers a sumptuous panorama of the town and surrounding coast.

🏛 Prvomajski trg
Northwest of Tartinijev trg is a maze of alleys and a trio of minor squares, of which the largest, Prvomajski trg, has an elaborate Baroque fountain. Built in 1776 on top of the town's balustraded cistern, the fountain is fronted by an imposing pair of statues symbolizing Law and Justice. A stone cherub holding an amphora stands on one corner of the balustrade. The guttering of a nearby house is fed into pipes that point down towards the cherub, so that rainwater from the gutter gushes out of the amphora.

Display of diving suits at the Museum of Underwater Activities

🐟 Piran Aquarium
Kidričevo nabrežje 4. **Tel** (05) 673 2572. **Open** daily. 🎫
Located beside the harbour is the Piran Aquarium (Akvarij Piran), with a large selection of fish and crustaceans indigenous to the Adriatic. A large tank has shark, grey mullet and sea bass swimming freely. Colourful, well labelled and educational, it is ideal for children to visit.

🏛 Sergej Mašera Maritime Museum
Cankarjevo nabrežje 3. **Tel** (05) 671 0040. **Open** Tue–Sun. 🎫
🌐 **pomorskimuzej.si**
On the southeastern side of the harbour, this museum (Pomorski muzej Sergej Mašera) recounts the town's history as a trading centre and fishing port. Many exhibits are displayed in glass-covered compartments on the floor.

The museum is dedicated to Yugoslav Navy Lieutenant Sergej Mašera, who drowned in April 1941 when he destroyed his ship off the Croatian coast to prevent it from falling into enemy hands.

🏛 Museum of Underwater Activities
Župančičeva 24. **Tel** (04) 168 5379. **Open** Jun–Sep: daily; Oct–May: Fri–Sun. 🎫 🌐 **muzejpodvodnih dejavnosti.si**

The small but absorbing collection in this museum (Muzej podvodnih dejavnosti) is dedicated to the history of diving in the Adriatic Sea, exhibiting deep-sea diving suits and helmets. A section is devoted to underwater warfare, with models of submarines and the uniforms of their crews on display.

Piran Town Centre
① Tartinijev trg
② Tartini House
③ Piran Art Gallery
④ St George's Cathedral
⑤ Town Wall
⑥ Prvomajski trg
⑦ Piran Aquarium
⑧ Sergej Mašera Maritime Museum
⑨ Museum of Underwater Activities

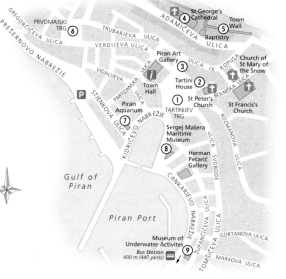

0 metres 100
0 yards 100

For keys to symbols *see back flap*

❷ Portorož

Road map A5. 2 km (1 mile) SE of Piran. 🚊 3,000. ✈ 🚌 from Koper, Ljubljana & Piran. 🛈 Obala 16; (05) 674 0231. 🖳 **portoroz.si**

Draped along a curve of Piran Bay, Portorož is Slovenia's biggest and most stylish beach resort. Despite the presence of a grand Habsburg-era hotel – the Kempinski Palace, built in 1911 (see p194) – most of Portorož dates from the post-World War II period; a number of modern hotels, cafés and casinos border the palm-lined main boulevard. There is a large crescent of beach made up of imported sand – there are no naturally sandy beaches on this part of the Adriatic. Boutiques selling major fashion labels and jewellery cater to an increasingly upmarket clientele.

As well as being very busy in summer, Portorož is a popular spa resort throughout the year, thanks to a warm microclimate and the therapeutic qualities of the local seawater.

The **Portorož Auditorium** (Avditorij) has a year-round programme of music, drama and film, and in summer, stages concerts in its outdoor amphitheatre.

🎭 **Portorož Auditorium**
Senčna pot 10. **Tel** (05) 676 6777.
🖳 **avditorij.si**

Black-winged stilt at the beautiful Sečovlje Salt Pan Nature Park

❸ Cape Seča
Rt Seča

Road map A5. 5 km (2 miles) SE of Piran. 🚌 from Portorož.

Dominating the horizon south of Portorož is Cape Seča, a hilly peninsula with holiday cottages, vineyards and olive groves. The olive-covered western flanks of the cape provide stunning views of the Sečovlje salt pans, which fill the bay that forms the border between Slovenia and Croatia.

A path leads around the cape from the southern side of Portorož's yachting marina on to an open stretch of seafront beneath grey-brown cliffs. Just beyond the cape's western-pointing tip is the Cactus Garden (Vrt kaktusov), a privately owned collection of

prickly plants that is open to the public during the summer months. Another route from Portorož goes over the ridge of the cape, passing **Forma Viva**, an open-air sculpture park. The park features over 130 works, many of which are strikingly abstract.

🏛 **Forma Viva**
Seča. **Tel** (05) 671 2080.
🖳 **obalne-galerije.si**

❹ Sečovlje

Road map A5. 9 km (6 miles) SE of Piran. 🚊 590. 🚌 from Portorož. Sečovlje Salt Pan Nature Park: **Tel** (05) 672 1330. **Open** 7am–7pm daily. 🖳 **kpss.si**

A small village just short of the Croatian border, Sečovlje is famous for the salt pans that stretch across the neighbouring Gulf of Piran. This arrestingly beautiful man-made grid of shallow pools is important both as a wildlife sanctuary and an industrial heritage site. Although salt extraction still takes place in a section of the pans, since 2001 they have been protected under the Sečovlje Salt Pan Nature Park (Krajinski park Sečoveljske soline).

The main entrance to the park is at the northern end of the pans and is easy to reach on

Visitors enjoying themselves at Portorož's popular promenade

For hotels and restaurants in this region see p194 and pp204–5

foot or by bike from Portorož. From the entrance, a dyke-top path leads towards the visitors' centre, which has a display on conservation issues. A second entrance at the southern end of the salt pans is by the Croatian border – the access road is in a no-man's land between the Slovene and Croatian frontier posts. This leads to the **Sečovlje Salt Museum** (Sečoveljske muzej), located in one of the blocks where seasonal workers used to live.

A unique area of man-made wetland, the pans are home to flora typical of salty marshland environments, and also serve as an important stop-off for migrating birds in spring and autumn. Nesting species include the yellow-legged gull, the common tern and the Kentish plover; white egrets often visit the area to hunt.

🏛 **Sečovlje Salt Museum**
Sečovlje. **Tel** (05) 671 0040. **Open** Jun–Aug: 9am–8pm daily; May, Sep & Oct: 9am–6pm daily. **Closed** Nov–Apr. 📷
📷 🖥 **pommuz-pi.si**

❺ Izola

Road map A5. 11 km (7 miles) NE of Piran. 🚗 14,600. 🚌 from Koper.
ℹ Sončno nabrežje 4; (05) 640 1050.
🎬 Kino Otok Film Festival (Jun).
🖥 **izola.eu**

A lively fishing port squeezed on to a thumb-shaped peninsula, Izola is a typical Mediterranean town of narrow alleys, shuttered windows and potted palms. It is one of the most pleasant spots in Slovenia for a seaside stroll, with its horseshoe-shaped harbour bordered by seafront gardens fragrant with lavender, sage and rosemary. Stretched around the peninsula's northern end is a sequence of concrete bathing platforms, each boasting views across the bay towards Koper and Trieste.

Dominating the high ground at the heart of the peninsula is the Church of St Maurus (Cerkev sv Mavra), with a striped orange-and-cream façade and a freestanding belfry. Below the church is the former palace of the Besenghi degli Ughi family,

Sail boats docked in the scenic harbour of Izola

sporting fancy wrought-iron window grilles and a stone balustrade adorned with carvings of human faces. It is now a music school.

Hidden in the alleys of the Old Town is the **Parenzana Railway Museum** (Muzej Ozkotirne Železnice Parenzana), celebrating the narrow-gauge railway line that once ran through Izola from Trieste in Italy to Poréč in Croatia. Closed in 1937, the Parenzana is remembered through old photographs and a model of a short stretch of the line displayed in the museum. The museum's collection of model locomotives recalls the days when the Izola-based toy manufacturer Mehanotehnika,

active from 1954 to 2008, produced train sets that were very popular with children across the former Yugoslavia. Today the railway line serves as a foot- and cycle-path.

🏛 **Parenzana Railway Museum**
Alme Vivoda 3. **Open** 9am–3pm Mon–Fri. 📷

❻ Ankaran

Road map A4. 28 km (17 miles) NE of Piran. 🚗 3,000. 🚌 from Koper.
ℹ Regentova 2; (05) 665 3000.
🖥 **obcinankaran.si**

Hugging the slopes of the Mirje peninsula just across the bay from Koper, the quiet settlement of Ankaran grew around a former Benedictine monastery, which was abandoned in 1641 after a plague. It became a hotel and camp site in the 1920s.

A huddle of holiday villas were subsequently built among the coastal pines and cypresses. Ankaran is a good base for undemanding coastal walks, with paths leading west towards Debeli Rt, a rugged cape made up of stone plates and boulders. Alternatively, the well-signposted Bebler Mountain Path (Beblerjeva planinska pot) climbs inland from the town's centre to the ridgetop village of Hrvatini, passing through olive groves, vineyards and pine forest.

Salt Pans of Sečovlje

Sečovlje has been known for salt production since the Middle Ages, although it was only in the 19th century that it became the region's main industry. Dykes were constructed across the bay, creating shallow pans in which seawater would evaporate, leaving pure salt crystals. The salt was then raked into piles and loaded onto barrows, before being exported all over the Mediterranean. Traditionally, the salt-harvesting season lasted from St George's Day on 23 April to St Bartholomew's Day on 24 August, when many families from the Piran region would converge on the salt pans to work until the harvest was over. The pans were neglected during the Communist period and the quality of the salt declined. Today, Sečovlje salt crystals, Piranske soline (*see p97*), make popular gastronomic souvenirs.

Sečovlje's famous salt pans

❼ Koper

Now Slovenia's main port, Koper began as a small Roman settlement known as Insula Caprea (Goat Island). It became a major trading centre under the Venetian Empire, and boasts an attractive Old Town rich in Venetian-influenced architecture. The city was home to a largely Italian-speaking population until it became part of Slovenia in 1954. The Italian heritage remains ever-present, street signs are bilingual and many of the locals speak Italian. Modern Koper is girdled with industrial zones and modern shopping centres, although the city centre remains a real historical gem, with an enjoyable network of medieval, pedestrianized streets at its heart.

🏛 Titov trg
Galerija Loža: **Open** 11am–5pm Tue–Sat, 11am–1pm Sun.

Many of central Koper's narrow alleyways meet at Tito Square, home to some spectacular historical buildings. The most eye-catching is the Praetorian Palace (Pretorska palača), a striking example of Venetian-Gothic style. Embedded in the façade are the coats of arms of leading Koper families and busts of prominent city administrators. Opposite the palace is the 15th-century Loggia, boasting Venetian-Gothic windows and a 16th-century statue of the Virgin and Child. Its ground-floor arcade is now a café. A side door leads to the first-floor **Galerija Loža**, a gallery for contemporary artists.

Detail on Loggia

🏛 Cathedral of the Assumption
Titov trg. City Bell Tower: **Open** 10am–1pm Sat & Sun.

On the eastern side of Titov trg is the Cathedral of the Assumption (stolnica Marijinega vnebovzetja), a pleasing amalgam of Romanesque and Baroque elements. On the right side of the transept is an animated painting of the *Virgin and Child Accompanied by Saints*, attributed to the Venetian painter Carpaccio, who is thought to have lived in Koper for some time. Hidden behind the main altar is the medieval sarcophagus of local protector St Nazarius, with an effigy of the saint on the lid. One side of the slab has a delicately carved relief of Nazarius holding a model of Koper, complete with city walls and cathedral spire. Slightly away from the cathedral is the Venetian-style **City Bell Tower**, a medieval defensive tower that was turned into a belfry in the 15th century. Steep steps lead up to a bird's-eye view of the city centre. Behind the cathedral is a 12th-century rotunda that was originally a baptistry.

🏛 Fontico
Trg Brolo.

One of the Old Town's most characterful buildings is the Fontico. A 15th-century grain warehouse, it is now occupied by municipal offices. The Fontico's busy exterior is studded with the crests of local merchant families, many bearing intriguing decorative details such as birds of prey and bare-breasted nymphs. Next door is the plain ochre Church of St Jacob (Cerkev sv Jakoba), a simple 14th-century Gothic structure.

De Ponte Fountain
Prešernov trg.

The delightfully elaborate Fontana da Ponte is located at one of the prettiest small squares in the Old Town's southern end. Dating from 1666, the fountain has an octagonal base spanned by an arch in the form of a balustraded bridge. On the southern end of the square

Red-tiled roofs in Koper's main square, with the harbour in the background

For hotels and restaurants in this region see p194 and pp204–5

Prešernov trg with the De Ponte Fountain

is the Muda Gate, a 16th-century archway with reliefs of the city's official symbol – a fiery-tongued sun with a smiling face.

Regional Museum

Kidričeva 19. **Tel** (05) 663 3570.
Open 9am–5pm Tue–Fri, 9am–1pm Sat & Sun.

Occupying the Belgramoni-Tacco Palace, the Regional Museum (Pokrajinski muzej) hosts a rich collection of fossils, archaeological finds and medieval stonework including several carved beasts salvaged from crumbling medieval churches. Overlooking the staircase are 17th-century portraits of the local Tarsi family. Paintings on display upstairs include a panorama of Koper in the 1600s, showing the salt pans that once surrounded the town, and a copy of the *Dance of Death* fresco from the Holy Trinity Church, Hrastovlje *(see p140)*. Exhibitions of historical interest are held in the Muzejska galerija, two doors further down the street.

Taverna

Carpacciov trg.
The western entrance to the Old Town is marked by the Taverna, a buttressed stone structure with open arches on each side. Originally a salt-storage warehouse, the building gets its name from the number of inns that were once clustered around it. It is now a venue for summer concerts. Diagonally opposite the Taverna is the market area.

VISITORS' CHECKLIST

Practical Information
Road map A4. 20 km (13 miles) NE of Piran. 23,700. Titov trg; (05) 664 6403. **koper.si**

Transport
from Ljubljana.
from Ljubljana & Trieste.

Ethnographic Collection

Gramšijev trg 4. **Tel** (05) 663 3570.
Open May–Sep: 10am–6pm Tue–Fri, 9am–1pm Sat.

Surrounded by an atmospheric maze of alleys, the Ethnographic Collection (Etnološka zbirka) fills a beautifully restored Venetian-Gothic house. The displays include utensils, costumes, dry-stone construction techniques of the Karst and a re-creation of a typical 19th-century kitchen.

Exhibit on the ground floor of Koper's Regional Museum

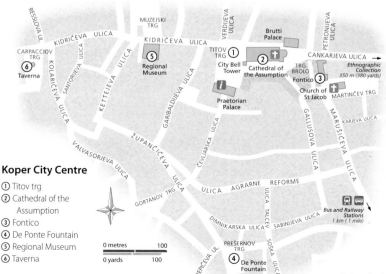

Koper City Centre

1 Titov trg
2 Cathedral of the Assumption
3 Fontico
4 De Ponte Fountain
5 Regional Museum
6 Taverna

0 metres   100
0 yards   100

For keys to symbols *see back flap*

Fifteenth-century frescoes in the Church of the Holy Trinity, Hrastovlje

❽ Hrastovlje

Road map A5. 20 km (13 miles) SE of Koper. 🚈 140. 🚌 from Koper. 🛈 Hrastovlje 4; (041) 398 368.

Located in the arid hills above the coast, the rustic village of Hrastovlje is home to one of Slovenia's most outstanding medieval treasures. Crowning a hillock a short distance from the rest of the village is the 12th-century **Church of the Holy Trinity** (Cerkev sv Trojice), a simple Romanesque structure sheltered behind a high defensive wall.

The church's interior is covered from floor to ceiling with dazzling frescoes painted by local artist John of Kastav in 1490. Painted over several times in the subsequent years, the frescoes were only discovered in 1949. Most famous of the friezes is the *Dance of Death* on the south wall, in which a jolly-looking company of skeletons lead the old and young, rich and poor alike towards the grave.

Many of the other scenes feature familiar stories from the Bible, but with the main characters clad in attire from the 15th century, providing a fascinating insight into the lifestyles of people in the late medieval period. Particularly imaginative are the scenes depicting the Book of Genesis, filled with exotic birds, beasts and plants; and the Journey of the Magi showing the three kings journeying with a retinue of richly clad followers on horseback. Ceiling panels carry delightful illustrations of local country life at different stages of the annual agricultural cycle and through the seasons.

🏛 **Holy Trinity Church**
Open 8am–noon & 1–5pm daily. 🅿

❾ Lokev

Road map A4. 38 km (24 miles) NE of Koper. 🚈 740. 🚌 from Sežana.

Surrounded by green pastures and limestone outcrops, Lokev is a typical Karst village of modest stone houses. It is famous for the local home-cured ham (*pršut*) that is sold in the shop at the huge drying shed (*pršutarna*). At the centre of Lokev is a castellated round tower built by the Venetians in 1485. The tower now houses the **Tabor Military Museum** (Vojaški muzej Tabor), a private collection containing mementos from both world wars. Exhibits include the uniform of General Svetozar Borojević, commander of the Austro-Hungarian forces on the Soča Front (*see p123*), and weapons used by the partisan brigades that liberated western Slovenia from fascist occupiers in 1945.

Environs
Located amid forest and scrub 2 km (1 mile) north of the village, **Vilenica Cave** (Jama Vilenica) was one of the first of the Karst caverns to become a tourist attraction, receiving visitors as early as the 17th century. However, it lost pro-minence when the nearby Postojna and Škocjan Caves were discovered. Visits to Vilenica were revived in 1963, and about 450 m (1,480 ft) of stalactite-encrusted passageways can now be seen as part of a guided tour. The Dance Hall, the biggest of Vilenica's chambers, serves as the venue for readings during the Vilenica International Literature Festival, which brings together Slovenian and Central European poets.

🏛 **Tabor Military Museum**
Tel (05) 767 0107. **Open** Jan & Feb: by appt; Mar–Dec: 9am–noon & 2–6pm Wed–Sun. 🅿

🏛 **Vilenica Cave**
Tel (051) 648 711. 🅿 🚫 Apr–Oct: 3 & 5pm Sun. 🎭 Vilenica International Literature Festival (Sep). 🌐 vilenica.com

Rock formations at the Vilenica Cave, near Lokev

Verdant archway in the Botanical Gardens, Sežana

⑩ Lipica

Road map A4. 48 km (30 miles) NE of Koper. 🚌 from Sežana.
W lipica.org

Located by the Italian border, the village of Lipica is synonymous with the Lipizzaner horses bred here since 1580. Established by the Habsburg Archduke Charles of Styria, the **Lipica Stud Farm** crossed Andalucian horses with local steeds, resulting in the graceful white Lipizzaner horses. The breed immediately found favour with the prestigious Spanish Riding School in Vienna, and has been considered aristocratic in the equine world ever since.

Today, Lipica has riding stables, two hotels, a casino, a nine-hole golf course and the Museum Lipikum (Muzej lipicanca). Many of Lipica's 400 horses can be seen grazing in the extensive paddocks that adjoin the stud farm. Tours of the stables allow visitors to see the beasts at close quarters, while presentations by the Classical Riding School show the highly trained horses performing complex routines. Ponies are available for rides, and horse-drawn carriage tours of the farm and pastures are on offer from April to October. Enthusiasts can book one-week courses ranging from horse riding for beginners to advanced dressage training.

Occupying a room in one of the older stable complexes is the **Avgust Černigoj Gallery** (Galerija Avgusta Černigoja), honouring Černigoj (1898–1985), the Modernist artist who spent the last years of his life at Lipica. The collection ranges from Constructivist paintings from the artist's youth to the collages he worked on in his later years. The gallery is designed according to the avant-garde aesthetics of Černigoj's early years, with grey metal staircases, bright red pillars and a circular viewing platform on the second floor.

Lipica Stud Farm
Tel (05) 739 1708. 🎨 📷 hourly; Apr–Sep: 10am–5pm Mon–Fri, 10am–6pm Sat & Sun; Oct–Mar: 10am–3pm daily.
W lipica.org

🏛 Avgust Černigoj Gallery
Tel (05) 739 1740. **Open** Apr–Sep: 10am–5pm Mon–Fri, 10am–6pm Sat & Sun; Oct–Mar: 10am–3pm daily. 🎨
W lipica.org

⑪ Sežana

Road map A4. 45 km (28 miles) NE of Koper. 🏢 12,600. 🚉 from Koper, Ljubljana & Nova Gorica. 🚌 from Nova Gorica. 🛈 Partizanska 63; (05) 731 0128. **W** sezana.si

An unassuming market town serving the hill villages of the western karst, Sežana is an important hub for travellers looking at visiting nearby attractions such as the Lipica Stud Farm and the Vilenica Cave. It also holds a variety of minor attractions in its own right, the most popular of which is the restful **Botanical Gardens**.

The gardens were laid out by the Scaramanga family, a Trieste-based trading dynasty who were enthusiastic horticulturalists, and collected plants from all over the globe. An elegant 19th-century palm house provides the garden's geometrically arranged flowerbeds with a focal point. Beyond the palm house lies an extensive arboretum, with a high number of evergreens that help to keep the gardens colourful all year round.

🌿 Botanical Gardens
Partizanska cesta 2. **Tel** (05) 731 1243. **Open** 7am–3pm Mon–Fri, 10am–4pm Sat & Sun. 🎨
W ksp-sezana.si

Lipizzaner Horses

Inspired by the need to produce a strong cavalry horse, Habsburg Emperor Maximilian II decided to breed white Andalucian horses with local horses. The experiment was continued by his brother Archduke Charles, who founded a stud farm at Lipica. After the break-up of the Habsburg Empire in 1918, the Austrians established a new Lipizzaner stud farm in Piber, Austria, while the Slovenians continued breeding the horses at Lipica. The horses are dark-coloured when young, and develop their distinctive off-white coats only after the age of five.

Typical white Lipizzaner horses grazing at the Lipica Stud Farm

⑫ Škocjan Caves

Škocjanske jame

Located in rolling countryside just outside the town of Divača, the Škocjan Caves are one of Slovenia's most spectacular karst features. The UNESCO World Heritage Site's labyrinthine complex of caverns and passageways is reckoned to be the world's largest network of subterranean chambers, and to this day, remains only partially explored. About 3 km (2 miles) of passageways are open to the public, accessible by a 90-minute guided tour. As well as a spectacular array of stalagmites and stalactites, visitors can marvel at underground waterways and rock bridges. The surrounding landscape, featuring limestone gorges, pastureland, traditional stone-built villages and deciduous forest, is a protected nature area.

Visitors outside the main entrance to the caves

Škocjan Village
The restored barns of Škocjan Village contain a number of museum collections, with a model of the cave system and Bronze Age archaeological finds among the exhibits.

Entrance

①

★ The Bowls
This sequence of cup-like formations, arranged in tiers and formed by the sediment left by dripping water, is one of the more unusual sights here.

KEY

① **Stalactites**, formed by constantly dripping water, hang from the ceiling of the caves.

② **Church of St Cantianus** is dedicated to the local patron saint. The name, Škocjan, is the local dialect for St Cantianus.

③ **Škocjan Village**

④ **Cerkvenik Bridge**

★ Cerkvenik Bridge
The most breathtaking moment for many visitors is the walk across this man-made bridge, hovering 45 m (148 ft) above the twisting underground Reka river.

Velika Dolina
Velika Dolina (literally, Great Valley) is where the Reka river disappears underground, carving out the chambers of the Škocjan Caves before re-emerging near the Adriatic Sea.

★ The Organ
This is one of the most alluring rock formations, so-called due to a ribbed curtain of limestone that resembles the pipes of a church organ.

Paradise Cave
Among Škocjan's set-piece caverns, the Paradise Cave is famous for the fluted pillars of glistening rock that connect the floor to the ceiling.

The bright and cheerful façade of the Veno Pilon Gallery, Ajdovščina

⑬ Vipava

Road map A4. 58 km (36 miles) N of Koper. 5,200. from Nova Gorica & Ljubljana. *i* Glavni trg; (05) 368 7041. **W** vipavska-dolina.si

Pressed against the sheer grey flanks of the Nanos ridge, the small town of Vipava stands at the centre of the Vipava Valley wine producing area. Dominating the main square is the ochre 17th-century mansion built by the Lanthieri Counts, who ruled over Vipava until World War I. A building on the town's main square houses the tourist information centre and the **Vinoteka**, where white wines made from the indigenous zelen and pinela grapes are available for sampling and purchase.

Beyond the square, Vipava's street plan of narrow twisting alleyways protects houses from the *burja*, the bone-chilling northeasterly wind that blasts down from the mountain ridges above. Alleyways behind the main square lead to an attractive waterside area near the source of the Vipava river, which emerges from the limestone slopes of Nanos mountain. From here, trails lead up towards the jagged ruins of Vipava's 13th-century

castle. For those keen to embark on longer hikes, several marked paths lead up towards Nanos's main ridge, beyond which lies a rolling plateau of evergreen forest and pastures. Perched on a small hill 2 km (1 mile) west of Vipava is the 7th-century **Zemono Manor**, a famously beautiful arcaded building, which now houses the Pri Lojzetu restaurant *(see p205).*

Vinoteka
Glavni trg 1. **Tel** (05) 368 7041. **Open** Jun–Sep: 9am–7pm daily; Oct–May: 10am–5pm Mon–Fri, 9am–2pm Sat.

⑭ Ajdovščina

Road map A4. 65 km (40 miles) N of Koper. 18,100. from Ljubljana & Nova Gorica. *i* Lokarjev drevored 8; (05) 365 9140. **W** tic-ajdovscina.si

The main town of the Vipava Valley, the semi-industrial Ajdovščina began life as a Roman fortified camp, ruins of which can still be seen around town. It became an important centre of milling and metal-working in the Middle Ages, its workshops powered by the gushing waters of the Hubelj river. More recently, Ajdovščina has become noted as the home of the Pipistrel aviation company, whose innovative gliders can frequently be seen at the airfield west of town.

Relics from Ajdovščina's ancient origins are most visible on the eastern side of the centre, where a surviving medieval gateway and adjoining section of Roman wall preside over a grassy park facing the river. Inside the gate lies a tightly woven web of narrow streets, where the **Veno Pilon Gallery** (Pilonova galerija) honours the locally born painter, Veno Pilon (1896–1970), with displays of paintings and mementos from his lifetime. The collection starts with Pilon's subtly dramatic watercolours of the Russian town of Lipeck, where he was interned as a prisoner of war during World War I. Most striking of Pilon's later works are the

Wine bottle, Vipava

Vista of vineyards from Zemono Manor, Vipava

The entrance gate to the ancient hilltop town of Štanjel

Expressionist portraits, in which the sitters are portrayed with asymmetrical faces, overlarge hands or elongated torsos.

A 30-minute walk on a well-signed and easy-going nature trail on the northern side of town leads to the source of the Hubelj river, which emerges from the rocky hillside in the form of a gushing waterfall.

⏷ Veno Pilon Gallery
Prešernova 3. **Tel** (05) 368 9177.
Open 8am–4pm Tue–Fri. 🖼 🅿
W venopilon.com

⑮ Vipavski Križ

Road map A4. 67 km (42 miles) N of Koper. 🚌 180.

Occupying a low ridge in the middle of the Vipava Valley, Vipavski Križ was an insignificant village until the late 15th century, when the Counts of Gorizia realized that they needed a forward line of defence to protect themselves against Ottoman attacks. Križ was quickly transformed into a fortress, with the ensuing influx of soldiers, builders and churchmen transforming it into a major regional centre.

Today, Križ is a sleepy settlement, with long stretches of defensive wall intact, and the stark remains of the fortress looming above the eastern end. Dominating the town is the 17th-century Capuchin Monastery Church (cerkev

kapucinskega samostana), famous for a monumental Baroque painting of the Holy Trinity which hangs upon the high altar. The monastery's **Library** contains a prized collection of manuscripts and prayer books.

⏷ Library
Open 9am–noon & 1–5:30pm Tue–Sat.

⑯ Štanjel

Road map A4. 59 km (37 miles) NE of Koper. 🚂 340. 🚌 from Nova Gorica & Sežana. 🚌 from Nova Gorica & Sežana. ℹ (05) 769 0056.
W stanjel.eu

The best-preserved of the ridgetop settlements to the southwest of the Vipava Valley is Štanjel, once an important way station on the trade route between Vipava and the coast. Sacked by Ottoman raiders in 1470, the town was refortified in the 16th century by the Kobenzl family.

The main approach to the town leads through the west gate, adorned with the deer and eagle motifs of Štanjel's coat of arms. Beyond lies a knot of narrow, unpaved alleys lined with sturdy cottages. Presiding over this stone warren is the arresting cone-shaped belfry of St Daniel's

Statue at the entrance to Štanjel

Church (Cerkev sv Danijela), a late-Gothic structure with Baroque altars.

On Štanjel's hill is the 16th-century Castle (Kaštel), much of which is in ruins; a restored lower section abuts a pleasant courtyard. Occupying one of the castle buildings is the **Lojze Spacal Gallery** (Galerija Lojzeta Spacala), housing a comprehensive collection of works by the Trieste-born artist Lojze Spacal (1907–2000), famous for his depictions of the Karst and the coast. Staff at the gallery also show visitors around the nearby Karst House (Kraška hiša), a traditional hill-village home. The ground floor was used as a storage room and barn, while the upper storeys served as living quarters.

Just beyond the Karst House, the town's eastern boundary is marked by the Kobdilj Tower (Kobdiljski stolp), a gateway topped with castellations. Running in an arc below the tower is Ferraris' Garden (Ferrarijev vrt), a landscaped park designed by architect Max Fabiani, featuring a lake with a Venetian-style ornamental bridge. The views from the garden are stunning.

Lojze Spacal Gallery
Grad Štanjel. **Tel** (05) 769 0197.
Open daily. 🖼 **W** spacal.net

Oval-shaped Tartinijev trg (Tartini Square) in Piran's Old Town ▶

Gorizia, as seen from the Franciscan Monastery of Kostanjevica, Nova Gorica

⑰ Nova Gorica

Road map A3. 85 km (53 miles) N of Koper. 🚇 13,900. 🚌 from Ljubljana. 🅘 Delpinova 18b; (05) 330 4600. 🅦 **novagorica-turizem.com**

The main administrative centre of western Slovenia, Nova Gorica owes its origins to post-World War II peace treaties which awarded the city of Gorizia to Italy but left the villages immediately to the east in Slovenian hands. The Slovenians decided to build a new town on their side of the border that would serve as an economic and social centre for the local rural population, and Nova Gorica (New Gorizia) was the result. Largely constructed in the 1950s under the guidance of urban planner Edvard Ravnikar, the town centre has a functional, grid-plan appearance. However, there is a surprising wealth of historical sights scattered throughout the suburbs.

Dominating a hill south of the centre, the **Franciscan Monastery of Kostanjevica** (Frančiškanski samostan na Kostanjevici) started out as a Carmelite foundation established in the early 17th century. Refounded by the Franciscans in 1811, it holds the burial vault of France's last

Bourbon king, Charles X (1757–1836), who reigned for six years until the revolution of 1830 forced him to take refuge in Habsburg-ruled Gorizia. The monastery's library contains many historic volumes, most notably a copy of Adam Bohorič's first-ever Slovenian grammar, published in 1584.

Around 4 km (3 miles) east of central Nova Gorica, Kromberk Castle is a Renaissance chateau surrounded by ornamental gardens. It provides a fittingly grand home for the **Nova Gorica Museum** (Goriški muzej), whose extensive art collection spans everything from Gothic altar panels to graphic prints by local artist Lojze Spacal (1907–2000). The museum's ethnographic and archaeological collections are housed in the **Villa Bartolomei** in Solkan, a leafy suburb made up of the summer villas of Gorizia's middle classes. The ethnography display is particularly engaging, including the kind of copper pots and pans that would have been used in a 19th-century Slovenian kitchen.

Spanning the Soča river on Solkan's northern boundary is Nova Gorica's most treasured architectural monument, the Solkan railway bridge (Solkanski

Coat of arms, Sveta Gora

most), opened in July 1906. The bridge's 85-m- (280-ft-) high central arch is the biggest of any stone-built bridge in the world. Despite being blown up by the Austrian army to prevent its capture by Italian forces in 1916, it was rebuilt by the Italians in 1927. The bridge is best viewed from the grassy banks of the Soča river.

Looming to the east of the Solkan bridge is Sveta Gora hill, its 684-m- (2,245-ft-) high summit crowned by the **Sveta Gora Monastery** (Frančiškanski samostan Sveta Gora) and its Pilgrimage Church of the Assumption. The church contains a 16th-century picture of the Virgin that is popularly believed to answer the prayers of the faithful.

🏛 **Franciscan Monastery of Kostanjevica**
Škrabčeva ulica 1. **Tel** (05) 330 7750. **Open** daily. 🅿 📷 🅦 **samostan-kostanjevica.si**

🏛 **Nova Gorica Museum**
Grajska 1. **Tel** (05) 335 9811. **Open** daily. 🅿 📷 🅦 **goriskimuzej.si**

🏛 **Vila Bartolomei**
Pod Vinogradi 2. **Tel** (05) 335 9811. **Open** 8am–5pm Mon–Fri.
🅦 **goriskimuzej.si**

🏛 **Sveta Gora Monastery**
Sveta Gora 2. **Tel** (05) 330 4020.
🕐 7am & 5pm Mon–Sat; 8am, 10am, 11:30am & 4pm Sun & holidays.
🅦 **svetagora.si**

⓲ A Tour of the Goriška Brda Region

Stretching northwest of Nova Gorica is the Goriška Brda region, characterized by green slopes and hilltop villages. It is one of Slovenia's foremost wine regions, famous for the light white rebula as well as international varieties such as Merlot and Chardonnay. Wine can be tasted at innumerable local establishments, ranging from big wineries in the main villages to family farmsteads out on country roads.

Tips for Drivers

Starting point: Nova Gorica.
Length: 45 km (28 miles).
Duration: Allow a full day.
Driving conditions: There are single-lane roads in the region; road crosses through Italy too.
Stopping-off points: The region is full of wineries. Among the most popular are Vinoteka Brda and Vinska klet Goriška Brda in Dobrovo.
Tourist information: Dobrovo: Grajska cesta 10; (05) 395 9594; **W** brda.si

⑦ Vipolže
Home to a ruined castle circled by cypresses, the village of Vipolže is sur-rounded by vineyards, olive trees and orchards.

① Nova Gorica
A 20th-century town, this is the administrative centre of the region.

⑥ Dobrovo
Goriška Brda's main settlement is also one of the most convenient places to sample and buy local wine.

⑤ Šmartno
The most attractive of Goriška Brda's villages, Šmartno is known for its local produce.

② Solkan Bridge
This masterpiece of engineering, with the largest single-span stone arch in the world, opened to railway traffic in 1906.

④ Vrhovlje pri Kojskem
Perched on a verdant ridge, Vrhovlje's pilgrimage church offers a wonderful panorama of the countryside.

0 kilometres 2
0 miles 2

Key

▬▬▬ Tour route
═══ Other road
—— Railway
▬▪▬ International boundary

③ Kojsko
This tranquil village is famous for the semi-fortified Holy Cross Church, home to a winged Gothic altarpiece.

For keys to symbols *see back flap*

⑲ Idrija

Road map B3. 102 km (63 miles) N of Koper. 🚗 12,000. 🚌 from Ljubljana. 🛈 Mestni trg 2; (05) 374 3916. 📅 Idrija Lace Festival (late Jun). 🌐 **visit-idrija.si**

Accessed via notoriously winding roads, Idrija's location at the base of a valley, amid green hills, is spectacular. Mining began here in 1490 when, according to local legend, a barrel-maker was soaking his wares in a nearby stream and discovered mercury. Idrija became the second-largest mercury-mining centre in Europe, providing 13 per cent of the global output.

Statue in the centre of the town

After mining came to a halt in 2008, the town became a major centre of industrial tourism.This mining heritage is apparent everywhere in Idrija – even the tourist office is housed in a former pit-head building, home to a lovingly polished 19th-century winding machine. The best place to view Idrija's industrial legacy is the **Town Museum** (Mestni muzej), housed in the Gewerkenegg Castle, perched on a hilltop above the centre. Lumps of ruddy ore along with displays of drilling equipment and photographs of helmeted workers illustrate the history of mining in the town. One section of the museum is devoted to the story of the manufacture of Idrija lace, a home industry begun by miners' wives to supplement modest family incomes, and still going strong today. The display includes everything from tablecloths to alluring lacy evening dresses. A first-hand experience of mining conditions is provided at **Anthony's Shaft** (Antonijev rov). This atmospheric network of tunnels, initially excavated in 1500, is located to the south of the castle. A tour of the shaft starts at the former administrative building known as the Šelštev House, where a video presentation introduces the growth of mining in the town. Visitors are then led down the shaft itself, where mining techniques of the past are demonstrated.

Several other industrial monuments are strewn around the centre of the town: the pit-head pavilion at Francis's Shaft (Jašek Frančiške) contains an absorbing display of mining machinery, while the nearby steep-roofed Miner's House (Rudarska hiša) reveals the cramped living conditions of 19th-century families. On the western outskirts of town is a large stone building containing the Kamšt, an impressive water-wheel built in 1790 to pump floodwater from the mineshafts below. With a diameter of 14 m (45 ft), it was the biggest waterwheel in Europe and was in use until 1948.

Immediately beyond the Kamšt is the Zgornja Idrijca Landscape Park, where a path runs alongside the Rake – a man-made water course that fed the waterwheel – below wooded hills. Keen walkers can follow forest trails towards the Klavže, 18th-century dams that controlled the flow of water on local mountain torrents, making it possible to float locally cut timber downstream.

Idrija has a major culinary claim to fame in the *žlikrofi*, ravioli-like pockets of pasta stuffed with potato, bits of bacon and onion. Freshly made *žlikrofi* is served in most of the local restaurants.

🏛 **Town Museum**
Prelovčeva 3. **Tel** (05) 372 6600.
Open 9am–6pm daily. 📷 📹
🌐 **muzej-idrija-cerkno.si**
Note: check here about access to Francis's Shaft & the Kamšt.

🏛 **Anthony's Shaft**
Kosovelova 3. **Tel** (05) 377 1142.
📹 10am, noon & 3pm Mon–Fri, 10am, noon, 3pm & 4pm Sat & Sun.
📷 📹 🌐 **antonijevrov.si**

Courtyard of the Gewerkenegg Castle, home to Idrija's Town Museum

For hotels and restaurants in this region see p194 and pp204–5

Cerkno village with the mountains in the background

⓴ Cerkno

Road map B3. 20 km (13 miles) NW of Idrija. 🚶 5,000. 🚌 from Idrija. *i* Mocnikova 2; (05) 373 4645. 🎭 Laufarija processions (Shrovetide), Cerkno International Jazz Festival (May). **W** turizem-cerkno.si

Stretched out beneath the 1,632-m- (5,354-ft-) high ridge of Mount Porezen, the village of Cerkno is a popular base for summer hiking and winter skiing. The main attraction in the village itself is **Cerkno Museum**, which contains an arresting collection of wood-carved carnival masks worn by the local pre-Lenten revellers, the *laufarji*.

The Cerkno tourist office can organize visits to the Divje Babe Cave, a major archaeological site rich in Neanderthal remains, between April and September. In 1996, archaeologists discovered what is claimed to be the world's oldest musical instrument, a 55,000-year-old flute carved from bear bone. The bone is exhibited in the National Museum of Slovenia, Ljubljana *(see p66)*, although the question of whether it is really a flute or simply a bone with holes in it is the subject of long-running academic debate.

🏛 **Cerkno Museum**
Bevkova 12. **Tel** (05) 372 3180.
Open 9am–3pm Tue–Fri, 10am–1pm & 2–6pm Sat & Sun.
W muzej-idrija-cerkno.si

⓴ Franja Partisan Hospital

Partizanska bolnica Branja

Road map B3. 25 km (16 miles) N of Idrija. **Tel** (05) 372 3180. **Open** Apr–Sep: 9am–6pm daily; Oct: 9am–4pm daily; Nov–Mar: pre-arranged groups only. 🎭 🅿 **W** muzej-idrija-cerkno.si

In the densely wooded and picturesque Pasica Gorge lies the Franja Partisan Hospital, a timber-built field hospital used by Slovenian resistance fighters during World War II. Active from December 1943 to 1945, the hospital's 13 wooden huts once housed wards that were fully equipped with x-ray machines, operating theatres and an electricity generator. Over 1,000 partisans and Allied soldiers were treated here during the war. Medical supplies, dropped by Allied aircraft throughout Slovenia, allowed this and other field hospitals to remain operational. Staff and patients were blindfolded on their way to and from the hospital to ensure maximum secrecy.

Converted into a memorial after the war, the site was named after partisan doctor Franja Bojc Bidovec (1913–85), the hospital's administrator from January 1944 until the end of the war.

The site was badly damaged by floods in September 2007. However, reconstruction and renovation are almost complete and the monument is open to visitors.

Wooden huts at the Franja Partisan Hospital

The Cerkno Laufarji

Some of Slovenia's strangest and most colourful carnival customs take place in Cerkno. The *laufarji* (runners) are local young men who cavort through the village in stylized costumes welcoming the spring. They appear on the first Sunday of the year and increase in number as the weeks go by. Their main task is to accompany the *Pust* – played by a local man clad in fir-tree branches, a symbol of winter that has to be confronted before spring can commence. The *Pust* is put on trial in the village square on the Sunday before Shrove Tuesday. He is then symbolically executed with a *bot*, a forester's hammer, on Shrove Tuesday. The *Pust* is policed by the *terjasti – laufar* with skull-like wooden masks featuring grotesque teeth – who also entertain the public by dancing and leaping.

Typical *laufar* mask and costume

㉒ Predjama Castle

Predjamski grad

There are few fortresses more dramatically situated than Predjama Castle, which sits halfway up a hillside carved into a huge cave. The site was fortified in the 13th century, although most of what can be seen today is the result of 16th-century rebuilding. Most famous of the castle's many owners was the 15th-century knight Erasmus Lueger, a bandit-like figure who was killed during a siege in 1484. In July, a tournament is held in the castle to celebrate the medieval period with jousts and parades.

Rocky entrance leading to the interior of the castle

Dining Room
The 16th-century furnishings and costumes, displayed in the restored dining room, provide an insight into the aristocratic lifestyles of the time when castles became residential chateaus.

★ Torture Room
The castle has a series of tableaux featuring wax dummies. This room shows a prisoner being tortured prior to interrogation in the inquisitor's room next door.

Drawbridge
Accessible via wooden bridges that could be hastily removed, Predjama was considered impregnable. A reconstructed drawbridge leads to the part that is located within the cave.

KEY

① **Karst caves** below the castle can be visited by guided tour.

② **Upper Vantage Point**

For hotels and restaurants in this region see p194 and pp204–5

Chaplain's Room
This room is one of several interiors redecorated to provide a flavour of castle life during the late 16th century, when Predjama was owned by the noble Kobenzl family.

VISITORS' CHECKLIST

Practical Information
Road map B4. 13 km (8 miles) NW of Postojna. 🛈 Postojna Caves Visitor Centre; (05) 700 0100. **Open** daily: Jul & Aug: 9am–7pm; May, Jun & Sep: 9am–6pm; Apr & Oct: 10am–5pm; Nov–Mar: 10am–4pm. 🚋 Tours of karst caves: May–Sep: 11am, 1, 3 & 5pm. 🎠 Erasmus Knights' Tournament (mid-Jul). 🆆 **postojnska-jama.eu**

★ Pietà in the Chapel
Located in the castle's Chapel of St Anne, a serene white space decorated with wooden pews and a simple cross, this tender and moving pietà from 1420 is one of the high points of late-Gothic art in Slovenia.

Castle entrance

★ Upper Vantage Point
Staircases ascend to the highest of the castle's five levels, from where the viewing terrace offers an extensive panorama of the valley below.

Erasmus Lueger

Born in Trieste, Erasmus Lueger became the owner of Predjama Castle in 1478. He fell foul of the authorities after killing one of the Emperor's kinsmen, and used the castle as a base from which to mount raids on the surrounding territory. In 1484, Baron Ravbar of Trieste laid siege to Predjama Castle for more than a year in an attempt to starve Erasmus into submission. The defenders brought in food through a secret tunnel, taunting Ravbar's men by tossing fresh cherries at them from the castle walls. Erasmus was ultimately killed by a cannonball, which hit the castle privy just when he happened to be squatting inside.

Portrait of Erasmus Lueger in Predjama Castle

㉓ Postojna Caves

Postojnska jama

Slovenia's most popular natural attraction, Postojna Caves constitute the longest subterranean system in the country, with over 20 km (12 miles) of chambers and tunnels. They were formed by the seeping waters of the Pivka river and its tributaries, which carved out several levels of underground galleries over a period of roughly three million years. The caves were first opened to visitors in 1819, with Austrian Emperor Francis I as the guest of honour. The site currently receives just under half a million visitors a year, making it one of the most popular natural attractions in Europe. Inside, magnificent formations of stalactites and stalagmites seem to stretch endlessly in all directions.

Visitors outside the main entrance to Postojna Caves

Subterranean Railway
The 2-km- (1-mile-) long underground railway offers an exhilarating introduction to the caves, speeding visitors through dramatically illuminated chambers. With the train swerving between dangling stalactites, it is almost like a fairground ride.

Stalactites, formed by constantly dripping water, hang from the cave ceiling.

Russian Bridge
Built by Russian prisoners during World War I, the Russian Bridge leads to the Macaroni Hall, which is covered with stunning pure-white stalactites.

Guided Tours
Lasting 90 minutes, guided tours begin with a train ride into the heart of the caves, followed by a walk through a series of halls with intricate rock formations.

★ Concert Hall
Before returning by train to the cave entrance, visitors emerge into the Concert Hall, a vast space where orchestral performances are occasionally held.

VISITORS' CHECKLIST

Practical Information
Road map B4. 53 km (33 miles) S of Ljubljana. **i** Jamska Cesta 9, Postojna; (05) 720 1610; **W** tdpostojna.si
Open Jan–Mar, Nov & Dec: tours at 10am, noon & 3pm; Apr & Oct: tours at 10am, noon, 2pm & 4pm; May, Jun & Sep: tours hourly 9am–5pm; July & Aug: tours hourly 9am–6pm.

W postojnska-jama.eu

Transport
from Ljubljana.
from Ljubljana.

Big Mountain
This 45-m- (147-ft)- high rocky mound was created when the ceiling collapsed.

★ White Passage
One of the series of chambers known as Beautiful Caves, the White Passage is crammed with impressive stalagmites and stalactites.

★ The Diamond
This huge stalagmite, also called "Brilliant", on account of its dazzling white surface and peculiar shape, is one of the highlights of the spectacular Winter Chamber.

Proteus Anguinus
The caves are the natural habitat of this rare amphibian, known as the human fish.

Entrance to the famous Postojna Caves

Exploring Postojna

The history of the town of Postojna, situated midway between Ljubljana and the Adriatic coast, is inextricably linked with that of the Postojna Caves, the famous sequence of caverns that can be entered from the western edge of town. Known since the Middle Ages, the caves were visited by the famous geographer Janez Vajkard Valvasor (see p95) in the late 17th century and became a destination for mass tourism in the 19th century.

The arrival of the railway in 1857 made the caves accessible to visitors from all over Central Europe. This also spurred the development of Postojna itself, which was transformed from a provincial market town into a major administrative centre. The town fell under Italian rule after World War I, and it became a heavily garrisoned military base on the frontier with the erstwhile Kingdom of Yugoslavia. Barrack buildings can still be seen on the outskirts of town. The **Postojna Regional Museum**, which occupies the former military garrison headquarters, has on display exhibits relating to the natural history, archaeology and ethnography of the entire Karst region.

Today, the caves remain Postojna's main attraction, drawing an average of half a million visitors every year. The caves are particularly rich in stalagmites, stalactites and other rock formations, thanks mainly to the region's high rainfall, which helps to produce the constantly dripping water from which stalactites are formed. The temperature in the caves is a constant 10° C (50° F); visitors are advised to wear warm clothing.

▥ Postojna Regional Museum
Kolodvorska 3. **Tel** (05) 721 1090. **Open** 9am–3pm Tue–Fri, 10am–1pm & 2–6pm Sat & Sun. **w** notranjski-muzej.si

❷ Pivka Cave
Pivka jama

Road map B4. 3 km (2 miles) N of Postojna. ◪ by appointment from the ticket office.

Just north of the entrance to the Postojna Caves is the lesser-known Pivka Cave. A steep descent via a stairway and a walk along the path that runs beside a submerged stretch of the Pivka river takes visitors to the caverns. A man-made passageway leads through to the neighbouring Black Cave (Črna jama), so named due to the smooth, black calcite rock that gives lustre to some of the caverns.

❷ Pivka Park of Military History
Park vojaške zgodovine

Road map B4. 16 km (10 miles) S of Postojna. **Tel** (031) 775 002. **Open** Jun–Sep: 10am–5pm daily; Oct–May: 10am–3pm Sat & Sun. ▨ ◪ ♿

Occupying the former Italian and subsequently Yugoslav barracks at the southern end of Pivka village is this major collection of military artifacts. Much of the exhibition is made up of artillery pieces and tanks used by Italian and German occupiers during World War II. Alongside these is military hardware used by the Yugoslav People's Army in the 10-day conflict of June/July 1991. A circular walking route named the Trail of Military History (Krožna pot vojaške zgodovine) runs up and down the neighbouring hills, passing fortifications dating from the interwar era, when the area was a highly militarized zone on what was then the Italian–Yugoslav border. The whole trail takes about 4 hours to negotiate, although visitors can choose a shorter 45-minute stretch that runs to Primož hill, site of an interwar Italian artillery fort.

A World War II tank

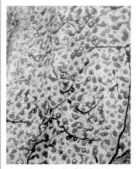

Unusual spotted walls of the Pivka Cave

Entrance to the spectacular Planina Cave

❷❻ Planina Cave
Planinska jama

Road map B4. 12 km (8 miles) NE of Postojna. **Tel** (04) 133 8696. Jun–Aug: 5pm daily; Apr, May & Sep: 3pm & 5pm Sat, 11am, 3pm & 5pm Sun. Oct–Mar: by appt only. **planina.si**

The Planina Cave is one of Slovenia's most spectacular water caves. The cave has passageways carved by the subterranean Pivka river, which flows here from Postojna Cave, and the Rak, which flows from the Rakov Škocjan Gorge. The rivers meet inside Planina to form the Unica river, which emerges from the cave's northern end. It is an important habitat for the amphibious *Proteus anguinus (see p23)*, which can be seen swimming in the rivers. Tours of the cave take visitors through the huge arched tunnel carved by the Unica before ascending to the Great Hall, so named because of its 70-m- (230-ft-) high ceiling. Further inside is the confluence of the Pivka and the Rak, with the Rak tumbling over a small waterfall. Deeper 4-hour explorations of the cave, including dinghy trips on subterranean lakes, are available if booked well in advance.

❷❼ Rakov Škocjan Regional Park

Road map B4. 7 km (5 miles) E of Postojna. **notranjski-park.si**

Rakov Škocjan is a rugged limestone canyon formed by the collapse of an underground tunnel carved by the rushing waters of the Rak river. Parts of the tunnel still survive in the form of two rock bridges, with the delicate 40-m- (140-ft)- high arch of the Small Natural Bridge (Mali naravni most) marking the eastern end of the gorge. The lower, but much longer, Great Natural Bridge (Veliki naravni most) lies 3 km (1 mile) further down. A well-marked trail runs between the two bridges. At the far end of the Great Natural Bridge, the Rak disappears into Tkalca Cave before joining the Pivka river in the Planina Cave.

❷❽ Lake Cerknica
Cerkniško jezero

Road map B4. 22 km (14 miles) E of Postojna. **notranjski-park.si**

Just south of the town of Cerknica is the "disappearing" Lake Cerknica, a broad karstic depression that fills with water during wet spells, especially during the spring thaw, but gradually dries as the water seeps away into its porous limestone underlay. The lake is in a constant state of growing and shrinking, and may disappear entirely during dry summers, when it becomes a reedy marsh. At its fullest extent the lake covers an area of 26 sq km (10 sq miles).

Lake Cerknica is a popular venue for boating and fishing in spring. It is surrounded by a network of quiet country roads, which make for ideal cycling terrain. The lake's popularity with ducks, corncrakes and wading birds has made it a major attraction for birdwatchers.

The "disappearing" Lake Cerknica during the dry season

㉙ Križna Cave
Križna jama

Road map B4. 30 km (19 miles) SE of Postojna. **Tel** (041) 632 153.
Open Apr–Sep. 🅿️ 📷 Apr–Jun: 3pm Sat & Sun; Jul & Aug: 11am, 1pm, 3pm & 5pm daily; Sep: 11am, 1pm & 3pm daily; 3–4 day notice advisable.
🆆 krizna-jama.si

Famous for its subterranean lakes, Križna Cave offers one of Slovenia's unique speleological experiences. Fed by underground water sources from both the Bloke and Cerknica plateaus, the 8-km- (5-mile-) long cave contains a string of 22 lakes, separated from each other by smooth rock barriers formed by mineral deposits.

The cave is not fully fitted with electric lighting so visitors are supplied with portable lamps on entering the cave, making the tour all the more atmospheric.

Guided tours last about an hour and begin with a trip through Bears' Corridor – so-called because of the huge number of skeletons of the prehistoric cave bear found here – before culminating with a boat trip on the first of the cave's lakes, a shallow body of water with sloping stone banks that resemble inviting

Egyptian room in Snežnik Castle

beaches at first sight. For visitors who wish to explore more, there are longer 4-hour tours, which use small dinghies to venture further into the underground lake and river system. This journey terminates at the Calvary Hall, where a submerged forest of stalagmites glitters beneath the crystal clear water. This longer tour is limited to four people per day so it is best to reserve well in advance.

The temperature inside the cave remains a constant 8º C (47º F) through the year and it is advisable to wear or carry some warm clothing.

The Križna Cave is also an important habitat for bats, with seven different species nesting here during winter.

㉚ Snežnik Castle
Grad Snežnik

Road map B4. 38 km (24 miles) SE of Postojna. **Tel** (01) 705 7814.
Open Apr–Sep: 10am–6pm daily; Oct–Mar: 10am–4pm Tue–Sun. 🅿️ 📷 hourly; obligatory. 📷

A Renaissance chateau rising behind picturesquely turreted walls, Snežnik Castle was owned by some of Slovenia's leading landowning families throughout the centuries.

The guided tours lead visitors through a series of historic interiors, each filled with a rich array of period furniture. Outside, the castle's verdant landscaped park is the perfect place for a relaxing stroll.

The castle's former dairy now houses the **Snežnik Dormouse Museum**, which informs visitors on traditional dormouse-hunting techniques, as well as different ways to cook the animal once it is caught. There is also a display of hats fashioned from dormouse fur.

🏛 Snežnik Dormouse Museum
Grad Snežnik. **Tel** (01) 705 7516.
Open mid-May–Oct: 10am–noon & 3–7pm Wed–Fri; 10am–1pm & 2–7pm Sat & Sun. 🅿️ 📷

㉛ Snežnik Plateau
Snežniška planota

Road map B4. 40 km (25 miles) SE of Postojna. 🅸 Loz; (08) 160 2853

Snežnik Castle is one of the main trailheads for mountain biking, horse riding and walking on the Snežnik Plateau, a typically

Well-lit section of the Križna Cave

rugged limestone landscape characterized by rocky outcrops, frequent abysses and dense forests. The plateau enjoys some of the highest precipitation in the whole of Slovenia, which mostly falls in winter as snow – hence the name Snežnik, which roughly translates as snowy.

Snow remains for much of the year on the upper slopes of the 1,796-m- (5,892-ft-) high Veliki Snežnik, the cone-shaped mountain at the centre of the plateau. Despite a bare, rocky summit, Veliki Snežnik is not a difficult climb for seasoned hikers.

Veliki Snežnik is a long day's walk from both Snežnik Castle and the other main starting point, Ilirska Bistrica. Alternately, visitors can drive to Sviščaki, a small settlement just east of Ilirska Bistrica, which has a mountain hut, and pick up the shorter trail to the mountain from there.

The other major holiday centre on the plateau is Mašun, midway between Snežnik Castle and Veliki Snežnik. It has B&B accommodation in the local farmhouses and a floodlit ski slope during winter.

❷ Ilirska Bistrica

Road map B4. 33 km (21 miles) S of Postojna. 🚈 5,000. 🚌 from Ljubljana. 🛈 Gregorčičeva 2; (05) 996 6278. 🌐 ilirska-bistrica.si

A quiet and uneventful town located on the road and rail route linking Ljubljana with the Croatian port of Rijeka, Ilirska Bistrica is best known as a starting point for walkers who wish to explore the nearby Snežnik Plateau.

At the centre of the town is St Peter's Church, which has a Gothic presbytery, a collection of 17th-century Baroque altars and paintings by 20th-century artist, Tone Kralj. Around the church lies an engaging huddle of 19th-century buildings.

The information centre in the town can help organize private accommodation here.

Remains of a castle in Mašun village

❸ Reka river valley

Road map B4. 37 km (23 miles) S of Postojna.

Rising on the south side of Snežnik Plateau, the Reka river flows northwest before disappearing into the Škocjan Caves (*see pp142–3*), only to emerge 33 km (21 miles) later on the Italian side. To the west

Reka river flowing through the Škocjan Caves

of Ilirska Bistrica, the river is particularly scenic.

The swift flowing waters were once used to power sawmills, such as in the **Novak Farmstead** (Novakova domačija) below Smrje village. The restored 19th-century mill has a waterwheel and a traditional farmhouse kitchen.

Just north of Smrje, the riverside village of Prem is a fine example of the stone-built settlements that once character-ized the area. The well-preserved **Prem Castle** (Grad Prem) offers fine views and contains a display of artifacts found at Bronze Age hill forts on the Brkini Plateau south of the river.

🏭 **Novak Farmstead**
Topolc 75C. **Tel** (05) 714 5987. **Open** by appt. 🌐 novakov-mlin.eu

🏰 **Prem Castle**
Prem. **Tel** (05) 710 1384. **Open** May–Sep: noon–7pm Sat & Sun. 🈯

The Škoromati of Hrušica

Located on the Brkini Plateau to the west of Ilirska Bistrica, Hrušica village is famous for preserving pre-Lenten carnival customs with pagan undertones. Revellers known as the *škoromati* run through the streets on the Saturday preceding Shrove Tuesday, clad in sheepskin jerkins, wooden masks and hats. They are led by the sinister *škopiti*, a black-clad figure wielding a huge pair of tongs. His job is to catch unmarried girls and smear them with ash, ensuring their fertility. On Ash Wednesday, an effigy known as the *Pust* is burned outside the village, guaran-teeing good fortune and healthy crops for the coming year.

Traditional masked *škopiti*

SOUTHERN AND EASTERN SLOVENIA

Bordered by Austria, Hungary and Croatia on three sides, and encompassing five of Slovenia's nine administrative districts, Southern and Eastern Slovenia is a melting pot of cultures and histories. The landscape here varies from subalpine hills to vast green plains and idyllic vineyards to virgin forests such as Kočevski Rog, full of deserted villages, brown bears and lynx.

Southern and Eastern Slovenia, because of its location between larger nations, has long been subject to a tug-of-war between European powers. The region's turbulent history began with the Bronze Age Hallstatt tribes. The Romans arrived in the 1st century AD, creating powerful military and merchant colonies such as Poetovio (Ptuj) and Celeia (Celje).

The Germanic aristocratic dynasties conquered swathes of territory in the early Middle Ages. The beleagured Slovenian aristocrats rallied briefly under the banner of the counts of Celje, but, with the assassination of Ulrich II in Belgrade in 1456, resistance crumbled. By the end of the century, the Habsburgs held sway over all territory except the land to the east of the Mura river, which was claimed by the Hungarian crown.

From the early 15th century, the regions that bordered Croatia were attacked by the Ottomans. These attacks lasted for two centuries, leading to the rapid fortification of feudal castles on the borders.

In addition to the Bronze Age archaeology, Roman antiquities, remote monasteries and Baroque fortresses, this region has more than its fair share of scenery. It is also home to Slovenia's most colourful festivals such as Kurent in Ptuj or the folk jamborees in Bela Krajina. The local wine culture established by the Romans continues in the east, and thermal spa resorts such as Dolenjske Toplice and Rogaška Slatina marry historic architecture with luxury wellness facilities. Maribor, Slovenia's second-largest settlement, has a range of shops and restaurants in its historic heart.

Swimming complex under a glass roof, Terme Čatež

◀ Magnificent Knight's Hall in Brežice Castle

Exploring Southern and Eastern Slovenia

Compared to Ljubljana, or the regions of Gorenjska and Primorska in the west, Southern and Eastern Slovenia is toured by fewer foreign visitors. This diverse region divides roughly into three areas. The north is characterized by the subalpine Pohorje massif, which extends from the west of Maribor to the pretty town of Slovenj Gradec. The area south of the Krka river valley is a land of small towns and folk customs, with border fortresses and sun-kissed wine hills along the eastern border. The region of Prekmurje beyond the Mura river is distinct due to centuries of Hungarian rule. Historic towns such as Ptuj, a cradle of civilization for two millennia, Celje and Maribor have modern hotels and are good bases for excursions. Charming country inns and splendid castle hotels provide an excellent incentive to explore the area further.

Sights at a Glance

Villages, Towns and Cities
1 Ribnica
3 Kočevje
6 Novo Mesto
8 Žužemberk
10 Črnomelj
11 Metlika
17 Rogaška Slatina
19 Celje pp174–5
20 Velenje
21 Slovenj Gradec
23 Dravograd
24 Šentanel
27 Laško
29 Slovenske Konjice
31 Maribor pp180–81
32 Ptuj pp182–3
35 Ormož
36 Ljutomer
38 Murska Sobota
40 Bogojina
41 Velika Polana
42 Lendava

Castles and Manors
15 Podsreda Castle
34 Štatenberg Manor

Monasteries
12 Pleterje Monastery
16 Olimje Monastery
28 Žiče Monastery

Tours
13 A Tour of the Krka Valley p169

Museums and Galleries
7 Gallery of Naive Artists
18 Rogatec Open-air Museum

Churches
2 Church of the Assumption
33 Church of the Virgin Protectress

Areas of Natural Beauty
5 Kolpa Valley

Spa Resorts
9 Dolenjske Toplice
22 Kope
37 Radenci
39 Moravske Toplice

Sites of Interest
4 Kočevski Rog
14 Bizeljsko-sremiška Wine Road
25 Peca Underground Mine
26 Roman Necropolis
30 Rogla

For hotels and restaurants in this region see pp194–5 and pp205–7

0 kilometres 15

0 miles 15

Kuzma

Gornji
Petrovci

716

Gorieko

440 232

**MORAVSKE
TOPLICE**

Cankova 39

Martjanci

**MURSKA
SOBOTA** 38

40 **BOGOJINA**

Filovci

RADENCI 37

Šentilj Trate

433

A1

436

437

Plintovec

PREKMURJE

442

Beltinci

A5

MARIBOR

31

Lenart

3

Cerkvenjak

**VELIKA
POLANA** 41

42 **LENDAVA**

3

Drava

ovenrč

Šelnica

Massif

ROGLA

*Rogla
1,517 m*

Radizel

A4

1

Miklavž

229

712

LJUTOMER 36

Juršinci

713

Jeruzalem

230

Mura

Drava

TAJERSKA

**SLOVENSKE
KONJICE**

29

A1

Žiče

32 **PTUJ**

**SLOVENSKA
Bistrica**

Ptujska
Gora

33 **CHURCH OF
THE VIRGIN
PROTECTRESS**

2

ORMOŽ

35

2

Središče
ob Dravi

Drava

Zavrč

28 **ŽIČE
MONASTERY**

Poljčane

34 **STATENBERG
MANOR**

9

18 **ROGATEC OPEN-AIR
MUSEUM**

107

**ROGAŠKA
SLATINA** 17

Podčetrtek

424

423

Pilštanj

Jurklošter

423

16 **OLIMJE
MONASTERY**

**PODSREDA
CASTLE** 15

Bizeljsko

nica

**BIZELJSKO-SREMIŠKA
WINE ROAD** 14

Sava

Žavratec

Krško

219

672

A2

220

Brežice

419

Cerklje

13 **A TOUR OF THE
KRKA VALLEY**

šentjernej

**TERJE
MONASTERY**

ETLIKA

Rosalnice

Theatre and concert hall, Lendava

Getting Around

There is an international airport at Maribor. The A1
motorway from Ljubljana provides access to all destinations to the east as far as Lendava, passing through
Maribor. Off the highways, travel is often slow due to
single-lane roads. There are good international rail
connections to Austria and Croatia from this region.
Maribor and Celje are the hubs of regional rail and bus
transport in the east, while Novo Mesto is the centre of rail
and bus transport in the south; links to villages are limited.

Key

═══ Motorway

━━━ Main road

═══ Minor road

─┴─ Railway

::::: Road tunnel

▬▬▬ International border

△ Peak

For keys to symbols *see back flap*

Quaint stone bridge over the Ribnica river

❶ Ribnica

Road map C4. 43 km (27 miles) SE of
Ljubljana. 🚶 9,200. 🚌 from Ljubljana.
ℹ Škrabčev trg 21; (01) 836 9355.
🎪 Dry Goods Fair (1st Sun of Sep).
🖥 ribnica.si

The modest market town of
Ribnica has long been renowned
for its woodcraft. The town's
cottage industry flourished
when, in an attempt to restore
prosperity in his kingdom after
Turkish raids, the Austrian
Emperor Frederick III (r.1452–93)
gave Ribnica free licence to trade
in his territory in 1492. As a result,
peddlers hawked locally made
spoons, butter pats, wicker
sieves, wooden buckets and
even toothpicks throughout
the Habsburg Empire.

A fascinating collection of
woodcraft as well as displays
on the peddlers' lifestyle are
highlights of the Municipal
Museum in **Ribnica Castle** (Grad
Ribnica), a restored Renaissance
stronghold situated on a river
islet. Visitors can purchase craft
souvenirs at the tourist office.

Located in front of the castle
is the Church of St Stephen
(Cerkev sv Štefana). Its two bell
towers, crowned with Classically
inspired obelisks and pediments, were designed by
the Modernist architect Jože
Plečnik (see p77).

Ⅲ Ribnica Castle
Škrabčev trg 40. **Tel** (01) 836 9335.
Open 10am–1pm & 4–7pm
Tue–Sun. 🏛

❷ Church of the Assumption
Cerkev Marijinega Vnebovzetja

Road map C4. 6 km (4 miles) W of
Ribnica; Nova Štifta 3. **Tel** (01) 836
9943. ♿

Perched on a hill and
shaded by ancient linden
trees in the tranquil
farming village of Nova
Štifta is the mid-17th-
century Church of the
Assumption, the most
revered pilgrimage
church of the Dolenjska
region. The church's
octagonal design, fronted
by a curious arcade and
capped by a lantern,
introduced the Lombardy
Mannerist style to Slovenia
and was later copied

Frescoed Holy Steps in the Church of
the Assumption

throughout Dolenjska. The
frescoed Holy Steps were added
to the rear of the church in
1780 to accommodate the
flood of pilgrims.

The church's plain interior
only heightens the impact
of the spectacular Baroque
furnishings decorated in
shades of ruby, emerald and
gilt. The carved high altar by
the 17th-century sculptor Jurij
Scarnos is especially rich – a
riot of gilded carvings on which
Mary is lifted heavenwards by
a flock of cherubs.

❸ Kočevje

Road map C4. 17 km (11 miles) SE of
Ribnica. 🚶 17,000. 🚌 from Ljubljana
& Novo Mesto. ℹ Trg zbora
odposlancev 72; (01) 893 1460.
🖥 **obcinakocevje.si**

During World War II,
the Kočevski Rog plateau
was a wellspring of
Partisan Resistance.
Kočevje – today, an
administrative centre
of the "Land of Forests"
("Dežela gozdov") on
the Kočevski Rog –
hosted the inaugural
assembly of the Dele-
gates of the Slovenian
Nation. This assembly,
held between 1 and
3 October 1943,
effectively led to the birth of
the modern Slovenian nation.

Tombstone,
Regional Museum

The parliament was held
at Šeškov dom, which is now
the **Regional Museum**
(Pokrajinski muzej). The hall
where the delegates convened
bears a banner that reads
Narod si bo pisal sodbo sam
(The nation shall choose its
fate alone). It also displays
superb reportage-style sketches
of the assembly as well as of
the Partisan Resistance by the
20th-century Novo Mesto-
born artist, Božidar Jakac.
A section in the museum
covers the lifestyles and the
sudden flight of the Germanic
Gottscheer population from
Kočevski Rog in 1941.

Another memento of partisan
activity is the heroic monument
to the Communist struggle,

Baza 20, the Partisan Resistance camp in Kočevski Rog

erected postwar in the central square, Trg zbora odposlancev.

Ⅲ Regional Museum
Prešernova 11. **Tel** (051) 269 972.
Open 8am–3pm Mon–Fri. 🅿 ♿
W pmk-kocevje.si

❹ Kočevski Rog

Road map C4. 37 km (23 miles) SE of Ribnica. **Tel** (07) 306 6025. ✉ Apr–Oct by the Dolenjska Museum in Novo Mesto. **W** dolenjskimuzej.si

The limestone plateau east of Kočevje is cloaked in one of Europe's last virgin forests, its pine and beech woods home to brown bears, wolves and lynx. Habsburg rulers resettled German immigrants, known as Gottscheers, in this remote region from the 14th century. The immigrants made the area one of the most developed in the region by the early 20th century but fled fearing reprisals at the outbreak of World War II.

The Partisan Resistance set up camp here in 1943 and established **Baza 20**, located 7 km (4 miles) west of the town of Dolenjske Toplice (*see p167*). Concealed in limestone depressions, this nerve centre for the anti-Fascist struggle was never discovered despite several attempts by the Nazis, and is preserved as the only serving headquarters of European wartime resistance. At its peak, around 200 people lived and worked in the 26 huts, which contained a hospital, workshops, a printing press and

barracks. All but two with display boards are empty, yet the silent forest makes the visit a haunting experience.

The base is now tainted by the partisans' massacre of thousands of pro-German Slovene Home Guard in the forest at the end of the war. Their mass graves were a secret until the 1970s and the exact number of people executed remains unknown.

❺ Kolpa Valley

Road map C5. 49 km (31 miles) S of Ribnica. 🅸 Osilnica 16; (01) 894 1594. 🚲 🏨 ⛰ **W** osilnica.si

Due to its natural beauty and one of the cleanest – and, in summer, warmest – rivers in

Europe, this tranquil river valley is a favourite holiday destination among Slovenians. Walking and fishing are popular, as is rafting on the gentle rapids of the Kolpa river that snakes along the Croatian border. The hub of all activity is Osilnica, 18 km (11 miles) west of the international border crossing. It has the only bank and supermarket in the area, as well as the Stane Jarm Gallery (Galerija Staneta Jarma), featuring works of local sculptor Stane Jarm (b.1931). Gallery visits can be organized at the tourist office.

East of Osilnica, in Ribjek, the diminutive Church of St Egidius (Cerkev sv Egidija) is a pretty shingle-roofed structure dating from 1681, with naive frescoes and painted glass windows, a traditional Slovenian folk art. It is said that the guard depicted on the right of the high altar is a commandant who fought in one of the many Turkish incursions of the 16th century.

Another folk hero of the valley is Peter Klepec, a shepherd boy who is said to have been given superhuman strength by local fairies. A legend relates that he uprooted the largest tree in the valley to defeat Turkish forces. This is depicted in a roadside sculpture by Stane Jarm a short distance west of Ribjek; the figure wields a tree and glares eastwards.

Rafting on the Kolpa

The clear Kolpa river provides delightful opportunities for rafting between April and September. While rafting on small whitewater rapids is possible early in the season, tranquil trips on inflatable rafts or canoes are possible in midsummer; the river is at its swiftest between Stari trg and Vinica. Hotel Kovač in Osilnica and Tine & Co on Stari trg organize rafting trips.

Visitors rafting on the Kolpa river

Impressive façade of the Town Hall, Novo Mesto

❻ Novo Mesto

Road map D4. 58 km (36 miles) E of Ribnica. 🚗 22,000. 🚉 from Ljubljana. 🚌 from Ljubljana & Dolenjske Toplice. ℹ️ Glavni trg 7; (07) 393 9264. 🏛️ Mon & Fri. **W visitnovomesto.si**

Located on the banks of the Krka river, Novo Mesto is the largest city in southeastern Slovenia and the capital of Dolenjska region. Although its name literally means New Town, historical evidence suggests that a settlement has occupied this spot since prehistory. Today's city was founded in 1365 by the Habsburg Archduke Rudolph IV (1339–65), who had christened it Rudolphswert. Novo Mesto blossomed into an important trading centre in the Middle Ages, and then into an industrial centre.

The modernity of the city's outskirts has not affected its historic centre. The oldest site in Novo Mesto is the Church of St Nicholas (Cerkev sv Nikolaja), built at the highest point on the river promontory. It features an altarpiece by the Venetian Renaissance artist Tintoretto (1518–94), as well as Slovenia's only Gothic crypt, built to prop up the presbytery and now a repository for bishops' tombstones.

The grand attraction of the town, however, is the **Dolenjska Museum** (Dolenjski muzej) beyond the church, which holds some of the richest ancient archaeological exhibits in the country. Particularly outstanding are the grave-finds of Celtic Hallstatt tribes of the late Iron Age, notably the armour of a high-ranking warrior, as well as exceptional situlae (bronze cremation urns) forged with vivacious images of warriors and hunters. An adjacent building showcases exhibits of regional ethnography.

Glavni trg, the former merchant centre, is a picturesque cobbled thoroughfare with several cafés and, at the centre, the 1903 **Town Hall** (Rotovž). The Franciscan St Leonard's Church (Fračiškanskan cerkev sv Lenarta), a block behind the town hall, has a Neo-Gothic and Secessionist façade and houses illuminated manuscripts in the attached library; the tourist office can arrange visits.

At the end of Glavni trg is **Jakčev House** (Jakčev dom), a gallery of works by the artist Božidar Jakac who was born in this riverside quarter. Displays rotate, but include charming

Situla at the Dolenjska Museum, Novo Mesto

images of Novo Mesto and the Dolenjska countryside as well as lively sketches made when the artist travelled to Europe and America in the 1920s and 30s.

🏛️ **Dolenjska Museum**
Muzejska ulica 7. **Tel** (07) 373 1130. **Open** 9am–5pm Tue–Sat, 9am–1pm Sun. 🅿️ **W dolenjskimuzej.si**

🏛️ **Jakčev House**
Sokolska ulica 1. **Tel** (07) 373 1131. **Open** 9am–5pm Tue–Sat, 9am–1pm Sun. 🅿️

❼ Gallery of Naive Artists
Galerija likovnih samorastnikov

Road map C3. 20 km (13 miles) NW of Novo Mesto; Goliev trg 1, Trebnje. **Tel** (07) 348 2106. 🚉 from Novo Mesto. 🚌 from Novo Mesto & Ljubljana. **Open** 10am–noon & 3–6pm Mon–Fri, 10am–noon Sat. 🅿️ **W galerijatrebnje.si**

The otherwise anonymous town of Trebnje warrants a visit for its Gallery of Naive Artists. Located above a shopping centre, Slovenia's only naive art museum displays the works of a village artists' collective established in the 1950s, modelled after the Hlebine school in northern Croatia. Characterized by sharp lines and bright clear colours, the art here depicts happy peasants, fairy-tale forests and bountiful fields. Their unconventional compositions are influenced by Slovenian folk arts such as painted beehive panels and oil-on-glass votive art. The gallery also displays works by affiliated international artists.

Paintings and sculptures at the Gallery of Naive Artists, Trebnje

For hotels and restaurants in this region see pp194–5 and pp205–7

Žužemberk Castle, as seen from the banks of the Krka river

❽ Žužemberk

Road map C4. 24 km (15 miles) W of Novo Mesto. 🚗 1,100. 🚌 from Ljubljana & Novo Mesto. 🎭 Medieval Days (mid-Jul). 🌐 zuzemberk.si

The geographical and administrative hub of the broad Krka river valley, this market town was built around a defence tower in the Middle Ages. **Žužemberk Castle** (Grad Žužemberk) was built in the 16th century by the Auersperg princes and retained offices, a court and prison cells until it began to collapse in 1893. It was reduced to a shell in 1945, but restoration, ongoing since the 1960s, has returned some of the visual impact of its five circular bastions. The castle now serves as a venue for concerts between June and September.

🏠 **Žužemberk Castle**
Grajski trg 1. **Tel** (07) 388 5180.
Open Jul & Aug: 10am–6pm Sat & Sun.

❾ Dolenjske Toplice

Road map D4. 13 km (8 miles) SW of Novo Mesto. 🚗 3,300. 🚌 from Novo Mesto. ℹ️ Sokolski trg 4; (07) 384 5188. 🌐 dolenjske-toplice.si

The oldest medicinal spa resort in Slovenia, Dolenjske Toplice lies at the foot of the Kočevski Rog plateau. Slovenian chronicler Janez Vajkard Valvasor *(see pp94–5)* recorded

tourists coming to bathe in its thermal spring waters in the mid-1600s, when the Auersperg princes promoted its warm and mud baths. The small town prospered at the close of the 19th century as a fashionable health resort of the Austro-Hungarian Empire.

Today, Dolenjske Toplice remains popular with visitors who come for medicinal cures; the 36º C (96.8º F) calcium-rich water is said to work wonders for rheumatism. Recreational visitors come to the Balnea Wellness Centre, which has a complex of pools, saunas and massage rooms.

Handicrafts at Primožič House

Spire of the Church of St Peter, Črnomelj, capital of the Bela Krajina region

❿ Črnomelj

Road map D4. 33 km (21 miles) S of Novo Mesto. 🚗 5,800. 🚆 from Ljubljana. 🚌 from Novo Mesto & Metlika. ℹ️ Trg svobode 3; (07) 305 6530. 🎭 Jurjevanje Folk Festival (mid-Jun). 🌐 belakrajina.si

The administrative capital of the Bela Krajina region is celebrated for a wonderful folk festival that attracts dancers and musicians from throughout Slovenia, as well as for its pre-Roman history. **Črnomelj Castle** (Črnomaljski grad), modified into offices and barely recognizable as a Romanesque stronghold from its façade, contains a small municipal museum. The **Church of St Peter** (Cerkev sv Petra), located diagonally opposite, is notable for its collection of fragments of Roman tombstones near the choir. Behind it, at the far end of the street, **Primožič House** (Primožičeva hiša) displays and sells regional handicrafts such as painted eggs *(pisanica)* and wickerwork.

🏛️ **Črnomelj Castle**
Trg svobode 3. **Tel** (07) 305 6530.
Open 8am–4pm Mon–Fri, 9am–noon Sat. 🚮

🏛️ **Primožič House**
Ulica Mirana Jarca 18. **Open** 8am–4pm Mon–Fri, 9am–noon Sat.

Tri Fare churches in Rosalnice, near Metlika

⓫ Metlika

Road map D4. 27 km (17 miles) SE of Novo Mesto. 🚉 3,400. 🚌 from Novo Mesto & Črnomelj. 🛈 Metlika Castle, Trg svobode 4; (07) 363 5470. 🍷 Vinska Vigred (3rd weekend of May). 🌐 **metlika-turizem.si**

Set in the lovely countryside, this wine-producing town near the Kolpa river is the most picturesque in the Bela Krajina region. Given the historic architecture in its town centre, it is hard to believe the town was frequently attacked and occupied by Turkish forces in the 15th and 16th centuries, and gutted by fire in 1705.

During the Turkish raids, Metlika Castle (Grad Metlika) was a Renaissance fortress; today's aristocratic manor is a result of renovation in the 18th century. A wing of the castle houses the **Bela Krajina Museum** (Belokranjski muzej), which has displays on the region. An audiovisual slideshow introduces the themes – local history, notably Hallstatt grave finds and Roman remains excavated near Črnomelj; and rural lifestyles and crafts, including winemaking and displays of the white embroidered folk costume after which Bela Krajina (literally, White Carniola), according to one theory, is named. The cellars house a wine bar serving local wines. Another wing of the castle contains the Slovenian Firefighting Museum (Slovenski gasilski muzej), which has displays of old fire engines; the country's first fire brigade was

established in Metlika in 1869. The heart of the old town is Mestni trg, a pretty square with small, pastel-coloured houses. At the square's end, fronted by the Maltese crosses of the Teutonic Knights and with a fresco of the Last Judgment, is the Church of St Nicholas (Cerkev sv Nikolaja).

Environs
Located just over 2 km (1 mile) east of Metlika in Rosalnice are the **Tri Fare** (literally, Three Parishes) – a trio of Gothic pilgrimage churches set side by side and enclosed within a low wall. Historians speculate that the churches may have been built to cater to a mixed denomination of Croats, Slovenians and Greek Orthodox worshippers or to cope with a surge in pilgrims in the early 1500s. The largest and smallest, the Lady of Our Sorrows and Ecce Hommó respectively,

Interior of a house, Open-air Museum, Pleterje Monastery

contain fine Baroque frescoes. The churches are usually locked; it is best to consult the tourist office in Metlika for the whereabouts of the keys.

🏛 **Bela Krajina Museum**
Trg svobode 4. **Tel** (07) 306 3370. **Open** 9am–5pm Mon–Sat, 10am–2pm Sun. 🅿
🌐 **belokranjski-muzej.si**

⓬ Pleterje Monastery
Samostan Pleterje

Road map D4. 17 km (11 miles) E of Novo Mesto; Drča 1, Šentjernej. **Tel** (07) 308 1225. 🕐 7:30am–5:30pm Mon–Sat. 🌐 **kartuzija-pleterje.si**

The Carthusian Order was permitted by the Count of Celje to found a monastery in this remote location in 1407. Today, white-cloaked monks remain in the monastery despite Turkish raids in the 16th century and the order's dissolution by Emperor Joseph II in 1784; the buildings were reclaimed in 1899. The monastery is screened by a high wall and visitors have access only to the Gothic Church of the Holy Trinity (Cerkev sv Trojice) – bare but for a medieval rood screen – and a shop that sells fruit brandies, wines, honey and beeswax candles made by the monks.

In an attempt to deflect attention from the monastery, an **Open-air Museum** (Pleterje Skansen) was built in an adjacent field. Historic buildings from the region were rebuilt here to re-create a traditional farmstead, centred around a snug 19th-century cottage with a "black kitchen" hung with smoke-cured meats and cabin-like bedrooms with corn-sheaf mattresses. A toplar or double hayrack and a small farmyard of animals complete the picture.

🏛 **Open-air Museum**
Drča 1, Šentjernej. **Tel** (07) 308 1050. **Open** Apr–Nov: 10am–5pm daily; Dec–Mar: 10am–4pm daily. 🅿
🌐 **skansen.si**

Bottle of pear brandy

⓭ A Tour of the Krka Valley

East of Novo Mesto, the Krka river snakes through a broad valley and passes a succession of large castles. These are a legacy of the Ottoman Turk expansion during the 16th century, when the Habsburg Emperor Ferdinand II established a military frontier (vojna krajina) to fight off raids from across the border. Modified later into palaces by feudal rulers, the strongholds on this route now house museums, galleries, spas and hotels.

Tips for Drivers

Starting point: Otočec, on the 419 from Ratež to Mokrice.
Length: 42 km (26 miles).
Duration: Full day.
Driving conditions: Single-lane country roads till Brežice.
Stopping-off points: There are restaurants at every stop-off en route that serve good traditional cuisine.

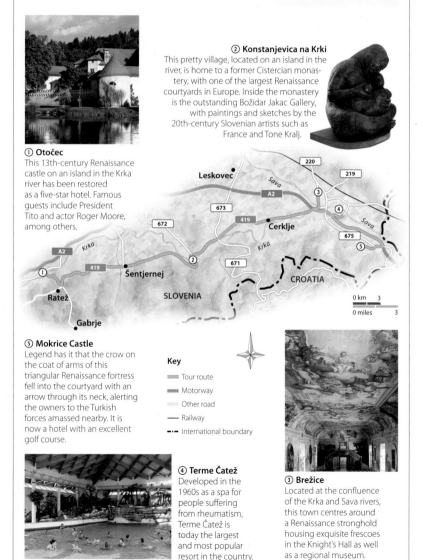

② Konstanjevica na Krki
This pretty village, located on an island in the river, is home to a former Cistercian monastery, with one of the largest Renaissance courtyards in Europe. Inside the monastery is the outstanding Božidar Jakac Gallery, with paintings and sketches by the 20th-century Slovenian artists such as France and Tone Kralj.

① Otočec
This 13th-century Renaissance castle on an island in the Krka river has been restored as a five-star hotel. Famous guests include President Tito and actor Roger Moore, among others.

⑤ Mokrice Castle
Legend has it that the crow on the coat of arms of this triangular Renaissance fortress fell into the courtyard with an arrow through its neck, alerting the owners to the Turkish forces amassed nearby. It is now a hotel with an excellent golf course.

Key

━━ Tour route
━━ Motorway
━━ Other road
── Railway
-∙- International boundary

④ Terme Čatež
Developed in the 1960s as a spa for people suffering from rheumatism, Terme Čatež is today the largest and most popular resort in the country.

③ Brežice
Located at the confluence of the Krka and Sava rivers, this town centres around a Renaissance stronghold housing exquisite frescoes in the Knight's Hall as well as a regional museum.

The 13th-century hilltop Podsreda Castle

⑭ Bizeljsko-sremiška Wine Road

Bizeljsko-sremiški vinorodni okoliš

Road map E3. 51 km (32 miles) NE of Novo Mesto. 🛈 Cesta prvih borcev 18, Brežice; (07) 499 0680. 🚲 🔄
🅦 **bizeljsko.si**

The lower Sava Valley area, north of Brežice *(see p169)*, is known for excellent sparkling and blended white wines cultivated in sandy, mineral-rich soils. The greatest concentration of winemakers lies 10 km (6 miles) north of Brežice on highway 219, around the villages of Stara vas, Brezovica and Bizeljsko. **Istenič** at Stara vas is one of Slovenia's premier sparkling wine producers and organizes cellar tours and tastings. A local attraction are the repnice cellars, cave-like sandstone cellars used by many winemakers. These were dug as natural refrigerators for farmers' crops, but their constant 6–8° C (43–47° F) temperatures and humidity proved ideal for laying down wines. Most of the repnice vineyards are located in Brezovica. The cellars also give refuge to bee-eating birds, which can be seen nesting between May and July near Bizeljsko.

🍴 Istenič
Stara vas 7. **Tel** (07) 495 1559. **Open** 1–8pm Mon–Thu, 1–10pm Fri, noon–10pm Sat, 10am–8pm Sun. 🍴 🚲
🅦 **istenic.si** Note: Book in advance.

⑮ Podsreda Castle

Grad Podsreda

Road map E3. 57 km (35 miles) NE of Novo Mesto; Podsreda 45. **Tel** (03) 800 7100. **Open** Apr–Oct: 10am–6pm Tue–Sun. 🚲 📷
🅦 **kozjanski-park.si**

With its sheer slab-sided walls and a perch on a high wooded spur above the valley, Podsreda Castle appears every bit the romantic castle. Originally erected in the 13th century and then owned by a succession of feudal dynasties, including the counts of Celje and Ptuj, this rectangular fortress was a near total ruin after World War II. Its impressive looks today are the result of

Black and golden altar at the church in Olimje Monastery

three decades of renovation; only the medieval kitchen looks as it did when the castle was built. Other rooms, which host an exhibition of glasswork, are bare and sometimes startlingly modern.

The castle's commanding position affords sweeping views of the lower Sava Valley all the way to the low mountains in Croatia.

⑯ Olimje Monastery

Minoritski samostan Olimje

Road map E3. 78 km (49 miles) NE of Novo Mesto; Olimje 82. **Tel** (03) 582 9161. ♿ Pharmacy: **Open** Mar–late Oct: 10am–7pm daily; late Oct–Feb: 10am–5pm daily. 🚲 🅦 **olimje.net**

Prettily located at the head of a valley near the Croatian border, Olimje Monastery is a squat Renaissance castle that was given to Pauline monks in the mid-17th century. The monks added a Baroque church to the original structure, in which they installed one of Slovenia's most extravagant religious artworks – an altar (1680), which fills the choir with jet-black and gilt carving.

The church also features Baroque frescoes by the Pauline monk Ivan Ranger (1700–1753), a leading Baroque painter of Central Europe, which rise to a trompe l'oeil lantern. Contemporary frescoes adorn a side chapel with an altar dedicated to St Francis.

The former south tower, just off the cloisters, contains what is claimed to be Europe's third-oldest pharmacy. This low-vaulted circular room retains a low Baroque cabinet and frescoes that depict physicians from Christianity and antiquity as well as scenes of Christ healing. The **pharmacy** has a vestibule where the Pauline monks sell herbal cures. The chocolatier, located on one side of the monastery gardens, is also popular with visitors.

Baroque fresco, Olimje Monastery Pharmacy

a cure for many ailments – spout within this hall. The hall also offers massages, aromatherapy and Fango mud treatments. Visitors can also spend time in the **Rogaška Riviera**, a complex of indoor and outdoor thermal mineral water pools.

🛈 Rogaška Riviera
Stritarjeva 1. **Tel** (03) 818 1950.
Open daily. **w** grandhotel-rogaska.com

Façade of the Grand Hotel Rogaška, Rogaška Slatina

🟊 Rogaška Slatina

Road map E3. 88 km (57 miles) NE of Novo Mesto. 🚌 5,500. 🚉 from Celje. 🚌 from Celje & Maribor. **🛈** Zdravilíški trg 1; (03) 581 4414. **w** rogaska-slatina.si

No other Slovenian spa town retains the air of its imperial heyday like Rogaška Slatina. Austro-Hungarians acclaimed the therapeutic power of the thermal waters after the Croatian viceroy Petar Zrinski was cured here in 1665. The arrival of Archduke Johann von Habsburg in 1810 propelled Rogaška Slatina into a fashionable resort frequented by Austro-Hungarian royalty and Viennese high society.

Its heart is the central park, Zdravilíški trg, with manicured lawns and immaculate flowerbeds. Here, the Habsburg-era health spa, Zdravilíški dom, now the Grand Hotel Rogaška (see p195), is one of the grandest Neo-Classical buildings in Slovenia and has an opulent ballroom in which composer Franz Liszt once entertained imperial spa-goers.

The original 19th-century drinking-temple lends its name to Rogaška Slatina's Temple mineral water, on sale throughout Slovenia. The focus of many of today's visitors, however, is the modern drinking hall (pivnica) at the far end of the square. Several mineral springs, including Donat – a potent magnesium-rich water, hailed as

🟊 Rogatec Open-air Museum
Muzej na prostem Rogatec

Road map E2. 8 km (5 miles) NE of Rogaška Slatina; Ptujska cesta 23. **Tel** (03) 818 6200. 🚉 from Rogaška Slatina. 🚌 from Rogaška Slatina. **Open** Apr–Nov: 10am–6pm Tue–Sun. **w** rogatec.si

The market town of Rogatec is home to the largest open-air museum in Slovenia. A short distance from the town centre, ten agricultural buildings gathered from Štajerska, a region in northern Slovenia, have been rebuilt to simulate a village, providing an insight into rural and religious folk-culture between the 18th and early 20th centuries.

The centrepiece cottage – the boyhood home of Slovenian poet Jože Šmit (1922–2004) – has hollowed

tree trunks for gutters. The windows of the room in the *hiška* (home), where the older daughters of the house slept, have hinged iron grilles to deter amorous suitors. Traditionally, the hinges were left unoiled so that it would be difficult to open the windows. The village also has a toplar (double hay-rack) unique to Slovenian rustic architecture, a pigsty fronted by a rack on which turnip and carrot leaves were dried for winter feed, and a cluttered 1930s grocer's store selling traditional souvenirs.

Demonstrations of domestic crafts such as baking, smithery and basket-weaving from corn husks are sometimes staged late on Friday or Saturday afternoons during the high season.

Agricultural buildings at the Rogatec Open-air Museum

Plague Column in the Main Square, Maribor ▶

⑲ Celje

The sobriquet "City of Counts and Princes" seems inconsistent with the modest appearance of Slovenia's third-largest town. Yet Celje, founded over Celeia, the administrative centre of the Roman province of Noricum during the 1st to 5th centuries, rose to become a regional superpower under the dukes of Celje in the Middle Ages. Until Count Ulrich II was assassinated by a rival in Belgrade in 1456, their feudal dynasty stood alone against the Habsburgs, an act of defiance that put their three-star crest onto the Slovenian flag. Modernization and damage during World War II erased the medieval glory, yet Celje's riverside core harbours appealing museums and a splendid castle. The largely pedestrianized Old Town is located on the bank of Savinja river.

Marian pillar in Glavni trg with St Daniel's church as the backdrop

🏛 Glavni trg

Ringed by cafés and shaded by plane trees, this picturesque cobbled square is a favourite place for locals to relax. It developed as the administrative heart of the Old Town and is surrounded by Baroque town houses of wealthy citizens. The house at No. 8 still retains its frescoes. A votive Marian pillar (1776) stands at the centre above statues of St Rok, protector against plague; St Florian, Catholic firefighter; and St Joseph, the patron saint of families and workers. The pillar itself was installed two centuries ago and became the place where criminals were publicly shamed.

Mounted into a town house behind the pillar is a Roman tombstone from Celeia.

⛪ St Daniel's Church

Slomškov trg.

Celje's principal church (Cerkev sv Danijela) stands on Slomškov trg, a square named to honour the 19th-century bishop, Anton Martin Slomšek, who was born near Celje and beatified in 1999. This large Gothic church was built in the early 14th century to replace a smaller predecessor when Celje's wealth and power had begun to rise.

Within the church's dark, atmospheric interior are several frescoes, including one of an Adoration procession that spans the presbytery arch, and fine tombstones of the Celje dukes in full armour in one aisle. The highlight of the church is the late-Gothic chapel – named Chapel of Our Lady of

Sorrows after its medieval pietà – to the altar's left.

Located behind the church is the Water Tower, the most impressive bastion of medieval defences, so-called for its riverside location.

🏛 Celje Regional Museum

Muzejski trg 1. **Tel** (03) 428 0962. **Open** Mar–Oct: Tue–Sun; Nov–Feb: Tue–Sat. 🔊 📷 obligatory. **w** pokmuz-ce.si

Located in a Renaissance palace, this museum (Pokrajinski muzej Celje) showcases the town's past from prehistory to the early 20th century and its ducal rulers. A ghoulish case contains 18 of their skulls – that of the ill-fated Ulrich II is almost sliced in half. The other star attraction is a painted ceiling (1600) that was uncovered

Beautifully painted ceiling of the Celje Regional Museum

For hotels and restaurants in this region see pp194–5 and pp205–7

during renovation of the ceremonial hall in 1926 and is so fragile that it is kept in dim light. Art historians dispute its attribution to the Dutch master, Almanach. Its trompe l'oeil is a spectacular work with guards and noblewomen gazing down at viewers from galleries that seem to fade into the distance, while images of the four seasons and battles frame the edges.

Elsewhere, rooms hold a selection of furnishings and oil paintings in styles ranging from Renaissance to Biedermeier. Other sections of the museum contain prehistoric archaeology, including the world's oldest needle and a lapidarium of votive slabs from Celeia.

🏛 Museum of Recent History

Prešernova 17. **Tel** (03) 428 6410.
Open 10am–6pm Tue–Fri, 9am–1pm Sat. 🅿 🆆 **muzej-nz-ce.si**

Located in the town hall, this museum (Muzej novejše zgodovine) offers an entertaining narrative of Celje from the late 19th century. Short films introduce local history and the "Street of Craftsmen" upstairs. There is a splendid re-creation of shops and ateliers in the mid-20th century with displays of tools and ephemera.

The museum also contains Herman's Den (Hermanov brlog), the only children's museum in Slovenia. Opposite the museum is a former Minorite monastery, nicknamed Old Pot (Stari pisker), that served as a World War II penitentiary. Nazis shot 374

VISITORS' CHECKLIST

Practical Information
Road map D3. 100 km (62 miles) N of Novo Mesto. 🚗 50,000. ℹ️ Krekov trg 3, (03) 428 7930; Old Castle, (03) 544 3690. 🆆 **celeia.info**

Transport
🚆 from Ljubljana, Maribor & Velenje. 🚌 from Ljubljana, Maribor & Murska Sobota.

hostages in six mass executions in its courtyard in 1941 and 1942.

🏰 Old Castle

Cesta na grad 78. **Tel** (03) 544 3690.
Open May & Sep: 9am–8pm daily; Jun–Aug: 9am–9pm daily; Oct–Apr: 9am–5pm daily. 🅿 🖥 🆆 **grad-celje.com**

The scale of one of Slovenia's largest castles, Stari grad, testifies to Celje's power under late-medieval counts. Originally a Romanesque stronghold on a sheer bluff southeast of the centre, the castle acquired its form during the late 14th century. The Celje counts built a palace and the four-storey defensive Friedrich Tower. After centuries of decay, it has been restored to some of its former glory and now doubles as an exhibition space. There are splendid views over Celje from a belvedere near the palace, and from the tower.

Historical performance in progress at the Old Castle

Celje City Centre

① Glavni trg
② St Daniel's Church
③ Celje Regional Museum
④ Museum of Recent History

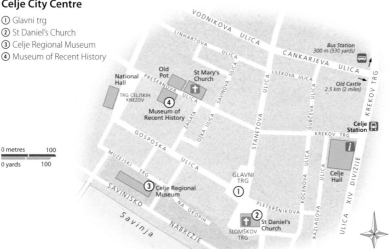

Collection of African masks, Velenje Museum

⑳ Velenje

Road map D2. 24 km (15 miles) NW of Celje. 🚗 33,800. 🚉 from Celje. 🚌 from Celje & Ljubljana. 🛈 Stari trg 3; (03) 896 1860. 🌐 velenje-tourism.si

Slovenia's fifth-largest town and one of the newest, Velenje is an interesting architectural piece of Communist Yugoslavia. It grew rapidly in the 1950s as the country's coal mining expanded. The town architect thought that since miners spent days underground, the town should be filled with light and space: achieved via tower blocks and squares. "Tito's Velenje", named in honour of Josip Broz Tito, was completed by 1959.

Velenje Castle (Velenjski grad) crowns a low hill to the south of town. The castle, first documented as a stronghold to control the north–south trade routes in the 13th century, was modified in the 16th century. The **Velenje Museum** (Muzej Velenje) hosts 10 different collections. The most absorbing relate to sacral and folk works, African art and ritual objects and modern Slovenian art.

The **Coal Mining Museum of Slovenia** (Muzej premogovništva Slovenije) offers tours to explore the shafts below.

🏛 **Velenje Castle & Museum**
Ljubljanska cesta 54. **Tel** (031) 752 418.
Open 10am–6pm Tue–Sun. 🅿
🌐 muzej.velenje.si

🏛 **Coal Mining Museum of Slovenia**
Stari Jašek, Koroška cesta. **Tel** (03) 587 0997. **Open** 8:30am–5pm Tue–Sun.
🅿 🗓 last tour 3pm. 🚻 🖼
🌐 rlv.si/muzej

㉑ Slovenj Gradec

Road map D2. 51 km (32 miles) NW of Celje. 🚗 8,000. 🚌 from Celje & Velenje. 🛈 Glavni trg 24; (02) 881 2116. 🌐 slovenjgradec.si

Reputedly the coldest town in Slovenia – four decades ago, schoolchildren would be sent home because the ink froze in their pens – this small town is better known as the birthplace of composer Hugo Wolf (1860–1903) and for its artistic heritage that dates to the 18th century, when a local workshop made sacred sculpture. A Modernist arts collective in the 1930s spawned the **Gallery of Fine**

Baroque altar of Church of St Elizabeth, Slovenj Gradec

Arts (Galerija likovnih umetnosti), a pastel-tinted medieval building with modern sculpture. The gallery hosts works by local 20th-century artists such as Jože Tisnikar and international names such as Ossip Zadkine, a Russian-born, Paris-educated Cubist. The building was originally the town hall and the exhibits of regional archaeology in the incorporated **Koroška Regional Museum** (Koroški pokrajinski muzej) are displayed in old cells. These include glass and jewellery from Colatio, a 3rd-century Roman settlement that preceded Slovenj Gradec.

The **Church of St Elizabeth** (Cerkev sv Elizabete) lies on Trg svobode, off Glavni trg. Its sombre late-Romanesque exterior conceals a late-Gothic interior with Baroque furnishings. Austrian sculptor Johan Jacob Schoy (1686–1732) carved an altar so large it just squeezes into the presbytery while the altarpiece is by Franz Strauss, leading artist of Slovenj Gradec's Baroque workshop.

The adjacent Church of the Holy Spirit (Cerkev sv Duha) contains fragments of Roman tombstone embedded in its walls and Gothic frescoes of Christ's martyrdom. The tourist office can provide access when mass is not in progress.

🏛 **Gallery of Fine Arts**
Glavni trg 24. **Tel** (02) 884 1283.
Open 9am–6pm Tue–Fri, 10am–1pm & 2–6pm Sat & Sun. 🅿 🖼
🌐 glu-sg.si

🏛 **Koroška Regional Museum**
Glavni trg 24. **Tel** (02) 621 2522.
Open 9am–6pm Tue–Fri, 10am–1pm & 2–6pm Sat & Sun. 🅿 🖼 🌐 kpm.si

Jože Tisnikar (1928–98)

Few Slovenian painters are as instantly recognizable as Jože Tisnikar. After an impoverished childhood as one of eight children to an alcoholic father, he took a job performing autopsies and preparing cadavers in the pathology department of Slovenj Gradec hospital. The experience shaped his work. *Autopsy* (1955) established the style of the self-taught artist: haunted and bleak.

The Flute Player, 1971, by Jože Tisnikar

The Romanesque Church of St Vitus, Dravograd

❷ Kope

Road map D2. 63 km (39 miles) N of Celje. **ℹ** Glavni trg 41, Slovenj Gradec; (02) 603 6555. **W** pohorje.org

A narrow road running east from Slovenj Gradec ascends slowly through villages to this small resort among the highest hills of the Pohorje massif. It is a popular destination for skiing as the snow cover can last from November to late spring, while in summer, hikers and families come for the clean, cool air and easy walking trails.

Hour-long walks from a car park at an altitude of 1,370 m (4,500 ft) ascend to the neighbouring peaks, Velika Kopa and Črni vrh. From the latter, at 1,540 m (5,060 ft), the path continues to hilltops Mali Črni vrh and Ribniški vrh to reach a pretty alpine lake covered with waterlilies.

❷ Dravograd

Road map D2. 60 km (37 miles) NW of Celje. **⚐** 3,400. **⚐** from Maribor. **⚌** from Maribor, Celje, Velenje & Slovenj Gradec. **ℹ** Trg 4 julija 50; (02) 871 0285. **W** dravograd.si

On the Austrian border, this small town wraps around the confluence of the Drava, Meža and Mislinja rivers. The location made it strategic for rafters, who bound felled logs at its quay then transported them as far away as Hungary, Romania and Serbia. Pleasure trips by raft *(flos)* are organized for groups *(see pp216–17)*.

Dravograd's name was tarnished in the last century, due to its association with a Gestapo prison in the basement of the town hall at Trg 4 julija. In its five cells, punishment and torture was meted out to Slovenian resistance fighters and troublesome Russian prisoners who were forced to build a hydroelectric dam on the Drava river. The cells can be accessed via the tourist office during weekday office hours.

Nearby in the town centre is the Romanesque Church of St Vitus (Cerkev sv Vida), built in 1170, when Dravograd first found mention in the records.

❷ Šentanel

Road map C2. 78 km (49 miles) NW of Celje. **⚐** 200.

This sleepy farming hamlet clusters around the Church of St Daniel, from where it gets its name, on a sun-drenched south-facing hillside. With good views, friendly locals and a lazy pace of life, Šentanel is a lovely destination at which to sample rural tourism, stop overnight in a traditional alpine farmhouse or sample the local cider *(mošt)* in the village-centre inns. Opposite the church are two farmsteads with a few small rooms on the ground floor and an attic storage space accessed by ladder. The village is also a popular base for some of the finest mountain biking trails.

Bicycle tour of the fascinating Peca Underground Mine

❷ Peca Underground Mine

Pdzemlje Pece

Road map C2. 46 km (29 miles) NW of Celje; Glančnik 8, Mežica. **Tel** (02) 870 0180. **⚌** from Dravograd & Črna na Koroškem. **ℹ** Park kralja Matjaža, Center 100; (02) 823 8269. **⚡ ⚙** Tue–Sun. **⌂** Museum: **Open** 9am–3pm Tue–Sun. **W** podzemljepece.com

Although the Romans are believed to have sourced lead ore from Mount Peca, it was not until 1665 that a mine was dug at Mežica to extract lead and zinc. Mining intensified in the early 20th century and when the mine ceased production in 1994, about 19 million tonnes (21 million tons) of ore had been extracted. Visitors can tour the mine by a train that descends 3.5 km (2 miles), or on bicycles. A **Museum** on the ground level focuses on miners' lifestyles and geology.

Traditional tourist farm, Šentanel

Mausolea at the Roman Necropolis, Šempeter

㉖ Roman Necropolis

Rimska nekropola

Road map D3. 12 km (8 miles) W of Celje; Ob rimski nekropoli 2, Šempeter. **Tel** (03) 700 2056. 🚆 from Celje. 🚌 from Celje. **Open** 1–15 Apr: 10am–3pm daily; 16 Apr–Sep: 10am–6pm daily; Oct: 10am–4pm Sat & Sun. 🅿 ♿ 🅦 **td-sempeter.si**

In 1952, villagers digging in an orchard in the town of Šempeter discovered a female statue, thereby unearthing a well-preserved Roman cemetery on the former Ljubljana to Celje road. The cemetery survived the reigns of the Roman Emperor Trajan and the Severi Dynasty (AD 96–235), but was abandoned around AD 270 when the Savinja river flooded. The silt preserved the 100-plus mausolea of Celeia (Celje) families, which have been reconstructed; the park is called Roman Necropolis.

The most impressive epitaph is the marble mausoleum of the Spectatii, a monument extending over 8 m (26 ft) high, built for a Celje dignitary and his family. There is an image of Medusa at the apex intended to protect their remains from grave-robbers, while on the base are reliefs of Roman civilization – images of hunting and sporting, depictions of the four seasons and one of a satyr flirting with a nymph.

The richest carving adorns the mausoleum of the Ennius family. The style of its reliefs dates it back to the mid-1st century AD. It is fronted by an image of Europa being carried out to sea by Zeus disguised as a bull. Canopied by a richly carved baldachin are images of Ennius family. Both monuments were created when Celje was at its most wealthy. The oldest tomb, that of Gaius Vindonius Successus, with images of Hercules leading Alcestis to the underworld, and the simple late 3rd-century tomb of Statucius Secundianus, reflect the rise then wane of a rich society. A section of the Roman road itself lies to the east of the cemetery.

Relief on a tombstone

㉗ Laško

Road map D3. 11 km (7 miles) S of Celje. 🏔 4,000. 🚆 from Celje. 🚌 from Celje. 🛈 Trg svobode 8; (03) 733 8950. 🍺 Beer & Flowers Festival (2nd week of Jul). 🅦 **lasko.si**

The road to the south of Celje follows the Savinja river to this small town famous as the home of the lager, Laško pivo. It was first brewed in 1825 by the owner of a honey and mead shop that grew into one of the largest breweries in Yugoslavia. The town's brewery *(pivovarna)* lies to the south of the medieval town centre and houses a small museum with displays on brewing techniques.

Laško's second claim to fame is its mineral springs. The Romans, medieval missionaries and the Austro-Hungarian Emperor Franz Josef I (r. 1848–1916) himself bathed in the 34° C (93° F) waters that bubble up just north of the Old Town. Today's spa resort is a modern complex named Wellness Park Laško (Zdravilišče Laško) with pools and a massage centre.

The town also boasts the fine early Gothic Church of St Martin (Cerkev sv Martina), which has a Romanesque tower.

㉘ Žiče Monastery

Žička kartuzija

Road map E2. 20 km (12 miles) NE of Celje; Stare Slemene 24, Loče. **Tel** (03) 759 3110. **Open** May–Oct: 9am–7pm daily; Nov & Feb–Apr: 10am–6pm Mon–Fri. 🅿 📷 🅿 📖 🅰 Apothecary: **Closed** winter.

Magical for its peace and isolation in the Valley of St John, Žiče Monastery might well be the most evocative ruin in Slovenia. The Carthusian monastery was founded in 1160 – the story goes that St John appeared in a dream to the Styrian ruler Otakar III of Traungau (1124–64), who had recently returned from the Crusades, and instructed him to create a self-sufficient community. The monastery withstood Turkish raids behind high defence walls in the 15th century and prospered until its dissolution by Emperor Joseph II in 1782.

At the heart of the complex is the shell of the Romanesque Church of St John the Baptist (Cerkev sv Janeza Krstnika) and an octagonal Gothic chapel that houses a model of the monastery. Surrounding

Swimming pool at the spa resort in Laško

Defensive towers guarding the entrance to Žiče Monastery

buildings have been restored and now house a museum with a lapidarium; the cellar of the acclaimed winemaker Zlati grič; and, in a defence tower, the **Apothecary** that sells medicinal liquors and herbal cures prepared to ancient Carthusian recipies. The Gostišče Gastuž (1467) by the entrance is reputed to be the oldest operating inn in Slovenia.

㉙ Slovenske Konjice

Road map D2. 19 km (12 miles) NE of Celje. 13,900. from Celje, Ljubljana & Maribor. Stari trg 29; (03) 759 3110. slovenskekonjice.si

Persevere through the modern suburbs and the Old Town lives up to the charm suggested by Slovenske Konjice's tagline "City of Flowers and Wine". Historic town houses, painted in shades of peach, cream and butterscotch with flowerbox-lined windows, stretch along the banks of a stream that is spanned by tiny bridges. A local tale explains that these early 18th-century houses survived where their medieval predecessors burned because their builders had incorporated sacred boulders from the Žiče Monastery in the walls. The village-like medieval core, Stari

trg, is enchanting. At Stari trg 15, the Riemer Gallery (Galerija Riemer) displays a private collection of period furniture and art amassed by a wealthy local businessman. Tours can be organized through the tourist office.

Bottle of Zlati grič wine

Another attraction is the Church of St George (Cerkev sv Jurija), an unusual two-nave Gothic construction with a frescoed Baroque chapel. Beyond it is the **Trebnik Manor** (Dvorec Trebnik), an erstwhile 17th-century residence, which now serves as a gallery and shop where organic herbal beauty products and foods are sold.

㉚ Rogla

Road map D2. 36 km (22 miles) N of Celje. from Zreče. Cesta na Roglo 15, Zreče; (03) 757 7100. rogla.eu

The rounded highlands north of Slovenske Konjice are the central section of the Pohorje massif extending west of Maribor. Once home only to isolated dairy farmsteads and a cottage timber industry, the lightly forested upland is known today for its ski resort on the summit of Rogla at 1,520 m (4,980 ft), north of the town of Zreče. Once the snow thaws, hiking and mountain biking take over on a variety of trails through alpine meadows and pine forests.

Shelves lined with goods at the Trebnik Manor shop, Slovenske Konjice

㉛ Maribor

Slovenia's second-largest city, Maribor occupies a strategic location on the Drava river. Settled by Slavs in the early Middle Ages, the city became an important trading centre. However, with the expansion of the Ottoman Empire, it assumed the role of a border fortress and trade declined. The city's fortunes improved with the construction of the Vienna–Trieste railway in 1846. Today, it has a mix of old and new architecture; the riverside quarter of Lent has the most attractive Baroque buildings.

Ornate west wing façade of the 15th-century Maribor Castle

🏛 Maribor Castle and Regional Museum

Grajska 2. **Tel** (02) 228 3551.
Open 9am–4pm Tue–Sat, 9am–2pm Sun. 🅰 Ⓦ **pmuzej-mb.si**

Dominating the northern end of Castle Square (Grajski trg), Maribor Castle (Mariborski grad) was built in 1478 to protect

Maribor from Ottoman attacks. Once the Turkish threat receded, the castle became an aristo-cratic residence. Today, it is home to the Regional Museum (Pokrajinski muzej), which displays folk costumes, military uniforms, furniture spanning several eras and Gothic and Baroque religious art. The building's 18th-century Rococo staircase, adorned with statues, is remarkable.

🏛 Cathedral of St John the Baptist

Slomškov trg. **Tel** (02) 251 8432.
Open dawn–dusk daily.

Just southwest of the castle, Maribor's medieval cathedral (stolna cerkev sv Janeza Krstnika) is predominantly Gothic in style, although a characterful Renaissance bell

tower was added in 1601. The interior decorations date mostly from the Baroque period, although some exquisitely carved medieval stone stalls remain in the choir. A chapel to the left of the main altar is dedicated to Bishop Anton M Slomšek, who promoted the Slovenian language at a time when Maribor was ruled by a German-speaking elite.

🏛 Main Square

The town's long, rectangular Main Square (Glavni trg) took shape in the 13th century, when Maribor was emerging as a major commercial centre in the region. On its northern

Maribor's Main Square with its Baroque Plague Column

Maribor City Centre

① Maribor Castle and Regional Museum
② Cathedral of St John the Baptist
③ Main Square
④ Lent
⑤ The Jewish Quarter

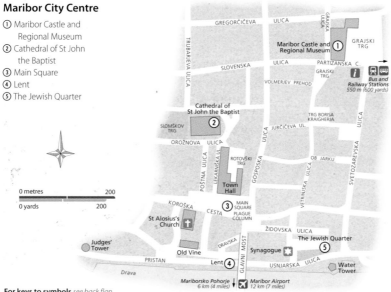

side is the Town Hall (Rotovž), with an onion-domed clock tower and an arcaded Renaissance courtyard at the back. In the square's centre is an ornate Baroque **Plague Column** (kužno znamenje), raised in 1743 to commemorate the 17th-century plague.

▦ Lent

Downhill from the city centre is the charming riverside Lent quarter, which was once a busy port from where rafts put together from local timber began their journey along the Drava and Danube rivers.

Today, Lent is a bustling neighbourhood, its well-preserved Baroque houses home to modern art galleries, cafés and bars. Growing along the façade of one of the water-front houses is the 400-year-old famous **Old Vine** (Stara trta), believed to be the oldest vine in the world. Marking Lent's western boundary is the **Judges' Tower** (Sodni stolp), a barrel-shaped medieval struc-ture with a curious mansard roof. To the east is the rather peculiar 16th-century **Water Tower** (Vodni stolp) featuring a pentagonal ground plan and a tall, tapering roof.

▦ The Jewish Quarter

Synagogue: Židovska 4. **Tel** (02) 252 7836. **Open** 8am–4pm Mon–Fri, 9am–2pm Sun. ▨ ☒ **pmuzej-mb.si**

Standing on a terrace immediately inland from the Water Tower is the Jews' Tower

Famous Old Vine growing against a house in the Lent quarter

(Židovski stolp), a quadrangular red-brick structure attached to a short stretch of the surviving city wall. The narrow lanes beside the tower were once home to Maribor's Jewish community, who were an important presence in the city from the 13th century until their extermination by the Nazis during World War II. The beautifully restored 14th-century **Synagogue** (sinagoga) now houses an exhibition devoted to local Jewish heritage.

Environs

About 6 km (4 miles) south of the Old Town is the Zgornje Radvanje suburb, from where a cable car *(vzpenjača)* takes visitors up to the **Mariborsko Pohorje** massif. This is the last upland before the Alps give way to the Pannonian plain; the lush

VISITORS' CHECKLIST

Practical Information
Road map E2.
57 km (35 miles) NE of Celje.
Ⓜ 116,000. ⓘ Partizanska 6;
(02) 234 6611. ⓔ Vodnikov trg:
Mon–Sat. ⓕ Lent Festival (late
Jun/early Jul); Festival Maribor
(classical music, early Sep); Wine
festivals (early Mar & late Sep).
ⓦ **maribor-pohorje.si**

Transport
✈ 🚆 from Ljubljana, Celje &
Dravograd. 🚌 from Ljubljana,
Celje, Ptuj & Murska Sobota.

meadows and pine forest offering a complete contrast to the jagged, bare mountains in the northwest.

Visitors can enjoy a number of outdoor activities here. Locals go skiing and snowboarding from December to March at the well-equipped resort, also called Mariborsko Pohorje, which offers 80 km (48 miles) of pistes.

It is also a popular destination for walking, hiking, horse riding, cycling and simply relaxing in summer. The well-marked 75-km- (46-mile-) long Pohorje Biking Transversal and Bike Park Pohorje is a world cup race venue catering to mountain bikers.

A number of hotels and restaurants as well as agents who organize outdoor activities are clustered around the upper terminal of the cable car. The massif can also be accessed by road.

Water Tower on the banks of the calm Drava river, Maribor

For hotels and restaurants in this region see pp194–5 and pp205–7

㉜ Ptuj

Scenically located on the banks of the Drava river, Ptuj is furnished with a wealth of monuments that testify to a history spanning two millennia. The town was founded in AD 69 as a self-governing Roman city-state named Colonia Ulpia Traiana Poetovio. At its height, 40,000 people lived in Poetovio, making it the largest Roman settlement in what is now Slovenia. The medieval town later blossomed under the governance of Austrian nobility and the archdiocese of Salzburg. Its influence, however, was weakened by the Ottoman Turkish attacks and then by fires in the 17th century. By the 1700s, Ptuj was just the provincial town it now appears to be at first glance.

The Church of St George and its neighbourhood, Ptuj

⊞ Mestni trg

The tidy main square, popular with locals for their morning coffee and evening drinks alike, has been the civic heart of Ptuj since medieval times. The grandest of the historic buildings on the square is the Germanic Neo-Gothic Town Hall, built in 1907 to replace the late-Gothic original. Statues on its corner oriel window depict the Roman emperor Trajan, who awarded Ptuj full colonial rights, and St Victorin, the town's first bishop in the early 4th century.

A statue on the votive column in the middle of Mestni trg depicts St Florian, protector against fire, as a Roman soldier. This statue is a replica of the original, which was erected in 1745 after four catastrophic fires hit the city in a span of 60 years. The St Florian Column seems to have worked at protecting the town from fires – the inferno in 1744 was Ptuj's last.

⌂ Minorite Monastery

Minoritski trg. **Tel** (02) 748 0310.
The Minorite Order set up this monastery (Minoritski samostan) when they arrived in Ptuj in 1261. Having survived the purges of autocratic Joseph II in 1784 and persecution by the Nazis, the order still remains in the monastery, which possesses what is said to be the oldest Baroque façade in Slovenia. Its interior has a beautiful summer refectory with rich stucco work and frescoes. In the library is one of only three surviving New Testaments by the 16th-century Lutheran Primož Trubar (see p39), who published the first books in the Slovenian language. Visits to the monastery can be arranged through the tourist office.

The adjoining modern church is a replica of the one destroyed by Allied bombs in 1945 – only the Gothic presbytery remains of the original. The gilded votive Marian pillar outside was erected in 1655 to safeguard against plague.

⌂ Church of St George

Slovenski trg. **Tel** (02) 748 1970. ⌂
Built in the 9th century over a Roman basilica, the Church of St George (Cerkev sv Jruija) is an atmospheric hybrid of late-Romanesque and Gothic styles whose walls are decorated with frescoes. The abundance of finely carved altars reveals the wealth of the medieval town – an *Adoration of the Magi* (1515) in the south aisle is a highlight. The church's most acclaimed sculpture is a 15th-century work that portrays its patron as a boyish knight. The sculpture is protected in a glass case in the vestibule.

The baptismal chapel at the rear of the south aisle contains a 15th-century colour-saturated polyptych of the death of the Virgin Mary by Konrad Laib, a Salzburg master influenced by Italian high art. One wing of the polyptych shows St Hieronymus wearing a red cape, holding a model of the original church.

Orpheus Monument
Slovenski trg.
This 5-m- (16-ft-) high Roman tombstone stands where it was unearthed sometime in the Middle Ages. Carved from white Pohorje marble for a 2nd-century mayor of Poetovio, and later used as a medieval pillory, this monument (Orfejev spomenik) is named after the worn relief of Orpheus, the legendary musician in Greek mythology. Here he is shown surrounded by the animals attracted by his songs of lament for Eurydice, his wife.

Frescoes in the summer refectory, Minorite Monastery

Carvings in the tympanum depict Selene, goddess of the moon.

More modest tombstones from Poetovio are mounted around the base of the City Tower (Mestni stolp) behind, a five-storey campanile that doubled as a watchtower during Turkish raids.

🏛 Dominican Monastery

Muzejski trg 1. **Tel** (02) 787 9230. **Open** 15 Apr–Nov: 9am–6pm daily. 🅿 🆆 pmpo.si

Thick floral stucco and sgraffiti, sculptures of friars and a candy-pink colour scheme give the Dominican Monastery (Dominikanski samostan) the most joyful façade in Ptuj. The decoration was added to the original Gothic building that housed the order after it arrived in Ptuj around 1230.

Inside, medieval frescoes in the cloister and Gothic vaults provide an atmospheric setting for the superb antique and medieval exhibits of the **Ptuj Regional Museum** (Pokrajinski muzej Ptuj).

🏛 Ptuj Castle

Na gradu 1. **Tel** (92) 787 9230. **Open** 9am–6pm daily. 🅿 📷 ♿

Like the Celts and Romans before them, the Salzburg archbishops built Ptuj Castle (Ptujski grad) on the high ground above the Drava river, in the 11th century. It was leased to the lords of Ptuj and was renovated into a palace by the Leslie Dynasty in the 17th century. A tour of the castle's rooms is included in the entry fee to the Ptuj Regional Museum. The lower floors house period furnishings and objets d'art. The floors above display musical instruments, costumes of Ptuj's famous Kurent carnival and devotional art.

Environs

Around 2 km (1 mile) west of Ptuj, a pavilion, signposted off Mariborska cesta, shelters the remains of the 3rd-century

Kurenti costumes, Ptuj Regional Museum

Mithra Shrine. Its finest sacrificial relief depicts the Roman sun god Mithras as he sacrifices a bull to create the world. Prize finds are displayed in the Dominican Monastery.

The Kurent

Somewhere between a fertility ritual and a rite of spring, the Kurent is named for its Kurenti – scary figures who dress in shaggy sheepskins, wear horns or a feather headdress and have beak-like noses and red tongues that hang to the chest. On Shrove Tuesday, the Kurenti gambol between houses, flailing wooden clubs and clanking cowbells to scare off evil and winter spirits. Spectators smash clay pots for good luck and some women give handkerchiefs to win favour with the male Kurenti.

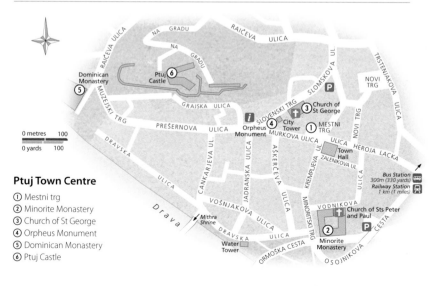

Ptuj Town Centre

① Mestni trg
② Minorite Monastery
③ Church of St George
④ Orpheus Monument
⑤ Dominican Monastery
⑥ Ptuj Castle

For keys to symbols *see back flap*

㉝ Church of the Virgin Protectress
Cerkev Marije Zavetnice

Road map E2. 11 km (7 miles) SW of Ptuj. **Tel** (02) 794 4231. ▦ from Ptuj. 🅸 Ptujska Gora 36; (02) 794 0027. Ⓦ **ptujska-gora.si**

Dating from the beginning of the 15th century, the Church of the Virgin Protectress is located above Ptujska Gora village. Funded by Ptuj's Lord Bernard III, the church was fortified during Turkish incursions in the middle of the century.

According to a local legend, the Virgin Mary draped her cloak over the hill as a black cloud to conceal the church from raiders – a miracle that elevated it to one of the most revered churches in Slovenia.

The story is probably related to the extraordinary *Virgin as Protector* (1410) high altar, the highlight of a beautifully spacious three-nave Gothic interior. Its centrepiece depicts a host of angels lifting the Madonna's dusty green cloak to reveal a kneeling crowd sheltered beneath. Among the 82 aristocrats, clergy and commoners depicted are Bernard III with his wife Valburga, presumably the two figures on the Virgin's left staring back at viewers. The south aisle contains a superb high-Gothic baldachin that was created to canopy the tomb of Celje's Count Frederick II;

Štatenberg Manor's emblem

the three-star crest of the Celje Dynasty – adopted in 1991 on the national flag – is just one feature among the exquisite carving. In the sanctuary, to the right of the main portal, is a finely executed Gothic fresco of St Dorothy and Jesus in the rose garden, with its donor depicted kneeling at the side.

㉞ Štatenberg Manor
Dvorec Štatenberg

Road map E2. Štatenberg 86, Makole. 18 km (11 miles) SW of Ptuj. **Tel** (040) 870 835. **Open** 10am–10pm Wed– Sun. 🏛 for tours only. 🅲 book in advance. 🖉 Ⓦ **dvorecstatenberg.si**

Set above the valley 9 km (6 miles) west of Ptujska Gora, this two-storey palace was commissioned by Count Ignaz Maria Attems in the early 18th century. Intended to replace a medieval castle in nearby Makole, it was designed by an Italian architect and served as a summer residence for the powerful aristocratic Styrian family.

The four-wing palace was created in one go and has not been altered by subsequent owners. While decades of neglect has left the exterior semi-derelict, the courtyard is a delight of restrained Baroque style. There is a restaurant on the palace's ground floor. The rest of the interior, much of which is in poor condition, can only be seen on tours.

Štatenberg Manor, with the garden in the forefront

The highlight is the ceremonial two-storey hall in the central wing, where the Attems held banquets and balls beneath a ceiling whose allegorical frescoes of mythology, arts and sciences are framed by stucco work. The surrounding English-style parkland, though neglected, is pleasant to explore, and angling is possible.

㉟ Ormož

Road map F2. 23 km (14 miles) E of Ptuj. 🚋 2,300. 🚌 from Ptuj & Murska Sobota. ▦ from Ptuj. 🅸 Kolodrorska cesta 9, (02) 741 5556; second office in castle.

A location on a terrace abutting the Slovenian border has put Ormož on the front line throughout modern history. Between the 15th and 17th centuries, the town was attacked by Hungarians and Ottoman Turks, prompting the lords of Ormož to fortify the 13th-century castle. **Ormož Castle** retains the Romanesque tower, but the Baroque courtyard palace is the product of renovation during peacetime in the 18th century. When the castle was being restored, allegorical Classical paintings were put up in its halls. These paintings are now located on the first floor and are the highlight of the small museum within the castle, which also has displays on the town's history. The museum's displays include photographs from the Ten-Day War (27 June–6 July 1991) when Ormož was again back on the barricades of Slovenia as tanks

Virgin as Protector relief, Church of the Virgin Protectress

For hotels and restaurants in this region see pp194–5 and pp205–7

of the Yugoslav Army invaded from Croatia (see p43).

The countryside north of Ormož is idyllic to explore at leisure. Isolated houses are scattered atop hills whose sun-drenched slopes nurture the vineyards of one of the country's premier wine regions. Details of the wine cellars (vinska klet) are available at the tourist office.

Environs
About 11 km (7 miles) north of Ormož lies the somnolent wine village, Jeruzalem. The story goes that it was christened by German Crusaders who were reminded of the Holy City by the local hospitality. They are said to have brought a pietà icon, a replica of which is on the altar of the Church of St Mary (Cerkev sv Marije).

🏛 **Ormož Castle and Museum**
Kolodvorska 9. **Tel** (02) 741 7290.
Open May–15 Oct: 8am–3pm Mon–Fri, 9am–2pm Sat; 16 Oct–Apr: 9am–4pm Mon–Fri, 9am–2pm Sat. 📷 📷

Nineteenth-century buildings in the main square, Ljutomer

Lush green vineyards found north of Ormož

🏛 Ljutomer
Road map F2. 44 km (27 miles) NE of Ptuj. 🚐 3,400. 🚉 from Ormož & Murska Sobota. 🚌 ℹ Jureša Cirila 4, (02) 581 1105; Glavni trg, (02) 584 8333. 🌐 **jeruzalem.si**

This region to the south of the Mura river has long been associated with horse breeding. This helps to explain why its administrative and cultural centre, Ljutomer, hosted

Slovenia's first horse-racing meet – only the second in the Austro-Hungarian empire – in 1875. Between April and September the racing society stages trotting races on two Sunday afternoons a month on a racecourse about 1 km (0.6 mile) north of the centre.

Ljutomer's heart is its spacious main square, Glavni trg, with a votive plague column of the Virgin Mary and saints Rok and Boštjan (1729). The **Ljutomer Museum** in the former town hall at the back of the square focuses on the Tabor Movement in Ljutomer (1868–71), when young Slovenian intellectuals initiated mass open-air forums (tabors) to rally support for a united Slovenia. More absorbing, perhaps, is footage from the oldest movies shot in Slovenia, filmed by cameraman Karol Grossmann in 1905.

🏛 **Ljutomer Museum**
Glavni trg 2. **Tel** (02) 581 1758.
Open 8am–3pm Mon–Fri. 📷 📷 📷

🏛 Radenci
Road map F1. 31 km (19 miles) N of Ptuj. 🚐 1,800. 🚌 from Ljutomer & Murska Sobota. 🌐 **zdravilisce-radenci.si**

Until the arrival of a young Austrian medical student, Karl Henn, in 1833, local peasantry believed the 30–33º C (86–91º F) waters that bubbled up from the ground at Radenci were

caused by the cooking of subterranean witches. Henn, by now a doctor, returned to the area in 1869 and began to export the naturally carbonated water to the imperial court in Vienna and the papal palace in Rome. Branded with a three-hearts logo, the water is popular throughout Slovenia.

The medicinal spa resort established by Henn in 1882, Zdravilišče Radenci, is located at the eastern fringe of a large wooded park east of modern Radenci. Its waters are believed to treat cardiovascular problems. Renovation has added Terme Radenci, a spacious modern spa hotel with a wellness centre and large thermal swimming pool. Both are open to visitors as well as guests.

Visitors at the thermal pool in the spa resort, Radenci

㊳ Murska Sobota

Road map F1. 47 km (29 miles) NE of Ptuj. 12,600. from Ljubljana & Ptuj. from Radenci, Maribor & Celje. Zvezna ulica 10, (02) 534 1130; Slovenska ulica 25, (02) 534 8822. **murska-sobota.si**

Until it was absorbed into the Kingdom of Serbs, Croats and Slovenes in 1919, Murska Sobota was a backwater of Hungary and, therefore, has few historical monuments. Today, the town is the capital of the Prekmurje region. The **Regional Museum** (Pokrajinski muzej) in Murska Sobota Castle (Murski grad) is worth a visit. An erstwhile residence of the counts of Murska Sobota, and notable for its ceremonial Baroque portal, this massively turreted Renaissance palace sits in an English-style parkland in the centre of the town.

The restored Baroque festive hall, with splendid frescoes and stuccowork, is arguably the highlight among the museum's archaeology and ethnology exhibits. One section has black pottery jugs crafted by potters in the northeastern village of Filovci, and displays on customs of the region. There is also footage of ferries that plied the Mura river until the 1930s – the region was cut off from Slovenia by road until a bridge was built over the river in 1924. One room details the liberation of Murska Sobota by Russia, after a second Hungarian occupation at the end of World War II. A Soviet-style victory monument in the town centre celebrates the Red Army's arrival in April 1945.

Baroque room in the Regional Museum, Murska Sobota

Visitors bathing in a thermal pool in Terme 3000, Moravske Toplice

Regional Museum
Trubarjev drevored 4. **Tel** (02) 527 1706. **Open** 9am–5pm Tue–Fri, 9am–1pm Sat & Sun.
pok-muzej-ms.si

㊴ Moravske Toplice

Road map F1. 54 km (34 miles) NE of Ptuj. 700. from Murska Sobota. Kranjčeva 3; (02) 538 1520. **moravske-toplice.com**

Several hot-water springs were discovered on the Prekmurje plains during the search for oil in the 1960s. This is where the spa town of Moravske Toplice was established. The mineral-rich waters here proved to be extremely popular with those seeking relief from rheumatism.

Every day in summer, hundreds of visitors come to the **Terme 3000** spa to take a dip in the waters, which emerge at over 70° C (158° F) but are cooled to around 36°–38° C (97°–100° F). The resort's complex of hotels and pools includes a medical facility, a wellness centre offering massages and saunas and a holiday area that is popular with young families.

Environs
The small village of **Martjanci** lies 2 km (1 mile) to the east of Moravske Toplice. Although its church appears to be an anonymous Gothic construction, its presbytery contains the finest medieval frescoes in the Prekmurje area. They were painted in 1392 by the artist Janez Aquila. The frescoes, which draw many visitors to the town, are intended to represent a heavenly Jerusalem. Apostles – St Peter with the key to the pearly gates, St James with his staff and scallop shell of pilgrimage and St George spearing a dragon – are depicted mingling with dying Crusaders while saints look on from the roof. Aquila chose a unique way to leave his signature on his work – he painted himself into the work as the tonsured monk kneeling in a corner.

Terme 3000
Kranjčeva ulica 12. **Tel** (02) 512 2200. **Open** daily.

㊵ Bogojina

Road map F1. 56 km (35 miles) NE of Ptuj. 570. from Murska Sobota.

Bogojina is a village of Hungarian-style L-shaped cottages, many of which are crowned by large nests of white storks. The village's main attraction is the **Church of the Ascension** (Cerkev Gospodovega vnebohoda), easily visible on a low slope on the northern outskirts. This parish church was remodelled by Slovenia's Modernist architect Jože Plečnik *(see p77)* in his idiosyncratic style; it is popularly known as Plečnik's Church (Plečnikova Cerkev). The church's spire is a cylindrical construction, like

an observation tower, crowned by a curious turret. The interior has been transformed from a single-nave Baroque construction into an impressive hall-like space that is broken only by a massive column of charcoal-grey marble in the centre. From this radiate four white-washed arches, all the more impressive for their simplicity. The most curious element of all is the wooden high altar. It has locally made pottery hanging from it, somewhat like the kitchen dresser of a Roman emperor. The church's oak-beamed ceiling is covered with ceramic plates glazed in the colours of the Prekmurje countryside – pale straw, moss green and terracotta.

Approach to the Church of the Ascension, Bogojina

❹ Velika Polana

Road map F2. 63 km (39 miles) NE of Ptuj. 🚏 800. 🛈 Velika Polana 2117; (02) 573 7327. 🌐 strk.si

From late spring, this village in southeast Prekmurje hosts more breeding pairs of white storks than anywhere else in Slovenia. Around 10 couples, who mate for life, migrate here, travelling 12,000 km (7,450 miles) from sub-Saharan Africa. For five months, until early August, these black-and-white birds stalk frogs and small rodents in the wetlands near the Mura river and then return at dusk to their nests – large baskets of twigs perched on roofs, chimneys and even telegraph

Stork's nest on a telegraph pole, Velika Polana

poles. These nests are repaired and expanded over successive migrations and can grow very heavy. Locals welcome the returning birds, believing they are a sign of good luck and a premonition of a new baby in the family, according to folklore.

Locally born writer Miško Kranjec (1908–83) eulogized the grasslands, woods, people and storks' nests in his works.

❷ Lendava

Road map F2. 72 km (45 miles) NE of Ptuj. 🚏 3,400. 🚌 from Murska Sobota & Moravske Toplice. 🛈 Glavna ulica 38; (02) 578 8390. 🌐 turizem-lendava.si

Equidistant from the Croatian and Hungarian borders, Lendava is the easternmost town in Slovenia. Founded by Romans on the Poetovio–Savaria route (today Ptuj–Szombathely), it developed into a medieval market town under Hungarian feudal rulers. The L-shaped **Lendava Castle** (Lendavski grad) sits on a terrace above the town. It houses a municipal museum whose displays include Bronze Age archaeology and folk art from Hetés, a Hungarian region known for its textiles.

On Glavna ulica are many Secessionist buildings that were built during a trading boom after the town was made the district centre in 1867. **No. 52**, distinct because of its canary-yellow colour, contains a

museum on contemporary trade and bourgeois lifestyle.

Much of the town's prosperity was driven by its large Jewish population. Although the Jewish community was deported by Hungarian forces during World War II, the town's **Synagogue** has been restored and is one of only two in Slovenia. Its square-shaped, galleried hall has a small display on the Jewish community and plays host to temporary art exhibitions. The building opposite the synagogue is a cultural centre designed by 20th-century Hungarian architect Imre Makovecz. Perched among vineyards above the town is the **Church of the Holy Trinity** (Cerkev sv Trojice). It has a mummified corpse on display, which, according to legend, is that of Captain Mihael Hadik, who died defending his hometown from Turkish forces in 1603 – a deed so noble that his corpse was preserved by its own sanctity. Although Hadik died in battle, his body was not found until 1733, preserved by the lime-rich soil.

🏛 **Lendava Castle**
Banffyjev trg 1. **Tel** (02) 578 9260. **Open** 8am–4pm Mon–Fri, 9am–2pm Sat. ♿

✡ **Synagogue**
Trg Györgya Zale 1. **Tel** (0) 577 6020. **Open** 10am–noon Tue–Sun. ♿

⛪ **Church of the Holy Trinity**
Lendavske gorice. **Tel** (02) 578 8330. **Open** 11–11:30am & 3:30–4pm Tue–Sun. **Closed** during snowfall. ♿ ⛪

Lendava Castle, perched above the town, Lendava

TRAVELLERS' NEEDS

WHERE TO STAY

As a small country, Slovenia doesn't boast a surfeit of places to stay, but it more than makes up for this in the quality of its accommodation. Hotels are continually being renovated to provide modern facilities, and bland business hotels have been refurbished with relaxed styles that also appeal to holiday-makers. Boutique-style accommodation in the form of small luxury hotels, often in historic buildings, have become popular too,

especially in Ljubljana. Yet much of the charm is in the country's smaller establishments and pensions – family-run hotels often make up in character what they lack in facilities. Better still are the tourist farms, isolated homesteads that offer simple rooms plus a chance to experience the hospitality and home cooking for which the country is renowned. The national tourist board website, www.slovenia.info, is a mine of information.

Hotels

Many of Slovenia's city hotels tend to be business-orientated – with prices to match – though it is possible to find some genuinely great places to stay, particularly in Ljubljana, which has seen a mini-explosion in cool design hotels. In the countryside, too, you'll find numerous boutique residences in historic buildings, three of the best being Vila Bled at Bled (see p193), Kendov dvorec (see p194) near Idrija and Grad Otočec (see p195). Grander establishments from the late 19th century can be found in Ljubljana, Bled and in contemporary spa resorts such as Rogaška Slatina and Dolenjske Toplice. Along the coast, too, there are a clutch of hotels occupying formerly grand buildings. Some of the most worthwhile hotels in Slovenia are the independent, family-run places in destinations such as Bled, the Soča Valley, Piran and Ptuj, where modest luxury, but lots of character and personal service, are the norm. Nearly all hotels have en suite rooms with air conditioning and Wi-Fi; larger hotels often feature a spa,

Otočec Castle, by the serene Krka River (see p195)

sauna and gym. Note that many hotels in coastal resorts such as Portorož close from November to March.

Hostels and Tourist Farms

Slovenia has a small, but superb, selection of hostels, many of which have cleverly utilized historic buildings; the best of these are in Ljubljana, Novo Mesto, Piran and the Karst (Pliskovica). Dormitory accommodation is often complemented by two- or three-bed en suite rooms, while facilities typically include a kitchen, laundry, common room and Wi-Fi.

Among the most relaxing – and certainly affordable – options are tourist farms (turistične kmetije). Affiliated to the **Association of Slovenian Tourist Farms**, these wonderful rural retreats offer homestays in everything from traditional alpine farms to modern houses with orchards. Accommodation is homely rather than luxurious and graded by "apples" – from one (basic rooms with shared facilities) to four (en suite rooms). Breakfast typically consists of produce from the farm itself, while dinners (for which you can pay extra) tend to be hearty and wholesome. Note that these farms are quite isolated, so you will usually need your own vehicle to reach them.

Another possibility is a room (sobe) or apartment (apartmaji) in a house, which is usually handled through private agencies. In large numbers on the coast and in the Julian Alps, these are categorized from one to three stars: a one-star offers shared facilities but provides a basin and the plusher three-star rooms have en suite facilities.

Mulej, a picturesque tourist farm in Bled (see p193)

◄ Hand-painted clocks at a flea market in Ljubljana

The opulent Kempinski Palace in Portorož, built in 1911 *(see p194)*

Camping and Mountain Huts

Slovenia has some wonderful camp sites *(kampi)*, with large clusters around Bled and Bohinj, as well as in the Soča Valley around Bovec and on the coast. Standards are universally high, whatever their size, though the larger sites are usually the most well appointed, typically offering restaurants, shops, sports facilities and play areas. Most camp sites open from late-April to October. Camping in the wild is strictly forbidden. The national tourist board's website, www.slovenia.info, has full details.

There are some 170 mountain huts *(Planinski domovi)* scattered around Slovenia's mountainous countryside, around a third of which are in Triglav National Park. Intended as overnight refuges for hikers, they are mostly basic shelters with bunk beds, though some do offer greater comfort and many offer refreshment, including basic hot meals. Most huts in the high Alps open from June to September only, while those at lower altitudes operate from April to October. All take reservations, but it is essential to secure a bed near the summit of Mount Triglav in July and August.

Rates and Reservations

Accommodation in Slovenia represents good value compared with much of Europe. Prices are highest in Ljubljana and Maribor, major resorts such as Bled and Bohinj, and along the coast. Rates peak from mid-June to August except in the capital, where rates are consistent. However, hotels in ski resorts such as Kranjska Gora or Mariborsko Pohorje have a second season from December to February, when rates are higher. A nominal tourist tax is charged per person per night in all hotels, and a 30 per cent surcharge is usually levied for stays of under three days in many resorts and farmstays. It is advisable to make a reservation year-round in Ljubljana and Maribor, both of which are consistently busy, and in summer at Bled, Bohinj and anywhere in Triglav National Park and on the coast.

Children

Most hotels accept children, so travel in Slovenia presents few difficulties. Tourist farms are a particular delight. Most types of accommodation can provide a cot or extra bed and have high chairs. Generally, only larger resort hotels offer baby-sitting services. Hotels offer a discount of 30 to 50 per cent for children up to the age of 14 to 17 staying in their parents' room. Toddlers – usually up to 3 or 4 years old – can stay free of charge.

Tents set up at a camp site in the Alps, Trenta

Travellers with Special Needs

Care for travellers with special needs is good in business hotels and large hotels in resorts, which usually have lifts and ramps. Elsewhere, accommodation options are limited. Few older hotels and tourist farms are suitable for those with restricted mobility. The **Paraplegics Association of Slovenia** provides further information on such accommodation options.

Recommended Hotels

The accommodation listed in this guide is a varied selection of the best types of places to stay in Slovenia. There are six themes in all: the first is luxury, top-of-the-range places that incorporate all the facilities and comfort you would expect of a four- or five-star hotel. Historic hotels are those that occupy celebrated buildings – such as a castle or Baroque mansion – while design hotels are generally smaller and typically manifest contemporary chic, often with a themed aesthetic. You will also find hostels, many of which in Slovenia are wonderfully conceived places. In the more rural areas, there are pensions and tourist farms, which are typically family-run, and offer a more restful option, as well as providing excellent value for money. Where an establishment has an exceptional feature, or has an outstanding view or offers impeccable service, it has been highlighted as DK Choice.

Where to Stay

Ljubljana

Old Town

Antiq Hotel €€
Historic   Map 2 D4
Gornji trg 3
Tel *(01) 421 3560*
w antiqhotel.eu
At this wonderfully idiosyncratic
town house, rooms feature chunky
wooden beds and plush carpets.

Hotel Allegro €€
Historic   Map 2 D4
Gornji trg 6
Tel *(059) 119 620*
w allegrohotel.si
This superbly restored period
building sports flamboyantly
designed rooms with reproduction
furniture and loud fabrics.

Maček €€
Pension   Map 2 D3
Krojaška 5
Tel *(01) 425 3791*
w sobe-macek.si
Positioned above the city's most
popular café (though it is well
insulated), the informal "Cat" guesthouse offers five cheerful rooms.

Lesar Hotel Angel €€€
Design   Map 2 D4
Gornji trg 7
Tel *(01) 425 5089*
w angelhotel.si
Class abounds at this hip hotel.
The bathrooms have gorgeous
tubs and underfloor heating.

DK Choice

Vander Urbani €€€
Design   Map 2 D3
Krojaška 6–8
Tel *(01) 200 9000*
w vanderhotel.com
The supremely cool Urbani is
tucked away down a tiny alley
near the river. It is actually four
interconnected medieval
town houses, with a total of
16 compact rooms manifesting
smooth grey and silver tones
and sleek furnishings.

New Town

Hostel Tresor €
Hostel   Map 2 D2
Čopova ulica 38
Tel *(01) 200 9060*
w hostel-tresor.si
A fine Secessionist building has
been transformed into a cutting-
edge hostel with spacious dorms
and modern communal areas.

Vila Veselova €
Hostel/Pension   Map 1 B3
Veselova 14
Tel *(05) 992 6721*
w v-v.si
This grand 19th-century villa
offers an assortment of colour-
themed dorms and private rooms.

Pri Mraku €€
Pension   Map 1 C4
Rimska 4
Tel *(01) 421 9600*
w daj-dam.si
In an enviable spot by the Križanke
open-air theatre, this enjoyable, if
slightly old-fashioned, place offers
rooms painted in warm colours.

Slamič €€
Pension   Map 1 C1
Kersnikova 1
Tel *(01) 433 8233*
w slamic.si
This delightful guesthouse offers
smooth, cream-coloured rooms,
with wrought-iron furnishings
and waxed wooden flooring.

Antiq Palace €€€
Luxury   Map 1 C3
Gosposka ulica 10
Tel *(08) 389 6700*
w antiqpalace.com
Unbridled luxury reigns in this
17th-century, former nobleman's
residence. Immaculately serviced
suites feature blond oak-parquet
floors and traditional furnishings.

Grand Union Hotel €€€
Luxury   Map 2 D2
Miklošičeva 1
Tel *(01) 308 1989*
w union-hotels.eu
This Art Nouveau property
houses executive and business-
style rooms in two adjoining
buildings. Gorgeous rooftop pool.

Tasteful bedroom at the 17th-century
Antiq Hotel, Ljubljana

Price Guide
Prices are based on one night's stay in
high season for a standard double room,
inclusive of service charges and taxes.

€   up to €80
€€   €80 to €130
€€€   over €130

Hotel Cubo €€€
Design   Map 1 C3
Slovenska cesta 15
Tel *(01) 425 6000*
w hotelcubo.com
Located opposite Kongresni trg,
in a fine pre-Cubist 19th-century
building, Cubo is one of the city's
ultra-sophisticated hotels.

Hotel Lev €€€
Luxury   Map 1 C1
Vošnjakova 1
Tel *(01) 433 2155*
w union-hotels.eu
This gleaming, Modernist high-
rise with ornately furnished
rooms features lots of oak.

DK Choice

Hotel Slon €€€
Historic   Map 1 C2
Slovenska cesta 34
Tel *(01) 470 1100*
w hotelslon.com
The "Elephant" is so-named
because it was at an inn on this
site, in 1552, that Emperor
Maximilian allegedly stayed,
with the aforementioned beast
in tow; it's somewhat more
luxurious today, with glass
doors leading into parquet-
floored bedrooms. The
breakfast room is magnificent.

Around the Centre

Hostel Celica €
Hostel   Map 2 F1
Metelkova 8
Tel *(01) 230 9700*
w hostelcelica.com
A brilliantly conceived hostel in
a former military prison, Celica
features artistic dorms and two-
and three-bed cells.

Further Afield

G Design Hotel €€
Design
Tržaška cesta 330
Tel *(01) 200 9100*
w gdesignhotel.si
This smart lodging offers the
latest design and technological
features; expect bamboo
memory foam matresses and
individual sensory ventilation.

The Alps

BLED: Mulej €
Tourist Farm **Map** B2
Selo pri Bledu 20
Tel *(04) 574 4617*
W mulej-bled.com
Stay in pine-furnished en suite
rooms at this friendly, family farm
a 15-minute walk from the lake.

BLED: Reka Hiša €
Pension **Map** B2
Obrne 17
Tel *(04) 576 0340*
W rekahisa.com
Situated by the rushing Bohinjsa
Sava, the easy-going "House on
the River" is an absolute delight;
terrific home-cooked food too.

BLED: Penzion Mayer €€
Pension **Map** B2
Zeleška cesta 7
Tel *(04) 576 5740*
W mayer-sp.si
Set above the lake, this farmhouse
offers big, comfy beds, parquet
flooring and pristine bathrooms,
plus a superb restaurant.

BLED: Vila Prešeren €€
Historic **Map** B2
Veslaška promenada 14
Tel *(04) 575 2510*
W sportina-turizem.si
Although known for its fabulous
restaurant, the villa rates highly
too, with rooms decked out in
fetching pinks, greys and blacks.

BLED: Grand Hotel Toplice €€€
Luxury **Map** B2
Cesta svobode 12
Tel *(04) 579 1000*
W sava-hotels-resorts.com
The *grande dame* of Bled hotels,
this magnificent establishment
offers decadent, antique-laden
rooms with unbeatable lake views.

DK Choice

BLED: Vila Bled €€€
Historic **Map** B2
Cesta svobode 26
Tel *(04) 575 3710*
W brdo.si
Set among its own stately
grounds, Tito's summer retreat
looks and feels much as it did
when the Yugoslav president
used to entertain world
leaders here; its wonderfully
evocative Socialist-era rooms
remain largely untouched,
except for some contemporary
elements. It has its own
private beach, where boats
can be hired for trips across
to the island.

Rustic Penzion Mayer, positioned above the lake in Bled

BOHINJ: Rustic House 13 €
Hostel **Map** A2
Studor 13
Tel *(031) 466 707*
W studor13.si
At this superbly renovated,
alpine-style house 3 km (2 miles)
from the lake, there's a mix of
small dorms and private rooms,
plus a lovely self-catering kitchen.

**BOHINJ: Bohinj Park
Eco Hotel** €€
Design **Map** A2
Triglavska cesta 17
Tel *(08) 200 4140*
W bohinj-eco-hotel.si
As the name suggests,
sustainability is the watchword
at this large hotel, which offers a
full complement of facilities and
an adjoining water park.

BOVEC: Dobra Vila €€€
Design **Map** A2
Mala Vas 112
Tel *(05) 389 6400*
W dobra-vila-bovec.si
A former telephone exchange is
now a romantic lodging with
stylish rooms – each one
assigned a random number.

KAMNIK: Malograjski dvor €€
Historic **Map** C3
Maistrova 13
Tel *(01) 830 3100*
W hotelkamnik.si
This restored 18th-century town
house contains appealing lime
green/lemon-coloured rooms
with antique furnishings. Enjoy
breakfast on the pretty terrace.

KOBARID: Hiša Franko €€
Design **Map** A2
Staro selo 1
Tel *(05) 389 4120*
W hisafranko.com
At this high-class retreat in the
countryside just outside town, the
rooms have sumptuous designer
beds, bamboo partitions and
muslin drapes as standard.

KOBARID: Hotel Hvala €€
Pension **Map** A2
Trg svobode 1
Tel *(05) 389 9300*
W hotelhvala.net
A long-standing, family-run hotel,
Hvala is known for its restaurant
but also has smart rooms.

DK Choice

KOBARID: Nebesa €€
Luxury **Map** A2
Livek 39
Tel *(05) 384 4620*
W nebesa.si
Nebesa, meaning "Heaven", is
pretty much what this place is:
high up on the mountainside,
with astonishing views across
to the Krn mountains, the four
chalet-style apartments are a
masterclass in interior design.

**KRANJSKA GORA:
Pension Lipa** €€
Pension **Map** A2
Koroška cesta 14
Tel *(04) 582 0000*
W hotel-lipa.si
At this warm, softly coloured
pension, balconied rooms afford
fantastic mountain views.

**LOGARSKA DOLINA:
Hotel Plesnik** €€€
Luxury **Map** C2
Logarska dolina 10
Tel *(03) 839 2300*
W plesnik.si
In the heart of this lush valley, the
Plesnik has cosy rooms in the hotel
and in a neighbouring alpine villa.

RADOVLJICA: Pension Lectar €€
Pension **Map** B2
Linhartov trg 2
Tel *(04) 537 4800*
W lectar.com
Centuries-old inn and former
gingerbread-maker, this place
has rooms with delightful, folksy,
hand-painted furniture.

For more information on types of hotels *see pages 190–91*

ROBANOV KOT: Govc-Vršnik €
Tourist Farm **Map** C2
Robanov kot 34
Tel *(03) 839 5016*
W govc-vrsnik.com
Guests are guaranteed a restful
stay at this tranquil tourist farm
set in a spectacular alpine valley.

TRENTA: Kekčeva domačija €€
Pension **Map** A2
Trenta 76
Tel *(041) 413 087*
W kekceva-domacija.si
In wonderful rural isolation, the
apartments in this farmstead have
an upstairs bedroom and down-
stairs living room and bathroom.

TRENTA: Pristava Lepena €€
Pension **Map** A2
Lepena 2
Tel *(05) 388 9900*
W pristava-lepena.com
This self-contained complex on
the edge of a forest has cosy log
cabins, swimming pools, tennis
courts and a first-rate riding
school with Lipizzaner horses.

Coastal Slovenia and the Karst

DUTOVLJE: Hostel Pliskovica €
Hostel **Map** A4
Pliskovica 11
Tel *(05) 764 0250*
W hostelkras.com
A preserved cultural site, this
restored farmstead possesses
classic Karst features, such as a
brilliant stone terrace.

GORIŠKA BRDA: Belica €€
Tourist Farm **Map** A3
Medana 32
Tel *(05) 304 2104*
W belica.si
This upmarket tourist farm offers
eight polished rooms that
overlook a beautifully manicured
lawn and have views across to
the Friulian Hills.

DK Choice

IDRIJA: Kendov dvorec €€€
Luxury **Map** B3
Na griču 2
Tel *(05) 372 5100*
W kendov-dvorec.com
Class and tranquility abound
at this renovated 14th-century
Kendov manor house that is
set among lush gardens. The
sumptuous, antique-laden
rooms are furnished with
gorgeous linens made from
the local Idrija lace. The food
here is truly sensational.

NOVA GORICA: Pri Martinovih €
Tourist Farm **Map** A3
Zagora 6, Deskle
Tel *(05) 395 3190*
W sloveniaholidays.com
Idyllically sited in a hamlet 11 km
(7 miles) from town, this gorgeous
little homestead is about as restful
a place as you could wish for.

NOVA GORICA: Hotel Perla €€€
Luxury **Map** A3
Kidričeva 7A
Tel *(05) 336 3000*
W hit.si
All glass and steel, the enormous,
super-luxurious Perla is Slovenia's
premier gaming venue; there's
no shortage of glitz here.

PIRAN: Hostel Val €
Hostel **Map** A5
Gregorciceva 38a
Tel *(05) 673 2555*
W hostel-val.com
Hidden away among a tangle of
alleys, this accomplished, long-
standing hostel has two-, three-
and four-bedded dorms plus a
self-catering kitchen.

PIRAN: Max Hotel €
Historic **Map** A5
Ulica IX korpusa 26
Tel *(05) 673 3436*
W maxpiran.com
This tall, narrow town house
snugly tucked away by St George's
Church is an intimate lodging
featuring a cosy breakfast
room, with bare brick walls
and quirky paintings.

PIRAN: Miracolo di Mare €
Pension **Map** A5
Tomšičeva 23
Tel *(05) 921 7660*
W miracolodimare.si
In a super alleyside location by
the harbour, the small but
appealing citrus-coloured rooms
are good value for money.

PIRAN: Hotel Tartini €€
Luxury **Map** A5
Tartinijev trg 15
Tel *(05) 671 1000*
W hotel-tartini-piran.com
Piran's most refined hotel offers
enticing balconied rooms with
glorious sea views, or rooms
facing the gorgeous main square.

PORTOROŽ: Grand Hotel Portorož €€€
Luxury **Map** A5
Obala 33
Tel *(05) 692 9001*
W lifeclass.net
You'll want for nothing at this
elegant establishment, with its
crisply decorated rooms and
extensive spa facilities.

Na Kluk', a country house among the hills,
Spodnja Idrija

PORTOROŽ: Kempinski Palace €€€
Luxury **Map** A5
Obala 45
Tel *(05) 692 7000*
W kempinski.com
This majestic seafront palace
once played host to the likes of
Archduke Franz Ferdinand. The
facilities are superb, but the high-
light is the lavish buffet breakfast
served on the stunning terrace.

SPODNJA IDRIJA: Na Kluk' €
Tourist Farm **Map** B3
Govejk 14C
Tel *(051) 43 5497*
W nakluk.si
Idyllically pitched amid verdant
hills, this large country house is
located near the mining town of
Idrija. It offers brightly coloured,
parquet-floored rooms.

TOMAJ: Škerlj €
Tourist Farm **Map** A4
Tomaj 53a
Tel *(05) 764 0673*
W skerlj.eu
This old farmhouse is situated
around a superb Karst stone
courtyard; the hospitality is
terrific, as is the home-made
wine and produce.

Southern and Eastern Slovenia

CELJE: Hotel Evropa €€
Luxury **Map** D3
Krekov trg 4
Tel *(03) 426 9000*
W hotel-evropa.si
A pristine 19th-century façade
conceals slick rooms typically
decorated in chocolate brown
and rich cream colours. The on-
site restaurant is excellent.

DOLJENSKE TOPLICE:
Hotel Balnea €€
Luxury Map D4
Zdraviliški trg 7
Tel *(07) 391 9400*
🅦 terme-krka.si
From the great-looking wood-
and-glass panelled atrium to the
retro-modern styled rooms, this
is a splendid option.

MARIBOR: Joannes €
Tourist Farm Map E2
Vodole 34
Tel *(02) 473 2100*
🅦 joannes.si
Although better known as a
winery, this three-roomed farm
in a hillside hamlet is delightful.

MARIBOR: Grand Hotel
Ocean €€€
Design Map E2
Partizanska cesta 39
Tel *(05) 907 7120*
🅦 hotelocean.si
Named after the first train to pass
through Maribor, in 1846, this
sparky boutique hotel offers
understatedly cool rooms decked
out in warm beige tones.

MARIBOR: Hotel Habakuk €€€
Luxury Map E2
Pohorska cesta 59
Tel *(02) 234 4333*
🅦 hotel-habakuk.si
An outstanding five-star hotel
nestled under the ski slopes,
Habakuk has magnificently
appointed rooms with smooth
lines, state-of-the-art technology
and even a pillow menu.

MOKRICE: Grad Mokrice €€€
Historic Map E4
Rajec 4
Tel *(07) 457 4240*
🅦 terme-catez.si
This beautifully proportioned
Renaissance chateau accommo-
dates a grand suite of rooms, the
best (and largest) of which are
those in the corner turrets.

MORAVSKE TOPLICE: Tremel €
Tourist Farm Map F1
Bokrači 28
Tel *(02) 545 1017*
🅦 kmetija-tremel.si
At this lovely renovated farmstead with beautifully furnished
rooms, the hosts cook and serve
delicious Prekmkurje cuisine.

DK Choice

MURSKA SOBOTA:
Sončna Hiša €€€
Design Map F1
Banovci 3c
Tel *(02) 588 8238*
🅦 soncna-hisa.si
One of the very few boutique
hotels in this part of Slovenia,
the effortlessly cool "Sun House"
offers five inspirational rooms,
each named so as to evoke
the style, or material, of that
particular room: for example,
Sea Memories, Limegrass and
Manhattan. Extra facilities
include a sauna and spa garden,
with sublime views of the
surrounding countryside.

NOVO MESTO: Hostel Situla €
Hostel Map D4
Dilančeva ulica 1
Tel *(07) 394 2000*
🅦 situla.si
Another superb Slovenian hostel,
Situla is named after a notable
archaeological find, and holds
artfully designed three- to
eight-bed dormitories as well
as private rooms.

OLIMJE: Penzion Amon €€
Pension Map E3
Olimje 24
Tel *(03) 818 2480*
🅦 amon.si
Crisp, modern rooms are complemented by a well-regarded winery
and restaurant, plus a fabulous
golf course. Great choice of local
and organic produce at breakfast.

ORMOZ: Dvorec Jeruzalem €€
Pension Map F2
Jeruzalem 8
Tel *(02) 719 4805*
🅦 dvorec-jeruzalem.com
This handsome 17th-century
manor house in the lush Jeruzalem
wine-growing region has rooms
with rich wood floors, mahogany
furniture and brass fittings.

OTOČEC: Šeruga €
Tourist Farm Map D4
Sela pri Ratežu 15
Tel *(07) 334 6900*
🅦 seruga.si
Both the rooms and the cooking
at this farm, set in isolated
woodland, are exceptional. The
gorgeous Granary guesthouse
is worth paying extra for.

OTOČEC: Grad Otočec €€€
Historic Map D4
Grajska cesta 2
Tel *(08) 205 0310*
🅦 grad-otocec.com
The rooms at this exclusive island
castle feature faux-Gothic
furnishings and large bathrooms.

PTUJ: Hotel Mitra €€
Design Map E2
Presernova ulica 6
Tel *(02) 787 7455*
🅦 hotel-mitra.si
This immaculate 16th-century
building is a so-called "Story
Hotel," by virtue of the fact that
each of the designer-led rooms
is themed on a Ptuj narrative.

PTUJ: Muzikafe €€
Pension Map E2
Vrazov trg 1
Tel *(02) 787 8860*
🅦 muzikafe.si
Quirky, fun and colourful sum up
this charming guesthouse, which
also boasts a retro-themed café.

ROGAŠKA SLATINA:
Grand Hotel Rogaška €€€
Luxury Map E3
Zdraviliški trg 14
Tel *(03) 811 2000*
🅦 terme-rogaska.si
Occupying the palatial Neo-
Classical bulding where Franz
Liszt used to play, the Grand is
the undisputed queen of this
spa town's hotels.

SLOVENJ GRADEC:
Rotovnik-Plesnik €
Tourist Farm Map D2
Legen 134A
Tel *(02) 885 3666*
🅦 rotovnik-plesnik.si
A warm welcome awaits at
this pretty tourist farm, where
they've even got a functioning
1970s jukebox.

Creatively styled room at Muzikafe guesthouse, Ptuj

For more information on types of hotels *see pages 190–91*

WHERE TO EAT AND DRINK

Slovenian cuisine is something of an unknown entity to a majority of foreigners. Nevertheless, you can eat very well here, whether at an international eatery in Ljubljana, a country restaurant where master chefs elevate seasonal and local produce to gourmet heights, or just at a village inn. A bad meal is rare in a country that takes fresh produce for granted, although it helps if visitors like hearty dishes. Apart from the national cuisine *(see pp198–9)*, you'll find ethnic dishes from the Balkans prevalent – particularly Serbian grilled meats and Croatian Adriatic fish – as well as Austrian and Italian cuisine; pizzas are ubiquitous. However, other European food is poorly represented, while Asian cooking tends to be limited to cities and large towns.

Types of Restaurants and Cafés

The term *restavracija* (restaurant) is used to define any formal establishment that offers fine local as well as international cuisine. As a rule of thumb, most are located in cities, large towns or, to a lesser extent, resorts. More widespread – and almost always more appealing in terms of its rustic atmosphere – is the *gostilna*. This roughly approximates to a British country inn and is just as varied in quality. Like celebrated British gastro-pubs, the finest Slovenian *gostilna* can provide the most memorable dining experiences in the country thanks to the efforts of master chefs who produce creative country cooking from seasonal and local ingredients. Others offer nothing more fancy than soups and schnitzels. Whether offering gourmet country cuisine or no-nonsense pub or bar food, the menus are usually traditional and at weekends many urban

Slovenians head out of town for a long lunch in a country *gostilna* – which is highly recommended. A *gostišče* is similar but also offers accommodation.

For a quick informal meal, there is the pizzeria – and with the country's proximity to Italy, these are invariably excellent – as well as the *okrepčevalnica*, or snack bar, which typically prepares Serbian meat snacks such as *čevapčiči* (meat rissoles with spicy sauce) or the filled filo pastry snack *burek*. A café (sometimes known as a *kavarna*) will invariably offer pastries, cream cakes and ice cream.

Vegetarians

Although meat dominates most Slovenian menus, there is a growing awareness of vegetarian needs and the majority of restaurants and *gostilna* will offer two or three worthwhile vegetarian dishes; aside from the usual soups, salads and omelettes, some

Slovenian specialities to look out for include *gobova rižota* (mushroom risotto), *ocvrti sir* (cheese fried in breadcrumbs) and *štruklji* (dumplings with cheese or fruit filling), which are delicious. Fish-eaters, meanwhile, will find life easier due to the wide variety of Adriatic and freshwater fish on menus.

Menus

Except in cafés and simple village inns, all restaurants and the majority of *gostilna* will provide an English translation of the menu. However, many places prepare extra dishes in addition to the standard menu, which will be chalked up in Slovenian on a blackboard or handwritten and presented with the menu at upmarket addresses. Since by definition these are the freshest dishes, generally prepared from whatever is in season and usually to local recipes, such offers are always worth investigating.

Outdoor seating at Sokol, Ljubljana *(see p200)*

Alfresco dining in Tartini Square, Piran

Prices, Tipping and Payment

Like most countries, the cost of a meal in Slovenia varies according to the location. Eating out in Ljubljana, Maribor, Bled and the coast area is far more expensive than elsewhere in the country. Many restaurants provide good-value set menus, which permit a choice from two or three dishes in each course. Similarly, the tasting menus of gourmet restaurants, usually with five to eight smaller dishes, can work out as good value. Look out, too, for *malica*, a light, two-course lunchtime meal usually costing no more than €5–6. Set lunches in major cities generally cost €7–10 for three courses. The price of alcohol varies, but beer is the cheapest drink.

Prices include tax but not always service. By and large, standards of service are high, with courteous and friendly staff, most of whom speak a high level of English. In a smart restaurant and upmarket *gostilna*, it is usual to add a tip of around 10 per cent for good service. In an inn, the standard practice is to round up the final sum, while loose change is perfectly acceptable in cafés. Credit cards are accepted in the majority of establishments, though some places might not accept American Express.

Opening Hours

Cafés generally open from 8am and *gostilna* from 11am, although many of those that serve as a hub for the local community may open around 9am. Restaurants usually open from noon, with a break from around 3 to 6pm; some city establishments open for dinner only. Dinner is eaten earlier in Slovenia than in neighbouring areas such as Dalmatian Croatia and Italy, usually around 7pm or even 6pm in remote country inns, some of which stop serving food by 9pm. Many inns and restaurants close on Mondays or Tuesdays.

Reservations

A prior reservation is essential only in the best restaurants. However, Friday and Saturday nights and Sunday lunchtimes are busy in highly regarded local *gostilna*, so a reservation is worthwhile if visitors want to eat at a particular place at a certain time or if they prefer a specific restaurant.

Children

Slovenians are fond of children and welcome them to all but the very choicest city restaurants. Most *gostilna* and restaurants can provide a high chair for toddlers and there will be light dishes for children particularly during the lunch period. Pizza and pasta or hamburger-like snacks such as *pleskavica* and *čevapčiči* are readily available and make for a good choice for children.

Recommended Restaurants

The restaurants listed in this book cover a range of cuisines and prices, and are the best of their kind in Slovenia. Traditional Slovenian cooking remains the dominant fare throughout the country, with strong regional dishes to the fore in certain parts, particularly in the Karst and coastal regions, and in Prekmurje to the east. There are also a number of restaurants listed that reflect the changing, and more innovative, trends in Slovenian cooking. International cuisine, although a fairly loose term, indicates places that serve dishes inspired by a variety of cuisines. These restaurants are increasingly coming to the fore, particularly in Ljubljana, although there are a handful of such terrific eateries liberally sprinkled throughout the remainder of the country.

The number of ethnic eateries is almost exclusively confined to the capital, though the Italian influence manifests itself strongly along the western fringes and down on the coast. Almost everywhere, however, you'll find some aspect of Balkan cuisine, typically of the Serbian grilled meat variety. With Slovenia's small slice of the Adriatic, and an abundance of lakes and rivers, high-quality fish and seafood is never far from the menu.

The highlighted restaurants, marked as DK Choice, have been chosen because they offer a unique experience – typically a combination of superb cuisine and a truly special atmosphere.

Dining room at Grad Otočec restaurant, Otočec, southeast Slovenia *(see p207)*

The Flavours of Slovenia

If Slovenia has surprisingly wide-ranging tastes for such a small nation, it is because its regional cuisines are shaped by neighbouring Italy, Austria, Hungary and the Balkans. Most of its best-loved dishes are rooted in the country's peasant past – the tenets of Slovenian cooking are simple, sturdy and meaty, and seasonal local produce is rightly celebrated. Small wonder, then, that the best Slovenian chefs retain a place for traditional recipes on their menus and, rather than striving to impress with high-concept cookery, let good ingredients do the talking.

Walnut potica

Freshly harvested wild mushrooms for sale in autumn

Country Cuisine

The frugal roots of much Slovenian cookery can be seen in the ingredients that make up many of its classic dishes. Vegetables such as potatoes, cabbage, squashes, turnips and pumpkins, which keep well through the winter months, appear in many forms. A national favourite is wild mushrooms, which are gathered and served fresh in autumn, then dried for use throughout the year.

Sweet dishes often feature orchard fruits, such as apples, cherries, pears and plums. Nuts, especially walnuts, and poppy, pumpkin and sunflower seeds, appear in many cakes and stuffed dumplings, often sweetened with local honey. Soured cream and soft curd cheese are widely used as well. The focus of most Slovenian meals, however, is meat, usually pork *(svinjina)*. Pork lard is often used to flavour side dishes, and sausage-making is a great tradition.

Perhaps the most distinctive Slovenian culinary feature is

Cottage cheese • Walnuts • Pumpkin • Poppy seeds • Carniolan sausage • Pears • Buckwheat

Selection of produce featured in many traditional Slovenian dishes

Slovenian Dishes and Specialities

Honey

Dine at a farmstay *(see p190)* or a restaurant that specializes in regional food and you will taste Slovenian cuisine at its most authentic and appealing. A typical starter is soup *(juha)* – often a hearty bowlful such as *jota* or mushroom soup *(gobova juha)*, sometimes served in a hollowed-out loaf as a bowl. The main course is generally of the meat-and-two-vegetables variety; pork is ubiquitous, often served as escalopes or schnitzel, but veal *(teletina)* and beef *(govedina)* are also popular, as is game in season, particularly venison *(srna)*, pheasant *(fazan)* and rabbit *(zajec)*. Freshwater trout *(postrv)* is delicious fried in cornflour or lightly smoked. Aside from fruit-filled *štruklji* and *prekmurska gibanica*, the classic Slovenian dessert is *potica*, a filling, ring-shaped cake made with nuts and honey.

Jota is a hearty soup made with sauerkraut, root vegetables, cured pork and red kidney beans.

Traditional, lavishly decorated cookies in a Radovljica bakery

the use of buckwheat; *žganci*, a buckwheat mash often served with mushrooms or pork crackling as a side dish, was dubbed "the pillar of Slovenia" in the 1800s.

Italian Influences

Flavours and cooking styles begin to change the further one travels west in Slovenia. In the Italian border region of Primorska, the food is noticeably lighter, and menus might feature home-made *njoki* (gnocchi) and *rižota* (risotto), often with wild mushrooms and herbs. Idrija is known for its ravioli-like *žlikrofi*, traditionally filled with potato, bacon, onion and chives. Arguably the most famous ingredient from this part of the country is *pršut*, a delicious air-dried ham, like Italian prosciutto, that originates in the Karst and Istrian Slovenia. In these southwesterly areas and along

the Adriatic coast, fish and seafood, fine wines, lashings of olive oil and excellent restaurants come as standard.

A Touch of Spice

Hungarian influences take over at the opposite end of Slovenia. Prekmurje, in the far east of the country, has a regional cuisine that is as distinctive as the Italianate food of west Slovenia, and nowhere is this more evident than in its use

Fresh fruits and vegetables on a stall in Ljubljana market

of paprika. This is the region of rich, spicy *golaž* (goulash) and steaming pots of *bograč* stew, a dish so highly revered that Lendava stages the Bogračfest cooking competition every August. Prekmurje's traditional autumn slaughter supports its reputation for fine hams *(šunka)* and pork sausages *(klobase)*, hot with paprika, aromatic with garlic, thickened with buckwheat or millet porridge, and served fresh or cured.

What to Drink

Water *(voda)* Sparkling water *(mineralna)* is standard unless still *(negazirana)* is specified.

Coffee *(kava)* As in Italy and the Balkans, this is served strong and black unless milk *(mleko)* is requested.

Tea *(čaj)* This is less common than coffee and always served black. Herbal tea is *zeliščni čaj.*

Beer *(pivo)* Slovenian beer – Union brewery's *Zlatorog* or *Laško* – is a thirst-quenching Pilsner-style brew.

Wine *(vino)* Whether white *(belo)* or red *(rdeče)*, Slovenian wines are of a high standard. Look especially for wines from the Goriška Brda region.

Pear brandy *(viljamovka)* This is a popular, often home-made fruit schnapps. Some of the best is distilled and sold at Pleterje Monastery *(see p168).*

Bograč, a spicy, meaty stew from Prekmurje, is named after its traditional earthenware cooking pot.

Štruklji are dumplings, stuffed with ground walnuts and spices. They are served as a side dish or a dessert.

Prekmurska gibanica is a pie with layers of filo pastry, cottage cheese, poppy seeds, walnuts and spiced apple.

Where to Eat and Drink

Ljubljana

Old Town

Čajna hiša €
Café **Map** D4
Stari trg 3
Tel *(01) 252 7010*
This wonderful and warming
barrel-vaulted teahouse serves
a delectable range of teas from
around the world, in addition
to sandwiches and salads.

Ribca €
Fish/Seafood **Map** D3
Adamič-Lundrovo nabrežje 1
Tel *(01) 425 1544*
Hidden under Plečnik's Market
Colonnade, this buzzing little fish
snack bar serves generous por-
tions of fried squid and sardines.

DK Choice

Julija €€
Mediterranean **Map** D4
Stari trg 9
Tel *(01) 425 6463*
The most enjoyable of Stari trg's
clutch of restaurants, Julija's
sparkling interior – all gilded
mirrors and blue-and-white tiled
walls – is a lovely spot in which
to indulge in predominantly
Mediterranean dishes, such as
octopus pasta and seafood
risotto. In summer, dine outside
on the cobbled street.

Marley & Me €€
Italian **Map** D4
Stari trg 9
Tel *(08) 380 6610*
Get in quick as there are just
a handful of tables in this
popular, minimalist restaurant.
Food is of a largely Italian bent.
Service is attentive.

Romeo €€
Mexican **Map** D4
Stari trg 6
Tel *(01) 426 9011*
The vivid-red-furnished Romeo
offers a tasty slant on Mexican
dishes, in addition to some
fabulous cocktails.

Sokol €€
Slovenian **Map** D3
Ciril-Metodov trg 18
Tel *(01) 439 6855*
This congenial, labyrinthine
gostilna is regularly packed
with diners seated at thick
wooden tables. It offers hearty,
meat-heavy Slovene fare and
a decent choice of light and
dark beers.

TaBar €€
European **Map** D3
Ribji trg 6
Tel *(031) 764 063*
The seasonal menu at this
fashionable bar offers a variety
of cold and warm tapas and
cheeses. Choose from the
extensive list of Slovenian wines.

Zlata Ribica €€
Fish/Seafood **Map** D3
Cankarjevo nabrežje 5
Tel *(01) 620 8834*
Occuying an enviable riverside
location, the "Golden Fish" serves
up reasonably priced fish dishes,
including some incredible
platters. Friendly service.

Gostilna na Gradu €€€
Slovenian **Map** D3
Grajska planota 1
Tel *(08) 205 1930*
Work up an appetite walking
up Castle Hill before settling
down to upscale traditonal
Slovenian country cuisine, such
as deer goulash.

Price Guide
Prices are for a three-course meal for
one, including half a bottle of house
wine, cover charge, tax and service.

€   up to €30
€€   €30 to €50
€€€   over €50

Most €€€
Slovenian **Map** D2
Petkovškovo nabrežje 21
Tel *(01) 232 8183*
Inventive, imaginative Slovenian
food is the focus at this high-end
establishment by the Butcher's
Bridge; expect the likes of home-
made buckwheat ravioli with
wild mushrooms.

DK Choice

Špajza €€€
Slovenian **Map** D4
Gornji trg 28
Tel *(01) 425 3094*
The pick of the Old Town
restaurants, relaxed Špajza is
essentially a cluster of elegant
small rooms decorated with
folksy bric-a-brac. This homely
setting complements the
expertly cooked food, including
smoked trout with horseradish
terrine, and horse fillet with
truffles. There's a great wine
selection too.

Valvas'or €€€
International **Map** D4
Stari trg 7
Tel *(01) 425 0455* **Closed** *Sun*
Named in honour of the eminent
Slovene historian (born across
the road), this sophisticated
restaurant has a tasteful designer
interior and a delicate blend of
Slovenian and international food.

New Town

Cacao €
Café **Map** D3
Petkovškovo nabrežje 3
Tel *(01) 430 1771*
Not only does this outdoor café
enjoy a cracking, tree-shaded
riverside location, but the ices are
wonderful. Kids and adults alike
will love this place.

Cantina Mexicana €
Mexican **Map** D3
Knafljev prehod 2
Tel *(01) 426 9325*
Vibrant, colourful and a heap of
fun, Cantina offers all the usual
Tex-Mex standards and a good-
time party atmosphere. It serves
up great cocktails too.

One of the elegant dining rooms at Špajza, in Ljubljana's Old Town

Foculus €
Pizzeria Map C4
Gregorčičeva 3
Tel *(01) 421 9295*
With a choice of over 60 types
of pizza on offer, including plenty
of vegetarian possibilities, there's
something for everyone at
this flamboyantly decorated
establishment. Speedy service.

Joe Pena's €
Mexican Map C2
Cankarjeva 6
Tel *(01) 421 5800*
This breezy Mexican restaurant
serves chimichangas, tacos and
fajitas, as well as some more
unusual offerings, such as hot
spiced red snapper. Good cocktails; try the strawberry margarita.

Kavarna Zvezda €
Café Map 2 D3
Wolfova 14
Tel *(01) 421 9090*
Savour fantastic ice cream as well
as superb cakes and pastries at
this consistently popular street-
corner café.

DK Choice

Le Petit Café €
Café Map C4
Trg Francoske revolucije 4
Tel *(01) 251 2575*
A little slice of Paris comes
to Ljubljana at this busy café
with its buzzing street-corner
terrace. Breakfast options
include eggs Florentine or
freshly baked croissants.
Make sure you don't miss the
opportunity to try a cup of
bela kava (white coffee), their
signature beverage. Later in
the day, wine becomes the
preferred drink of choice.

Sarajevo 84 €
Balkan Map C2
Nazorjeva 12
Tel *(01) 425 7106*
Try classic Balkan standards such
as *čevapi* (minced meat kebab)
and *pleskavica* (meat patty) at
this fun, subterranean Bosnian
restaurant. The interior is decked
out in sporting paraphernalia
that hark back to the 1984
Olympic Games in Sarajevo.

Ambient €€
International
Čufarjeva 2
Tel *(01) 430 2756* **Closed** *Sun*
This funky, bright orange bistro
has a comfortable, loungey
interior that attracts a hip
young crowd. The gourmet
steak dishes stand out.

Čajna hisa, a teahouse in Ljubljana's Old Town

Bistro Monstera €€
European Map C3
Gosposca ulica 9
Tel *(04) 425 4251*
Run by acclaimed TV chef Bine
Volčič, this restaurant is open all
day from breakfast onwards. Using
the freshest seasonal ingredients,
the dishes on offer change
regularly. At weekends there is a
seven-course tasting menu.

Šestica €€
Slovenian Map C2
Slovenska cesta 40
Tel *(01) 242 0855*
This old favourite spans the full
gamut of the Slovenian kitchen,
including stuffed grilled squid
from the Adriatic and goulash
from Prekmurje.

Shambala €€
Asian Map C4
Križevniška 12
Tel *(01) 184 3833* **Closed** *Sun*
If you only eat at one Asian
restaurant, make it this one. It
has a gorgeous interior and its
choice menu features the likes of
Vietnamese salad rolls, Japanese
tempura and Thai red curry.

Gostilna AS €€€
Mediterranean Map C2
Čopova 5a
Tel *(01) 425 8822*
Dining in Ljubljana doesn't
get much classier than at this
expensive, Mediterranean-
influenced restaurant. Try the
fillet of turbot with champagne
sauce. There's also an adjoining
affordable bistro.

JB Restavracija €€€
European Map D2
Miklošičeva 17
Tel *(01) 430 7070* **Closed** *Sun*
This is the leading destination
in town for Mediterranean and
Central European fusion, with a
small, seasonally changing menu
featuring the best local ingre-
dients. Well-stocked wine cellar.

Sorbara Steak House €€€
International Map D4
Gallusovo nabrezje 31
Tel *(01) 425 4251*
Set on the banks of the Ljubljanica
River, Sorbara offers a good-value
set lunch menu. The organic Black
Angus beef steak is a speciality.
The menu also includes Wagju
beef, bison steak and burgers.

Around the Centre

Kavarna SEM €
Café Map F1
Metelkova 2
Tel *(01) 300 8700* **Closed** *Mon*
The Slovene Ethnographic
Museum's stylish café is an ideal
place to recharge and refresh.
There's also a cool programme of
musical and cultural happenings.

Okrepčevapnica Harambaša €
Balkan Map D4
Trnovski Pristan 4a
Tel *(041) 843 106*
Feast on classic Bosnian dishes,
such as *cevapčiči* with *kaymak*
(beef rissoles and creamy
cheese), then round things off
with a cup of Turkish coffee and
a piece of Turkish delight.

Curry Life – Hotel Park €€
Indian Map F2
Tabor 9
Tel *(041) 344 004*
Formerly the Figovec, which had
served traditional Slovenian fare
since 1776, Curry Life now brings
some spice to the city's culinary
scene. Try the tender lamb
dishes. There are good vegetarian
options, too. Popular for lunch.

Gujžina €€
Regional Map D3
Mestni trg 19
Tel *(01) 439 7040*
This marvellous, countrified
restaurant specializes in Prekmurje
cuisine, so expect *bograč* (stew),
buckwheat porridge and scrump-
tious *gibanica* (cheese pastry).

For more information on types of restaurants *see pages 196–7*

Pri Škofu €€
International **Map** D5
Rečna cesta 5
Tel *(01) 426 4508*
A real gem, hidden down a residential side street, this informal restaurant doesn't have a menu as such; instead you'll be offered a selection of different dishes that might include black risotto or pepper-encrusted tenderloin.

Yildiz Han €€
Balkan **Map** E5
Karlovška cesta 19
Tel *(01) 426 5717* **Closed** *Sun*
In a gorgeous villa just behind Castle Hill, the low tables, cushioned seats and hanging carpets look great, and the food is full of flavour. There are hookahs available on the terrace and belly dancers at weekends.

Further Afield

Pri Kopač €€
Slovenian
Tržaška 418, Brezovica
Tel *(01) 365 3066* **Closed** *Sun & Mon*
This long-established eatery offers superb fare. Its trademark rustic dishes include roast veal, pork knuckle and the house favourite – *Ljubljanski zrezek* (veal or pork-stuffed schnitzel covered in mushroom sauce).

Gostilna pri Danilu €€€
Slovenian
Reteče 48, Škofja Loka
Tel *(04) 515 3444* **Closed** *Mon & Tue*
Arguably one of the best restaurants in the country, this place serves exquisite traditional cuisine with a modern twist. The seasonal menu also includes good vegetarian options. Excellent wines.

The Alps

BLED: Gostilna pri Planincu €
Slovenian **Map** B2
Grajska cesta 8
Tel *(04) 574 1613*
Walkers and cyclists love this alpine-style pub/restaurant, which has been serving up hearty, meat-heavy dishes and big jugs of beer since 1903. Portion sizes are large.

BLED: Šmon €
Café **Map** B2
Grajska cesta 3
Tel *(04) 574 1616*
This is *the* place to sample the Bled speciality, *kremna rezina*, a deliciously thick, creamy pastry. The other pastries and cakes on offer are also worth trying, as is the superb home-made ice cream.

Gostilna Mihovc, a classic country inn dating from 1888, Bohinj

BLED: Chilli €€
Mexican **Map** B2
Cesta svobode 9
Tel *(04) 574 3027*
This fun, colourful place serves up authentic Tex-Mex dishes that are best enjoyed with a cocktail on the terrace. The burritos are one of the highlights on the menu.

BLED: Ostarija Peglez'n €€
Fish/Seafood **Map** B2
Cesta svobode 19
Tel *(04) 574 4218*
This pleasant place has a homely rustic design, with wicker blinds and old coffee pots and ceramics hanging from the walls. Indulge in some of the lake's best seafood. Try the mixed platter.

BLED: Okarina €€€
International **Map** B2
Ljubljanska cesta 8
Tel *(04) 574 1458*
The offbeat interior, with Indian paintings and textiles, sits well with this elegant restaurant's accomplished fusion menu, much of which is prepared in a traditional tandoor clay oven.

DK Choice

BLED: Prešeren €€€
Mediterranean **Map** B2
Velaška promenada 14
Tel *(04) 575 3710*
It's the stunning waterside location that really sets this place apart, so arrive early to get one of the prime lakeside tables on the wood-decked terrace. The menu is mainly Mediterranean in design, with risottos, pastas, salads and bountiful fish dishes. Even if you're not eating here, it's a great place to come for an early morning coffee to watch the lake spring into life.

BLED: Topolino €€€
International **Map** B2
Ljubljanska cesta 26
Tel *(04) 574 1781* **Closed** *Tue*
This is a sophisticated slow-food restaurant, so allow yourself plenty of time to enjoy dishes like steamed shrimp over puréed carrots with caramel sauce.

BOHINJ: Don Andro €
Italian **Map** A2
Ukanc 20
Tel *(05) 995 5787* **Closed** *Mon*
A rather fine *spaghetteria* at the lake's westernmost shore, Don Andro affords marvellous mountain views from its open terrace. The Karst-influenced pasta dishes are well worth investigating.

BOHINJ: Pizzerija Ema €
Pizzeria **Map** A2
Srednja Vas v Bohinju 73
Tel *(04) 572 4126*
Ema is an unassuming little place with well-crafted pizzas prepared in a wood-fired oven and friendly staff. The portions are huge. There's also a children's playground and peerless views across the valley.

BOHINJ: Gostilna Mihovc €€
Slovenian **Map** A2
Stara Fužina 118
Tel *(05) 922 6786*
At this classic country *gostilna*, where hearty home-style cooking is the focus, try Bohinj sausage in minced lard, or buckwheat dumplings with crackling. Good value for money.

BOHINJ: Gostilna Rupa €€
Slovenian **Map** A2
Srednja Vas 87
Tel *(04) 572 3401* **Closed** *Mon*
This *gostilna* is rather touristy, but hugely enjoyable nevertheless, especially on Thursdays in

summer when you can feast on roast suckling pig to the sounds of a live folk band.

BOVEC: Martinov Hram €€
Slovenian Map A2
Trg golobarskih žrtev 27
Tel *(05) 388 6214* **Closed** *Mon*
Try local specialities such as Soča trout, and cottage cheese and chives, alongside a long menu of grilled Balkan meats, at this warm and classy inn with a vine-covered terrace.

KAMNIK: Kavarna Veronika €
Café Map C3
Glavni trg 6
Tel *(05) 997 0949*
This charming patisserie, nestled directly below Mali Grad, is where the locals meet and gossip over coffee and cream cakes.

KOBARID: Gostilna Breza €€
Slovenian Map A2
Mučeniška ulica 17
Tel *(05) 389 0040* **Closed** *Wed & Thu*
Breza is a hidden gem. Take a table on the flowery summer terrace and feast on succulent lamb, game and grilled fish.

KOBARID: Kotlar €€
Fish/Seafood Map A2
Trg svobode 11
Tel *(05) 390 1110* **Closed** *Tue & Wed*
Tasty fish from the Adriatic is served here and complemented by a stellar wine list. The curvaceous, nautically themed bar is the centrepiece.

DK Choice

KOBARID: Hiša Franko €€€
International Map A2
Staro selo 1
Tel *(05) 389 4120* **Closed** *Mon & Tue*
Franko's has become a real foodie destination thanks to the chef's brilliant menu of superb imaginative dishes, such as roebuck fillet with chocolate and sage sauce and rhubarb, and marble trout with ceviche of celery and pink pepper. There's an outstanding wine cellar – Valter, the owner, can offer more than 350 bottles. Sit on the tree-shaded terrace in summer.

KOBARID: Topli Val €€€
Fish/Seafood Map A2
Trg svobode 1
Tel *(05) 389 9300*
The "Warm Wave" restaurant, inside the Hotel Hvala, offers a gamut of treats, like crayfish cocktail and black risotto with cuttlefish. Lovely desserts, too.

KRANJSKA GORA:
Gostilna Cvitar €€
Slovenian Map A2
Borovška cesta 83
Tel *(04) 588 3600*
This charming, historic tavern serves solid Slovenian fare such as veal stew with buckwheat dumplings. The pedestrian-facing terrace is a great spot to watch the world go by.

KRANJSKA GORA: Miklič €€
International Map A2
Vitranška 13
Tel *(04) 588 1635*
As accomplished as the hotel it's part of, Milklič serves a thoughtfully created menu of international dishes, invariably accompanied by seasonal spit-roast specials.

DK Choice

KRANJSKA GORA:
Skipass €€€
Slovenian Map A2
Borovška cesta 95
Tel *(04) 582 1000*
Chef Mojmir Šiftar brings age-old Slovenian recipes into the modern era. The food is beautifully presented and shows evidence of the culinary influences of Austria and Italy. Try the caramelized scallops served with cauliflower purée and pumpkin caponata.

LOGARSKA DOLINA:
Gostilna Raduha €
Slovenian Map C2
Luče 67
Tel *(03) 838 4000* **Closed** *Mon & Tue*
Owner Martina Breznik is one of the country's more enlightened chefs, though it's the relatively simple home-smoked trout (both cold and warm) that people head here for. Excellent wine list and good service.

The interesting architecture of Gostilna Raduha set in lush grounds, Logarska Dolina

RADOVLJICA:
Gostilna Kunstelj €€
Regional Map B2
Gorenjska cesta 9
Tel *(04) 531 5178* **Closed** *Mon & Thu*
This mellow *gostilna* offers dining in one of three themed rooms: poets, hunters and golfers. There's a good wine collection.

RADOVLJICA:
Gostilna Lectar €€
Regional Map B2
Linhartov trg 2
Tel *(04) 537 4800* **Closed** *Tue*
At this centuries-old inn, good old-fashioned Gorenjska cuisine marries with an old-world atmosphere. Try smoked sausages with sauerkraut, and buckwheat fritters with cottage cheese.

VRSIC PASS: Pristava Lepena €€
Slovenian Map A2
Lepena 2
Tel *(05) 388 9900*
Despite its seclusion high up in the Lepena Valley, people come here from far and wide to sample the trout, plucked from the Soča and grilled on an open fire.

Gostilna Lectar, a centuries-old inn in Radovljika

For more information on types of restaurants *see pages 196–7*

The charming exterior of Belica, Goriška Brda

Coastal Slovenia and the Karst

GORIŠKA BRDA: Belica　€€
Slovenian　**Map** A3
Medana 32
Tel *(05) 304 2104*　**Closed** *Mon*
Boasting sublime views across to the Friulian hills in Italy, the setting at sundown is unbeatable, while the food – not least the home-made salamis, sausages and ribs – is delicious. Excellent wine, too.

GORIŠKA BRDA: Klinec　€€
Regional　**Map** A3
Medana 20
Tel *(05) 304 5092*　**Closed** *Mon–Wed*
One of Goriška's finest wineries also has a first-class restaurant, rustling up exquisite, traditional Karst and Italian cuisine using fresh herbs and produce from the garden. There are wonderful views across the vineyards from the terrace. The staff are attentive.

HRASTOVLJE: Gostilna Švab　€€
Regional　**Map** A5
Hrastovlje 53
Tel *(05) 659 0510*　**Closed** *Mon & Tue*
Classic Istrian and Karst dishes dominate the menu in this village inn close to the famous church. Start with a platter of home-cured meats before moving on to a bowl of truffle pasta.

IDRIJA: Gostilna Kos　€€
Regional　**Map** B3
Tomšičeva 4
Tel *(05) 372 2030*　**Closed** *Sun*
The welcoming Blackbird Inn is as good a place as any to try the local speciality, *žlikrofi* (potato- or mushroom-filled ravioli parcels). Tasty pizza and pasta dishes too.

IZOLA: Gostilna Gust　€
Italian　**Map** A4
Drevored 1 Maja
Tel *(051) 383 666*
If it's good enough for the Italians, then you know you're in the right place. A fine pizzeria with more than 30 varieties on offer, Gust is also renowned for its desserts.

IZOLA: Marina　€€
Fish/Seafood　**Map** A4
Velki trg 11
Tel *(05) 660 4100*
With superb views overlooking the marina, delicious grilled fish, and one of the best-stocked wine cellars on the coast, there's much to like about this place.

KOPER: Loggia　€
Café　**Map** A4
Titov trg
Tel *(05) 673 2689*
Housed in one of the square's many fine Venetian-Gothic buildings, this is the perfect spot to sit and sip the finest coffee in town.

KOPER: Istrska klet　€€
Slovenian　**Map** A4
Zupančičeva 39
Tel *(05) 627 6729*　**Closed** *Sat*
A dark woody interior and checked tablecloths set the tone for plates of seafood nibbles and wines straight from the barrel. To start, don't miss the bean soup. Efficient service.

KOPER: Skipper　€€
Fish/Seafood　**Map** A4
Kopališko nabrežje 3
Tel *(05) 626 1810*
There are few more pleasurable activities than sitting down to the day's freshest catch with a glass of chilled white wine, but that's exactly what you can do at the beachfront Skipper.

DK Choice

KOPER: Gostilna za Gradom　€€€
Fish/Seafood　**Map** A4
Kraljeva 10
Tel *(05) 628 5505*　**Closed** *Mon*
Despite its tricky location out in the western suburb of Semedela, it is well worth the effort to get to this sublime restaurant. Darko, the owner, is a gracious host, and goes that extra mile to ensure that dining here is a truly memorable experience. Much of the food is playful without being pretentious, such as bread urchins.

LOKEV: Muha　€
Regional　**Map** A4
Lokev 138
Tel *(05) 767 0055*　**Closed** *Thu & Fri*
Tuck into terrific regional dishes washed down with a glass of local teran or Refošk wine in the Karst's oldest inn, dating from 1679.

NOVA GORICA: DAM　€€€
Fish/Seafood　**Map** A3
Vinka Vodopivca 24
Tel *(05) 333 1147*
Popular with Italians from just across the border, this high-end eatery conjures up superb seafood dishes, including tuna tartare and sashimi of sea bass. Consider the good fixed-price gourmet menu.

NOVA GORICA: Pikol　€€€
Fish/Seafood　**Map** A3
Vipavska 94
Tel *(05) 302 2562*　**Closed** *Tue & Wed*
Housed in a purpose-built wooden pavilion on the edge of a forest next to a pond, Pikol is another fantastic seafood restaurant. The dishes are simply superb. Try the six-course meal.

PIRAN: Pirat　€
Fish/Seafood　**Map** A5
Zupančičeva 24
Tel *(05) 673 1481*
Pirat is a pleasant antidote to Piran's tourist restaurants, with no-frills seafood served in copper bowls and excellent daily menus.

PIRAN: Pizzeria Petica　€
Pizzeria　**Map** A5
Zupančičeva 6
Tel *(05) 901 4279*
Arguably, Petica doles out the finest pizza anywhere on the coast. There's a great buzz about the place too. Impeccable service.

Tables set in the sophisticated dining room at Proteus, Postojna

Outdoor seating on the pretty courtyard of Majerija, Vipava

PIRAN: La Bottega dei Sapori €€
Fish/Seafood **Map** A5
Kajuhova 12
Tel *(05) 992 0474* **Closed** *Mon*
Occupying a plum location on
lovely Tartini Square, this place
serves accomplished Istrian-
influenced seafood dishes.

PIRAN: Pri Mari €€
Fish/Seafood **Map** A5
Dantejeva 17
Tel *(05) 673 4735* **Closed** *Mon*
With folksy furnishings and
maritime prints, Pri Mari is one
of the best places on the coast
to try grilled and baked fish.

PIRAN: Verdi €€
Fish/Seafood **Map** A5
Verdijeva 18
Tel *(05) 673 2737*
This cosy old-town restaurant
impresses with its remarkable
collection of Lojze Spacal prints
and its succulent seafood dishes.

PORTOROŽ: Cacao €
Café **Map** A5
Obala 14
Tel *(05) 674 1035*
Sporting a cool, loungey interior
and a fabulous beach-facing
terrace, Cacao is an ultra-stylish
café that livens up come sundown. The delicious ice cream
comes in a variety of flavours.

PORTOROŽ: Mignon €
Café **Map** A5
Obala 33
Tel *(05) 674 9040*
Cracking beachfront café doling
out delicious coffee and cakes,
and, some say, the best home-
made ice cream in town.

PORTOROŽ: Staro Sidro €€
Fish/Seafood **Map** A5
Obala 55
Tel *(05) 674 5074* **Closed** *Mon*
The Old Anchor is a restful, rather
old-fashioned place that's been
around for aeons, but its fish
menu remains highly creditable.

PORTOROŽ: Tomi €€
Fish/Seafood **Map** A5
Letoviška 1
Tel *(05) 674 0222*
Away from the tourist hubbub,
this sunny restaurant offers a
canopied terrace with unrivalled
views of the water, and a strong
menu featuring exotic starters
such as truffles and crab. Don't
miss the crêpes for dessert.

POSTOJNA: Minutka €
Balkan **Map** A4
Ljubljanska cesta 14
Tel *(05) 720 3625*
Feast on juicy Serbian grilled
meats like *pleskavica* and *čevapi*,
or perhaps a stew of *prebranac*
(beans), in this cheerfully
serviced restaurant in the centre
of town.

POSTOJNA: Proteus €€€
International **Map** A4
Titov trg 1
Tel *(40) 457 483*
Named after Postojna's mysterious
cave-dwelling creature, Proteus
is a glitzy affair whose chef
rustles up ingenious dishes such
as stuffed rabbit with pistachios
in a pork net.

ŠTANJEL: Grad €€
Regional **Map** A4
Štanjel 1A
Tel *(05) 769 0118* **Closed** *Mon & Tue*
Occupying the atmospheric
courtyard of this wonderful
village's derelict 16th-century
castle, Grad offers a menu almost
exclusively devoted to the local
Karst cuisine.

VIPAVA: Majerija €€
Slovenian **Map** A4
Slap 18
Tel *(05) 368 5010* **Closed** *Mon–Thu*
This delightful white stone-built
farmstead offers tasty home-
made creations such as pork-
filled ravioli with fresh veggies
from the garden. Excellent home
brews too.

DK Choice

VIPAVA: Pri Lojzetu €€€
International **Map** A4
Dvorec Zemono
Tel *(05) 368 7007* **Closed** *Mon &
Tue*
One of Slovenia's most highly
regarded restaurants, Pri Lojzetu
is located just outside Vipava
in the cellar of a striking 17th-
century Palladian-style manor
house. The food here is elevated
to almost an art form, with taste
and colour combinations that
you are unlikely to find
anywhere else in Slovenia, such
as citrus-cured beef on a cheese
mousse with pea purée and
smoked pancetta. The
ambience and service are
absolutely first-class too.

Southern and Eastern Slovenia

**BIZELJSKO-SREMIŠKA:
Pri Peču** €€
Slovenian **Map** E3
Stara vas 58
Tel *(07) 452 0103* **Closed** *Tue*
This snug cocoon of old stone and
wood lies on a country lane in one
of the country's lesser-known wine
regions. Here you'll find an unfussy
menu of smoked meats and some
fish, plus lots of great wine.

BREŽICE: Aquarius €
Café **Map** E3
Bizeljska ulica 4
Tel *(07) 499 2505*
One of the more unusual venues
around, this sprightly café
occupies the four small circular
floors of the old water tower,
easily recognized owing to its
shocking-pink colour.

DK Choice

**BREŽICE: Ošterija
Debeluh** €€€
International **Map** E3
Trg Izgnancev 7
Tel *(07) 496 1070* **Closed** *Sun*
In such a small town, it's a
pleasant surprise to come
across such an upmarket restaurant as this one, appropriately
titled "Fat Man". The beautifully
lit interior features pastel-
painted walls and elegant
tables, while all the dishes, for
example roast duck with
peaches, or foal steak with
sautéed foie gras, are carefully
paired with wines from the
nearby Bizeljska-Sremska region.

For more information on types of restaurants *see pages 196–7*

Pavus Grad Tabor restaurant, housed in Tabor Castle, Lasko

CELJE: Oaza Café   €
Café   **Map** D3
Glavni trg 13
Tel *(040) 377 995*
Sit back in this great-looking café/tearoom, with modern decor and a chilled-out vibe, and enjoy the finest coffee in town. The breakfasts are very popular, too.

CELJE: Francl   €€
Slovenian   **Map** D3
Zagrad 77
Tel *(03) 492 6460*   **Closed** *Tue*
A popular weekend destination for locals looking to escape the city, Francl specializes in locally caught game, plus fish and stews. There are wonderful vegetarian dishes as well.

CELJE: Gostilna Amerika   €€
Balkan   **Map** D3
Mariborska cesta 79
Tel *(03) 541 9320*
The name is slightly odd for this determinedly Balkan establish-ment, where a meat-fest awaits, typically grilled over charcoal and served in huge portions. If you can't decide what to have, go for the mixed platter. The home-made bread is delicious.

CELJE: Gostilna pri Kmetec   €€
Slovenian   **Map** D3
Zagrad 140a
Tel *(03) 544 2555*   **Closed** *Mon*
The main reason to come here is for the views, which stretch as far as the Kamniško-Šavinjske Alps, but the food is very commendable too, not least the roasted wild boar.

CELJE: Stari Pisker   €€
International   **Map** D3
Savinova 9
Tel *(03) 544 2480*   **Closed** *Sun*
Mouthwatering steaks and burgers are the order of the day down in the brick-vaulted Old Pot Inn. Wash them down with a local beer. There is a good selection of wines, too.

ČRNOMELJ: Gostilna Muller   €€
Slovenian   **Map** D4
Ločka cesta 6
Tel *(07) 356 7200*   **Closed** *Mon*
Perched over the Lahinja river, Muller is a very popular venue among townsfolk, and being so close to the Croatian border ensures that grilled meats dominate the menu.

JERUZALEM: Vinski Hram   €€
Slovenian   **Map** F2
Jeruzalem 18
Tel *(02) 719 4504*
Overlooking sweeping vine-covered terraces, this guesthouse has a decent restaurant which, although largely catering to passing coachloads, is worth stopping at for lunch.

LASKO: Pavus Grad Tabor   €€€
International   **Map** D3
Cesta na Svetino 23
Tel *(03) 620 0723*   **Closed** *Mon & Tue*
Enjoy superb dining at this upmarket place, housed in Tabor Castle high above town. Try dishes like deer loin with poached pear and a black walnut and herb soufflé.

The elegant dining room for events at Gostilna Pec, Maribor

LENDAVA: Lovski Dom   €€
Regional   **Map** F2
Lendavske gorice 238a
Tel *(02) 575 1450*   **Closed** *Mon*
Grab a table inside the thatched barn before tucking into solid regional staples like *ciganska pečenka* (gypsy roast pork) and *bograč* (spicy goulash).

MARIBOR: Cajnica   €
Café   **Map** E2
Slovenska ulica 4
Tel *(02) 250 2986*
At this peaceful, old-world teahouse, with a wonderfully cluttered interior of nostalgic furnishings, you can enjoy a wide choice of brews from around the world. There's good coffee too.

MARIBOR: Gril Ranca   €
Balkan   **Map** E2
Dravska ulica 10
Tel *(02) 252 5550*
The surrounds are spartan and the service functional, but this place serves the best Bosnian grilled meats for miles around, and the river views are terrific.

MARIBOR: Kavarna Q   €
Café   **Map** E2
Gorkega 45
Tel *(02) 805 1390*
This sleek, modern restaurant-cum-café is best known for its chicken dishes, but there's plenty more besides, including calorific cakes and ice cream. Great atmosphere and friendly staff.

MARIBOR: Gostilna Pec   €€
International   **Map** E2
Spodnja Selnica 1, Selnica ob Dravi
Tel *(02) 674 0356*
A little way out of town, but the setting, under a vine-covered terrace beside the Drava, is lovely, and the food is top-notch. Try the deer fillet or duck breast.

MARIBOR: Pri treh ribnikih   €€
International   **Map** E2
Ribniška ulica 9
Tel *(02) 234 4170*
Maribor's oldest restaurant is named after the three ponds on which it's located, though the menu is by no means exclusively dedicated to seafood and fish.

MARIBOR: Novi svet pri Stolnici   €€€
Fish/Seafood   **Map** E2
Slomškov trg 5
Tel *(02) 250 0486*
Novi svet is fitted out in the style of a Dalmatian *konoba* (pub), with fishing gear strung across the walls and ceiling. Fresh fish is flown in daily from the Adriatic.

MOKRICE: Grad Mokrice €€€
International Map E4
Rajec 4
Tel *(07) 457 4240*
Experience refined dining in the Renaissance castle and golf resort hotel. The distinguished menu features delights like *oves sčrno trobento* (oatgrain and black trumpet mushrooms).

MURSKA SOBOTA: Rajh €€
Regional Map F1
Soboška ulica 32
Tel *(031) 705 007* **Closed** *Mon*
Fantastic regional flavours, such as Prekmurje ham with buckwheat salad and *gibanica* (a cottage cheese-based cake with walnuts, poppy seeds and apples), dominate the menu at Rajh.

NOVO MESTO: Čajarna Krojač €
Café Map D4
Grajski trg 17
Tel *(07) 337 0160*
This café serves an appealing range of teas and a short menu of sandwiches and baguettes, the best of which are those stuffed with *pršut* (home-cured ham).

NOVO MESTO: Gostišče Loka €€
International Map D4
Zupančicevo sprehajališče 2
Tel *(07) 332 1108* **Closed** *Sun*
Hidden away underneath the Šmihelksi Bridge, this is the choice place to eat in town, with a menu covering all bases, from pizza to pasta and grilled meats to fresh river fish.

OLIMJE: Amon €€
Slovenian Map E3
Olimje 24
Tel *(03) 818 2480*
Rough-plastered walls and chunky tables and chairs recycled from old wine presses set the tone for this distinguished restaurant serving upmarket country meals.

DK Choice

OTOČEC: Grad Otočec €€€
International Map D4
Grajska cesta 2
Tel *(07) 384 8900*
There are few more romantic places to eat in Slovenia than this Relais & Chateaux hotel's posh restaurant – all brown leather, silver trays and white linen-topped tables. It's certainly not cheap, but the food, including quail soup, and steak with truffles, is exquisite. The restaurant's unique island setting rounds things off perfectly.

PTUJ: Muzikafe €
Café Map E2
Vrazov trg 1
Tel *(02) 787 8860*
This uber-cool hangout combines a sunny stone terrace with a funky retro furnished interior – check out the cinema seats. Coffee, cakes and, often, great live music.

PTUJ: Amadeus €€
Slovenian Map E2
Prešernova ulica 36
Tel *(02) 771 7051*
Steak in sour cherry or plum sauce, and buckwheat *štruklji* are just two of the house specialities at this warm and classy venue.

PTUJ: Gostilna Ribič €€
Fish/Seafood Map E2
Dravska ulica 9
Tel *(02) 749 0635* **Closed** *Mon*
At this understatedly stylish riverside restaurant, you can sample all manner of Adriatic seafood and freshwater fish. The pergola terrace is inviting.

ROGAŠKA SLATINA: Kaiser €€€
Slovenian Map E3
Zdravilíški trg 14
Tel *(03) 811 4710*
The gorgeous cherry-wood furnishings recall the *belle époque* grace of the resort's heyday, while the conservatory is modern and stylish. The food is upscale modern Slovenian.

ŠENTANEL: Gostilna Marin €
Slovenian Map C2
Šentanel 8
Tel *(02) 824 0550*
The emphasis at this tourist farm is firmly on country-style home cooking, typified by *kmečka pojedina* (a feast of sausages, buckwheat mash, larded beans and potatoes).

SLOVENJ GRADEC:
Gostilna Murko €
Slovenian Map D2
Francetova cesta 24
Tel *(02) 883 8103*
This family-run guesthouse with a super restaurant offers dishes such as *pečenice* (sausages cooked in wine). Enjoy with a glass of home-made brandy.

DK Choice

SLOVENSKE KONJICE:
Zlati Gric €€€
International Map D2
Škalce 86
Tel *(03) 758 0361* **Closed** *Sun*
This fine restaurant is spectacularly set on a small rise amid lush vineyards. Its pastel peach walls and woody interior give a peaceful country air and the terrace is shaded by birch trees. Rich, red-meat dishes form the mainstay of an appetizing menu and are best savoured with a bottle of Blaufrankish, cultivated in these very hills.

TREBNJE: Gostilna Rakar €€
Fish/Seafood Map C3
Gorenje Poikve 8
Tel *(031) 441 066* **Closed** *Tue*
The most sophisticated dining place in the region, Rakar boasts Adriatic dorade and langoustines, alongside locally caught trout, on its menu.

ZUŽEMBERK: Gostilna
Pri Gradu €€
Fish/Seafood Map C4
Grajski trg 4
Tel *(07) 308 7290*
This *gostilna* is just down from the castle. The food here is simple, but Pri Gradu is the hub of village social life and makes for a decent pit stop if passing through.

Kavarna Q, a contemporary eatery in Maribor

For more information on types of restaurants *see pages 196–7*

SHOPPING IN SLOVENIA

Slovenia tempts visitors to spend at every turn. The chain stores are the backbone of shopping in towns, but you will find the abundant smaller workshops in the capital and tourist destinations more interesting. Here you will discover goods that make excellent souvenirs: laceware and folk craft such as *pisanice* (painted eggs), crystal glassware from Rogaška Slatina and paintings or jewellery crafted by artisans who draw on traditional styles. While you may find crafts at markets, their mainstay is seasonal foodstuffs, much of it organic. Home-made fruit brandies, honey and seed oils are worth a try. Notwithstanding the growth of malls, most shopping is in pedestrian precincts which feature a department store or two, high-fashion brands, an ice cream parlour and cafés.

Paintings for sale in a street, Kranj

Opening Hours

As a rule of thumb, shops open from 8am to 7pm on weekdays and until 1pm on Saturdays. However, this will vary depending on the size of the town and location. Major chain stores in city shopping centres may open on Sunday morning, while many shops on the coast keep more Mediterranean hours in summer, with about one or two hours' break for lunch and late evening opening. Similarly, shops in smaller towns often close from 12:30pm until 2pm. Apart from the large chains in shopping centres, the only shops that are open on Sundays are some of the bakeries, and even then only for a few hours in the morning. Everything is shut on public holidays. Outside of these hours, the only places to purchase supplies are large petrol stations on major routes, most of which have basic supermarkets, and kiosks at major train stations.

Prices and Payment

Prices in shops are fixed and it is not accepted practice to haggle in major stores. Owners of craft studios may be open to negotiation, although remember that the owner may well be the artist, too. Though prices are usually displayed in markets and street stalls, it is permissible to attempt to negotiate a lower price for goods if done with goodwill – gentle humour is more persuasive than tough talk in Slovenia.

In department stores, shopping centres and independent shops in large towns, it is possible to pay in cash or by using an internationally recognized credit card. In the smaller shops and in places such as markets, payments are always made in cash.

VAT Refunds

Visitors from non-European Union countries can obtain a refund on the value-added tax (DDV) levied on purchases by requesting a form at the point of sale. This is filled out by the seller, then certified by customs authorities upon presentation of the original receipt as you exit the country. Note that to qualify for a refund, goods must be unopened and taken out of the country within three months of purchase. The tax – 20 per cent of the purchase price – is refunded by the institutions indicated on the tax-free purchase form. Refunds cannot be requested for mineral oils, alcohol and alcoholic beverages or for tobacco products.

Markets

The street markets of Slovenia are wonderfully colourful and lively places to browse. In large towns these are generally held on weekdays, and occasionally on Saturday morning, and display a fine array of seasonal produce from local farmers, plus a small quota of imported

Façade of the Citypark mall, Ljubljana

foods. No visit to Ljubljana is complete without a stroll around the excellent open-air Market *(see p54)* located near St Nicholas's Cathedral. Alongside fruit and vegetables, you can expect to find honey and beeswax, excellent charcuterie stalls and often patterned *medeni kruhek* (honey bread) fashioned into rings or hearts. Ljubljana and Maribor *(see p180)* have enjoyable flea markets on Sundays and the last Saturday of the month respectively. These are great places to unearth unusual Slovenian items from a bygone era.

Shopping Centres

High streets aside, the hubs of modern shopping in cities and large towns are the large shopping centres located in the more modern outskirts beyond the old centres. Here you will find a variety of fashion chain stores, perhaps a department store, and usually a branch of the national supermarket giant, Mercator.

Handicrafts and Modern Goods

With a tradition of trade guilds it can trace to medieval times, Slovenia boasts a wide array of regional crafts that make novel souvenirs. Local tourist information centres often sell a selection of goods or can point you to a studio. Common novelty items in the alpine

Traditional beehive paintings on sale in a souvenir shop

Small wine shop in a family-owned cellar in Medana, Goriška Brda

northwest include tall brimmed hats or pipes from the Bohinj area. Radovljica, with its apiary museum, is a good source of painted beehive panels *(see p115)* decorated with witty folk designs, while nearby Kropa is celebrated for decorative wrought-iron pieces. Idrija *(see p150)* is renowned for lace handicrafts made with great skill and patience. Ribnica is the home of *suha roba* (traditional household wares crafted from wood and wicker), while the Bela Krajina region specializes in traditional rustic crafts such as *pisanice* (painted Easter eggs) and wicker baskets; try a store in Črnomelj *(see p167)*.

Modern Slovenian brands stocked countrywide include lead crystal glass, manufactured in Rogaška Slatina, and stylish Lisca lingerie. Though not unique to Slovenia, the traditional alpine Sunday-best clothes such as collarless jackets and dirndl-bodiced skirts, sold in upmarket traditional stores, also make unusual gifts.

Necklace made of felt

Food and Wine

Slovenian herbal teas, sea salt skimmed from pans near Portorož *(see p136)*, *bučno olje* (nutty pumpkin-seed oil) and apiarian products such as honey, beeswax and propolis are sold throughout Slovenia. Mass-produced examples are

sold in supermarkets, but higher quality produce is available from specialist shops or from markets, where it is sold by producers. In the Alps, look out for cheeses produced by alpine farmers in Triglav National Park. Shops at the monasteries of Pleterje *(see p168)* and Stična *(see p93)*, whose monks maintain a centuries-old tradition of self-sufficiency, sell herbal and apiarian produce as well as herbal remedies. However, Pleterje monastery is most celebrated for fruit brandies produced from the monastic orchards and said to be beneficial to health; bottles of *viljamovka* (pear spirit), with a whole fruit inside, make excellent gifts. Mass-produced fruit and berry liqueurs are sold in wine shops and supermarkets. The finest Slovenian wines are rarely exported and are good souvenirs: Simčič and Movia wines are highly rated by sommeliers.

Shoppers at one of the local pastry shops, Piran

ENTERTAINMENT IN SLOVENIA

From professional opera to punk, metal and jazz ensembles to alpine polka groups, Slovenia has a small but diverse entertainment scene. Inevitably, the wellspring of culture is the capital, Ljubljana – whether for music, theatre, opera or nightclubs. For such small cities, Ljubljana and Maribor boast an impressive cultural scene throughout the year, though the main institutions reduce their output in July and August. Maribor's scene is supported by its large student population. Many of the small towns and villages boast their own folk heritage ensembles which stage regular performances. Particularly memorable are the outdoor cultural festivals staged throughout the country – from Ljubljana's Jazz Festival and the folk extravaganza at Črnomelj to the reggae and rock festivals at Tolmin, there is some form of entertainment for everyone.

Entrance to the Kolosej theatre, Koper

Information and Tickets

Local tourist information centres are the most reliable sources of information on entertainment in Slovenia. Their offices stock flyers and posters for upcoming events and their websites generally publish dates of festivals and major concerts. The website of the Slovenian Tourist Board (see p217) is also useful for planning. In Ljubljana the "Kažipot" section of the daily newspaper *Delo* offers up-to-date listings. Tickets are available at the door or in advance at the box office of venues such as Križanke (see p73). Major venues also allow online booking and collection from the box office.

Theatre and Film

Plays are almost universally staged in the Slovenian language, which will marginalize the theatre as a source of entertainment for all but the most ardent theatregoer.

On the plus side, Slovenian theatre has a penchant for visual flair, so performances are often enjoyable nonetheless. The Slovene National Theatre (see p99), a splendid Art Nouveau edifice that hosts the national theatre company in Ljubljana, is the nation's premier stage. Its secondary arm, the

Performance by the contemporary Maribor Puppet Theatre

Slovene National Theatre Maribor has an excellent reputation nationwide, while the Prešernovo gledališče Kranj supports its own city theatre. Other theatres include the Mladinsko Theatre (Slovensko mladinsko gledališče) and Gledališče Glej (see p99). Puppet theatre (Lutkovno gledališče) is a charming tradition that excels in fantastical visuals. Dedicated venues are the Ljubljana Puppet Theatre and the Maribor Puppet Theatre.

All large towns have multiplex cinemas (kino) such as Kolosej. Foreign films are shown in their original language with Slovenian subtitles. Of special interest is the Ljubljana International Film Festival (LIFFe), which hosts a fortnight of international cinema in November.

Classical Music, Opera and Dance

Five professional orchestras operate in Slovenia. It may come as a surprise to many visitors to learn that the nation's elite orchestra, the Slovenian Philharmonic (see p72), is one of the oldest in Europe, having been formed in 1701. The Cankarjev dom, an arts and conference centre in Ljubljana, also hosts classical concerts, including international artistes. The Slovene National Opera and Ballet (see p99) are the leading companies in their fields and share a splendid historic Opera House in the

Poster of the annual Mladi Levi festival, held at the Bunker Institute

capital. Again, a secondary offshoot of the company performs in Maribor, sharing a venue with the national theatre. Slovenian mezzo-sopranos Bernarda Fink, born to Slovenian parents in Buenos Aires, and Marjana Lipovšek, are great cultural ambassadors for Slovenian opera, and both regularly perform in Slovenia. The Exodos and the Mladi Levi international festivals have a reputation for daring contemporary pieces.

Rock, Jazz and Folk

Slovenian rock music came roaring into the public consciousness with the birth of a Ljubljana punk scene in the late 1970s. Bands Laibach and Pankrti were deemed a civil threat and suppressed by the authorities. Re-formed and as confrontational as ever, the former still tours. Other

heavyweights of the Slovenian rock and pop scenes include evergreen stadium rock group Siddharta; Vlado Kreslin, who create tuneful folk pop, and ethno-pop singer Magnifico. The student population in the two main cities continues to support a thriving alternative live scene; Ljubljana's Metelkova Mesto *(see p81)* is a counterculture legend with associations such as **Menza pri koritu** promoting culture and the arts. The capital's Orto Bar *(see p99)* hosts national rock bands and DJs in its nightclub. In Maribor, **Klub MC Pekarna** is the bastion of student rock bands and local DJs. Tolmin-based music festivals **Metalcamp** and **Overjam International Reggae Festival** draw thousands of music fans to the Soča Valley in July.

Both Ljubljana and Maribor have jazz venues that host Slovenian groups plus touring foreign artists; Ljubljana's Cankarjev dom is the main stage for major international names. The Jazz Club Gajo *(see p99)* organizes music events during the summer. Events such as the Ljubljana Jazz Festival are also a must for any visiting jazz fan.

Lovers of traditional music are spoiled for choice in Slovenia. The country retains a strong folk tradition that can be heard in the music of groups such as Terra Folk (actually a quartet of classically trained musicians) or Katalena, who blend folk and jazz. No country festival is complete without a folk group, especially in the Bela Krajina and Prekmurje regions – the Jurjevanje festival at Črnomelj

is the high point of the folk calendar. In the alpine area, visitors can hear chirpy accordion music. No group is more famous than the gold-disc selling, but now retired, Avsenik Brothers, whose polkas are copied across Germanic Europe. Ansambel Saše Avsenika, a band formed by an Avsenik grandson, still performs in a polka style.

DIRECTORY

Theatre and Film

Kolosej
Šmartinska 152, Ljubljana.
Tel (01) 520 5500.
W kolosej.si

Ljubljana Puppet Theatre
Krekov trg 2, Ljubljana.
City Map E3.
Tel (01) 300 0970. W lgl.si

Maribor Puppet Theatre
Vojasniski trg 2, Maribor.
Tel (02) 228 1978. W lg-mb.si

Mladinsko Theatre
Vilharjeva 11, Ljubljana.
Tel (01) 300 4900.
W mladinsko.com

Prešernovo gledališče Kranj
Glavni trg 6, Kranj.
Tel (04) 280 4900. W pgk.si

Slovene National Theatre Maribor
Slovenska ulica 27, Maribor.
Tel (02) 250 6100. W sng-mb.si

Classical Music, Opera and Dance

Cankarjev dom
Prešernova cesta 10, Ljubljana.
City Map C3. **Tel** (01) 241 7100.
W cd-cc.si

Opera House
Župančičeva 1, Ljubljana.
City Map C2. **Tel** (01) 241 5959;
(01) 241 5960. W opera.si

Rock, Jazz and Folk

Klub MC Pekarna
W pekarna-net

Menza pri koritu
W menzaprikoritu.org

Metalcamp
W metaldays.net

Overjam International Reggae Festival
W overjamfestival.com

Façade of the Cankarjev dom with the Ivan Cankar monument in front

OUTDOOR ACTIVITIES AND SPECIALIST HOLIDAYS

Visitors who revel in scenery and the great outdoors are spoiled for choice in Slovenia. The country's diverse landscape ranges from snowcapped mountains and lush wine slopes towards the coast and virgin woods. Triglav National Park and the Kamniško-Savinjske Alps offer ample opportunities for walking, hiking, cycling and paragliding during summer and for skiing and snowboarding in winter. The country's numerous rivers are popular with fishing enthusiasts as well as with those interested in adventure sports such as hydroboarding and canyoning; sailing, windsurfing and diving are popular in coastal Slovenia. The numerous spas in the country also attract a large number of visitors every year and offer patrons a wide variety of thermal cures as well as therapeutic massages.

Walking and Hiking

No one should contemplate a visit to Slovenia without good walking shoes. There are walking trails everywhere and one can take anything from a stroll along the boardwalk at Vintgar Gorge *(see p114)* to a month-long hike along Slovenia's alpine spine. All routes, except themed trails, are indicated by a white dot within a red circle. Themed trails currently have their own symbols, although a programme to replace these with a new symbol – a white dot within a yellow circle – began in 2010. Nevertheless, maps are advisable for all but the shortest tourist trail. Produced by the **Alpine Association of Slovenia** (Planinska zveza Slovenije), these maps are available in Ljubljana and at visitor centres

or agencies. The decision about where to go is limited only by the traveller's imagination and stamina. Mountain routes are clear of snow and the weather is usually stable from mid-June to September, although conditions in the Alps change rapidly year-round.

The most popular destination for walking in Slovenia is Triglav National Park *(see pp116–17)*. The most famous hike is the two-day ascent of Mount Triglav. Lake Bohinj *(see pp118–19)* offers an excellent base for all walks in the National Park; local agencies organize hikes during the season. Logarska dolina *(see p126)* is a good base for excursions into the Kamniško-Savinjske Alps. The **Slovenian Mountain Guide Association** provides detailed information

on guides and hiking. Other popular walking areas include the subalpine Pohorje massif, accessible from Kope *(see p177)*; Rogla *(see p179)*; Maribor *(see pp180–81)*; the Karst; the high meadows of Velika Planina *(see p125)* and Robanov kot *(see p126)*. The **Slovenian Tourist Board** publishes *Hiking in Slovenia*, a brochure providing a good overview of options. The trekking guide publisher Cicerone produces two guides to walking in Slovenia – *Trekking in Slovenia* and *The Julian Alps of Slovenia*.

Slovenia has also developed the 500-km- (310-mile-) long Slovene Alpine Trail, from Maribor via the Slovenian Alps to Ankaran on the Adriatic coast. The walk takes around 30 days to complete.

Breathtaking views while hiking in the Alps

Skiers at Stari Vrh resort, a small skiing area close to Škofja Loka

Rock Climbing

Bled *(see pp112–13)* and Lake Bohinj are the focus for rock climbing, known as *športno plezanje* (sports climbing), in Slovenia. All the 340-plus routes in this spectacular limestone area are bolted and offer a good range of climbing grades, the majority in the 5a to 7b range according to the French Free Climbing Grading System. The ideal time to visit Bled for rock climbing is from May to October. Beginners are advised to book a trip with an activities provider in Bled or Bohinj.

Other destinations for climbing include Osp, east of Koper *(see pp138–9)*, and around Celje *(see pp174–5)*. Sidarta publishes details of 3,600 routes in 84 areas in its guidebook the *Slovenia Sports Climbing Guidebook*.

Skiing and Snowboarding

Skiing is a very popular sport in Slovenia; one in five Slovenians ski and the most popular pistes are those in the alpine areas of Gorenjska and on the Pohorje massif. Of the 48 ski centres in the country – which combined, provide upto 50,000 skiers with over 272 km (169 miles) of pistes – 15 qualify as resorts. Only a few are as developed or offer skiing as challenging as that in Austria, Italy or the French Alps. However, this means fewer skiers, lower prices and a large variety of slopes *(see pp30–31)* in a small area.

Depending on the weather, the skiing season generally runs from late November to March or April, and sometimes even early May on the high slopes of Kanin in the Soča Valley. The peak season is from late December to mid-February. Cable cars or ski pulls, ski hire and ski coaching are available at all resorts.

The most popular resort for foreign visitors is Kranjska Gora *(see p120)*, which has 30 km (19 miles) of pistes ranging from easy to moderate. In the northwest, Krvavec, northeast of Kranj *(see p124)*, is well equipped and popular with skiers from Ljubljana at weekends; visitors should be prepared for long queues. Vogel, beside Lake Bohinj, has off-piste routes and superb views, as does Kanin near Bovec *(see p122)*, offering the only pistes over 2,000 m (6,562 ft) high. Slovenian skiers also enthuse about Cerkno *(see p151)*; none of its 18 km (11 miles) of trails are higher than 1,300 m (4,265 ft) but the downhill skiing is famously challenging.

The most popular slopes to the east are at Rogla and Mariborsko Pohorje *(see p181)*. The latter has the largest ski area in the country with 220 ha (544 acres) laid with 80 km (50 miles) of pistes, of which 10 km (6 miles) make up Europe's longest night run. Snowboarding is popular at Krvavec, Vogel – which has a

dedicated snowboard park – and Rogla, all of which have half-pipes and jumps. Popular off-piste ski areas include those around Komna, above Lake Bohinj, and the foothills of Mala Mojstrovka, above Vršič Pass *(see pp120–21)*; a local guide is recommended for both areas.

Cross-country skiing is a delight. Trails are laid out through picturesque glades or fairy-tale snowy forests and are usually free. The best-known trails are on Pokljuka plateau, although the unspoiled valley of Logarska dolina is peerless for scenery.

Further details of resorts are available in *Skiing in Slovenia*, a brochure brought out by the Slovenian Tourist Board. Each resort also has its own individual website, which generally offers maps of pistes, contacts, links to local schools, information on hire companies and often a webcam showing snow conditions. Links to all resorts are available on the **Active Slovenia** website.

Golf

The first golf course was laid for the King of Yugoslavia at Bled in 1937, but was neglected by subsequent rulers. Redesigned in 1972 by golf architect Donald Harradine and in 2016 by Swan Golf Designs, the **Bled Golf & Country Club** is the nation's premier course, with its 6,278 m (6,865 yard), par 72, 18-hole course set against the backdrop of the Alps. It has a par 36 nine-hole course as well.

Guests are also welcome to courses at Lipica *(see p141)* – open year round – Volčji Potok near Kamnik, Diners Golf & Country Club Ljubljana, Mokrice, Ptuj, Moravske Toplice, Slovenske Konjice and Podčertek, among others. Clubs can be hired at all courses except in Slovenske Konjice. The Slovenian Tourist Board website provides information on courses, details of major courses, contacts and addresses, hole breakdowns and maps.

Teeing off in Lipica

Cycling

Mountain biking and cycling are very popular in Slovenia. Quiet country roads through diverse landscapes present opportunities for superb scenic touring. This variety also means there are opportunities for cyclists of all abilities and ages. All children under 14 must wear a helmet while cycling on Slovenian roads.

There are lovely country routes to explore around Bled and Bohinj and the gravel tracks that circuit these lakes also offer great opportunities for cycling. Other destinations include the wine hills of Goriška Brda *(see p149)* or around Jeruzalem *(see p185)*, the little-visited roads of Idrija *(see p150)* and the Karst, as well as Prekmurje, the flattest region of Slovenia. Twisting mountain roads such as those around Vršič Pass or ascents to the ski resorts at Kope or Rogla pose a challenge even for experienced cyclists.

With abundant uplands crisscrossed by old cart tracks, options for mountain biking abound in Slovenia. Bike Park Pohorje in Mariborsko Pohorje is the venue for the downhill Mountain Bike World Cup. Challenging free-ride routes in bike parks in Bovec and Kranjska

Visitors cycling in Slovenia

Gora satisfy those seeking adventure in the Alps. Less challenging dirt tracks lie in the Koroška hills around Jamnica, west of Dravograd *(see p177)* – visitors can even cycle underground through the disused Peca Underground Mine *(see p177)*, near Mežica, and on the subalpine meadows at Velika Planina, which is accessible by cable car.

The Slovenian Tourist Board has information on 14 cycling regions in its brochure *Cycling in Slovenia*. Its website is also a mine of information for cyclists. Bikes can be hired via tourist agencies throughout the country. Most agencies stock maps of biking routes and the staff can advise on cyclist-friendly hotels and camp sites, which receive one- to five-wheel accreditation instead of star ratings. Agencies in premier cycling regions such as Bled and Bovec organize guided trips. One of the agencies that provides information on guided tours, trails and accommodation is **Mountain Bike Nomad**.

The best weather for cycling is between May and late September. July and August can be hot, especially in central and eastern Slovenia; the Alps, however, are cooler.

Children taking horse riding lessons in Roznik Hill, Ljubljana

Horse Riding

Slovenia's most famous equestrian exports are the Lipizzaner horses bred at Lipica *(see p141)* since the 17th century. The **Lipica Stud Farm** offers riding classes as well as tours – a must-do for any horse enthusiast.

Smaller, local riding schools and tourist farms that provide riding for guests are located throughout Slovenia and managed by the Ljubljana-based **Slovenian Equestrian Association**. The tourist board website provides information on accredited schools. Its *Friendly Countryside* brochure of tourist farms uses icons to indicate those that offer riding for guests.

Paragliding

With numerous hills and mountains to use as launch pads, Slovenia has taken to paragliding with enthusiasm. The finest venues for a flight are Krvavec; Mount Vogel, where a 1,200-m (3,937-ft) height difference between the take-off and landing points ensures flights of around 20 minutes; and the Mangart or Kanin mountains near Bovec. The last two enjoy superlative views of Mount Triglav and Triglav National Park.

For visitors, paragliding is only possible in tandem with an experienced instructor. The activities agencies **Pac Sports** and **Avantura** in Bohinj and Bovec respectively are of good repute.

Fishing

Slovenia's unpolluted rivers and lakes offer great sport for fishing enthusiasts. The fishing season runs from April to October. Visitors are required to possess a licence issued by the **Fisheries Research Institute** of Slovenia (Zavod za ribistro Slovenije). Available at the local tourist boards and select hotels, these cost between 30 and 100 euros a day depending on the area, although catch-and-release permits are cheaper. Rods can

Fishing in the Pivka river, near Postojna Caves

only be hired by visitors who opt for guided trips. Indigenous fish species vary according to whether rivers drain into the Danube basin or the Adriatic Sea. Those in the former, which accounts for three-quarters of the rivers in Slovenia, include brown trout, the grayling and the huchen – a relative of the taimen and salmon. Rivers that drain into the Danube include the Krka around Žužemberk *(see p167)* and the Kolpa.

The prize catch of rivers draining into the Adriatic is Europe's largest trout species, the marble trout. The premier Adriatic fishing ground is the Soča river, renowned as a fly-fishing venue from June onwards; other forms of fishing are banned in some sections.

Visitor paragliding in the Slovenian Alps, Tolmin

The Sava Bohinjka river and Lake Bohinj offer good sport for char, mostly from boats, while Lake Bled is famous among anglers for its trophy carp, which weigh over 20 kg (44 lb).

Information about each area, including links to local clubs, which manage 94 per cent of Slovenian fishing waters, can be found on the Slovenian Tourist Board website.

Sailing and Windsurfing

Though overshadowed by the islands of neighbouring Croatia, Slovenia's 47-km- (29-mile-) long coastline permits it to promote itself as a Mediterranean yachting destination. The majority of yacht charter companies are based at Izola *(see p137)*, home to one of three Slovenian marinas; the others are at Koper and Portorož *(see p136)*. Visitors who want to hire a yacht need to present proof of their sailing qualifications. It is also possible to charter a yacht along with an experienced captain – some companies offer sailing lessons with the hire – or take a day trip along the coast. Again, Izola is the principal base for day trips along the coast.

If the coastline is limiting for yachtsmen, it is ideal for those visitors who are new to windsurfing. Winds rarely rise above a gentle breeze in summer and the sea temperatures are warm. Outlets hiring out windsurfing equipment line the beachfront at Portorož.

Adventure-sports enthusiasts kayaking on the Soča river

Rafting, Kayaking and Canoeing

The Soča river is the premier adventure destination for Slovenians, ranking among the top five whitewater rafting and kayaking destinations in Europe. Sections of the river have rapids ranging from easy to difficult, with the added appeal of a turquoise river and impressive alpine scenery. Bovec and Kobarid (see p122) are the hubs of activity and several watersports agencies in the towns organize 1.5–2 hour trips. The season runs from April to October; April and early May, when the river is swollen with snow thaw, are best for experienced rafters. In August and early September, the river is safe for families.

Among Slovenians, rafting is popular on the Kolpa river, where the midsections provide gentle, unchallenging rapids. There are agencies such as **Soča Rafting** and **Bovec Rafting Team** that hire out rafts to paddle at leisure.

Canoeing is a relatively new activity in Slovenia. You can hire canoes from agencies that serve the Kolpa, and from the shores of Lake Bled and Lake Bohinj. Canoeing along the Ljubljanica river, through Ljubljana to the Ljubljana Marshes (see p92), is a marvellous trip.

Hydroboarding and Canyoning

These are new additions to the roster of adventure sports in Slovenia. Many aficionados consider hydroboarding – racing through rapids with a large float – the most extreme watersport in the country. A wetsuit and protective helmet are obligatory.

Canyoning treats the river gorge as a giant adventure playground. Snug in a wetsuit and wearing a helmet, visitors can swim through rock pools, sluice down waterfalls, and abseil over low cliffs to negotiate a river canyon.

The Soča river and its tributaries are the focus for both activities. Due to their inherent dangers, a guide is compulsory; agencies such as Soča Rafting and Bovec Rafting Team organize trips between April and October.

Diving

The sea between Piran (see pp134–5) and Strunjan is the first choice for Slovenian scuba divers due to the variety of its marine flora and fauna. Other sights include wrecks of cargo vessels and warships sunk during World War II. The Piran-based company **Sub-net** rents equipment, leads guided trips to dive sites and runs Professional Association of Diving Instructors (PADI) scuba courses from April to October. Diving is also possible in Slovenia's rivers and lakes. Lake Bled is the focus of scuba diving for novices, with local agencies such as **3glav Adventures** organizing trips. The **Slovenian Diving Federation** publishes lists of accredited instructors on its website.

For expert divers, Slovenia's many karst springs offer the opportunity for cave-diving adventures. Scuba divers are still exploring the karst sump of the Wild lake (Divje jezero) near Idrija; in 1997 divers descended to 170 m (558 ft), yet did not reach the bottom.

Deep-sea diving in the Adriatic Sea off the coast at Piran

Spa Tourism

Slovenia has a tradition of spa tourism that can be traced back to Roman days. Today, alongside private spa facilities in upmarket hotels throughout the country, there are around 15 dedicated health and spa resorts where wellness is the priority. There are two resorts on the coast at Portorož and Strunjan. The others are at natural thermal springs in Dolenjska and Prekmurje.

Since the early 2000s, "taking the waters" has shifted from simply meaning a health cure to pampering. Consequently, most resorts now provide a hedonistic range of exotic massages and beauty treatments as well as medicinal facilities, which are typically for rheumatism or cardiovascular complaints. This shift is reflected in the move by spas to use the Italian word *terme* or wellness rather than *toplice*, the Slovenian word for spa.

The slick Balnea Wellness Centre at Dolenjske Toplice *(see p167)* typifies the move. Others, such as Moravske Toplice *(see p186)* and Terme Čatež on the outskirts of Brežice *(see p169)*, with their numerous warm swimming pools, promote themselves as family holiday destinations.

The best-known spa resort is Rogaška Slatina *(see p171)*, which retains the architecture and grandeur of its time as a fashionable Austro-Hungarian spa resort in the late 1800s.

Visitors at the spa in Dolenjske Toplice

DIRECTORY

Walking and Hiking

Alpine Association of Slovenia
Dvoržakova 9, Ljubljana.
Tel (01) 434 5680.
🇼 pzs.si

Slovenian Mountain Guide Association
Dvoržakova 9, Ljubljana.
🇼 zgvs.si

Slovenian Tourist Board
Dimičeva 13, Ljubljana.
Tel (01) 589 8550.
🇼 slovenia.info

Skiing and Snowboarding

Active Slovenia
🇼 activeslo.com (in Slovenian only).

Golf

Bled Golf & Country Club
Vrba 37 a Lesce, Bled.
Tel (01) 537 7711.
🇼 golfbled.com

Diners Golf & Country Club Ljubljana
Smlednik 200.
Tel (051) 262 226.
🇼 golf-ljubljana.si

Cycling

Mountain Bike Nomad
Jamnica 10, Prevalje.
Tel (02) 870 3060.
🇼 bikenomad.com

Horse Riding

Lipica Stud Farm
Lipica 5, Sežana. **Tel** (05) 739 1580. 🇼 lipica.org

Slovenian Equestrian Association
Celovška cesta 25, Ljubljana.

Tel (01) 434 7265.
🇼 konj-zveza.si
(in Slovenian only).

Paragliding

Avantura
Trg golobarskih žrtev 19, Bovec. **Tel** (041) 718 317; (041) 832 774.
🇼 avantura.org

Pac Sports
Ribčev laz 50, Lake Bohinj.
Tel (040) 864 202.
🇼 pac-sports.com

Fishing

Fisheries Research Institute
Sp. Gameljne 61, Ljubljana-Šmartno. **Tel** (01) 244 3400.
🇼 zzrs.si

Rafting, Kayaking and Canoeing

Bovec Rafting Team
Mala vas 106, Bovec.

Tel (041) 338 308.
🇼 bovec-rafting-team.com

Soča Rafting
Trg golobarskih žrtev 14, Bovec.
Tel (041) 724 472.
🇼 socarafting.si

Diving

3glav Adventures
Ljubljanska 1, Bled.
Tel (04) 163 8184.
🇼 3glav.com

Slovenian Diving Federation
Celovška cesta 25, Ljubljana.
Tel (01) 433 9308.
🇼 spz.si
(in Slovenian only).

Sub-net
Prešernovo nabrežje 24, Piran.
Tel (041) 746 153.
🇼 sub-net.si

SURVIVAL GUIDE

PRACTICAL INFORMATION

Slovenia was always the most progressive of the Yugoslav nations. Its acceptance into the European Union in 2004 and integration into the European Monetary Union in 2007, coupled with the growth of tourism, has left it well prepared to welcome visitors. Economic integration has simplified border formalities and monetary issues for tourists. Major investment in infrastructure – motorways, roads and a reliable rail service – has made transport quick and easy. Most of the Slovenians themselves are eager to promote their nation. Every town, large and small, has an enthusiastic tourist information centre that helps to source accommodation and provides information about local attractions as well as activities. In addition, most Slovenians speak a second language – English is popular among the younger population and German among the older generation.

When to Visit

Slovenia's location, where the Alps, the Adriatic Sea and the Pannonian plain converge, results in a diverse climate. The southwest is characterized by a Mediterranean climate of hot summers and mild winters. The northwest is typically alpine, with warm summers, cold winters and heavy snowfall. The north and east have the dry, airless hot summers and bitter winters typical of a continental climate. Mean national temperatures over 24 hours are 20º C (68º F) in summer and 0º C (32º F) in winter.

The busiest tourist season is between June and August, when popular destinations such as Ljubljana, the Adriatic coast and Lake Bled are crowded. Resorts are at their busiest from late July to mid-August. That said, Ljubljana's café society is also at its most effervescent and the high Alps at their most accessible for hiking at this time; the alpine plateaus provide relief from the often suffocating heat in the centre and east. Summer is also the busiest time for festivals and most towns stage some form of summer event.

November is the wettest month of the year, especially in the Alps, and many coastal hotels close for winter. However, mountain resorts prepare for the start of the ski season that is in full swing throughout the country by December and January. Winters are at their mildest on the coast but are extreme in the continental north and east, compensated for by the lowest precipitation in the country.

Crowds thin and prices fall in spring (April to early June) and autumn (mid-September to early November), both of which are lovely times to visit. The countryside begins to bloom during the former while the latter sees it luxurious and fruitful.

What to Pack

What you pack depends on when and where you visit. A waterproof jacket is recommended at all times (albeit lightweight in summer). Walking boots are essential and alpine hikers should come prepared for adverse conditions even during the summer.

Visitors enjoying the sun on the promenade at Portorož

◄ Cable cars to help skiiers reach higher alpine slopes at the Krvavec Ski Resort, Kamnik–Savinja Alps

Tourist information counter at Ljubljana Airport

Passports and Visas

Slovenia became a member of the European Union on 1 May 2004. Consequently, holders of full, valid EU, US, Canadian, Australian and New Zealand passports do not need a visa to enter Slovenia for up to 90 days.

There are no border controls in the EU, although the police may conduct checks at major border crossings with Austria, Italy and Hungary. A passport or photo ID is sufficient from Croatia. Always check the latest entry requirements with the Slovenian embassy in your country before leaving.

Travel Safety Advice

Visitors can get up-to date travel safety information from the **Foreign and Commonwealth Office** in the UK, the **State Department** in the US and the **Department of Foreign Affairs and Trade** in Australia.

Embassies and Consulates

The embassies or consulates of most countries including **Australia**, the **UK**, **Canada** and the **US** are located in Ljubljana.

Customs Information

Customs regulations have been harmonized with EU standards: EU nationals over 17 years can import a limitless amount of goods, but only for personal use. Reasonable limits for entrants within the EU are 800 cigarettes/400 cigarillos/200 cigars/1 kg (35 oz) of tobacco; plus 10 litres (21 pints) of spirits, 90 litres (190 pints) of wine and 110 litres (233 pints) of beer.

Non-EU arrivals have to pass through customs inspections at Brnik Airport. These are generally cursory but are subject to the following cap on imports: 200 cigarettes/ 100 cigarillos/50 cigars/250g (9 oz) of tobacco; 1 litre (2 pints) of spirits, 4 litres (9 pints) of wine; perfumes and electronic goods up to €430 value. A maximum of €10,000 can be imported in cash; larger sums must be declared on arrival. On leaving, non-EU travellers can apply for a refund on Slovenian VAT (DDV) if they can prove a one-day, single-retailer spend of over €70 (see p208).

Visitor Information

A well-developed network of tourist information centres caters to visitors' needs. Denoted by "TIC" (Turističnoinformacijski center), these are generally run by city, town or regional authorities and manned by friendly staff who speak excellent English. Apart from information on local accommodation, attractions, tour and activity providers, most of the centres provide maps of their region free or for a nominal fee. Most also stock excellent brochures from the national tourism coordinator, the **Slovenia National Tourist Office**. Its main office beside the Triple Bridge (see pp52–3) in Ljubljana's Old Town bursts with information about the country. Private tourist agencies fill in the gaps in towns where there is no official bureau, often located around rail or bus transport hubs.

Most destinations in Slovenia maintain a website and provide pages in English and often a searchable database of entertainment and festivities, accommodation listings and details of tourist sights. The national tourist office's website is also a wealth of information.

Opening Hours

Public and private offices operate from 9am to 4 or 5pm on weekdays. Banking hours (see p226) generally include an hour's break from 12:30pm. Post offices (see p229) and pharmacies tend to operate slightly longer hours. Standard shop opening times are from 8am to 7pm on weekdays and until 1pm on Saturdays, although these vary with the size of the town; those in large city shopping centres may open on Sunday mornings, for example. Bear in mind that 24-hour petrol stations on major routes have basic supermarkets and that country petrol stations generally operate shop hours, so may close on Sundays. Museums and galleries typically open from 9 or 10am until 5 or 6pm from Tuesdays to Sundays; details are provided with each entry. Odprto means open, zaprto means closed.

Supermarket at a petrol station in Bled

Ticket booth at Tolmin Gorge

Admission Charges

A small charge is levied for entry to most museums and galleries in Slovenia. Expect to pay a couple of euros at small town museums and up to four euros for showpiece galleries in towns and cities. Entry to churches and to Triglav National Park is free.

Language

The south Slavic tongue of Slovenia is not the easiest language, even to anyone with a smattering of other European languages. This is apart from the fact that there are about 40 or so dialects.

Fortunately, most people in Slovenia speak at least one other language, so visitors should be able to make themselves understood easily. The standard of English is excellent among the younger generation – seek out a student or young person if you need to ask for help – and German is common among older citizens and around the Austrian border. Italian is widely understood in the border areas. Nevertheless, attempting a few local words (*see pp250–52*) is appreciated.

Religion

Although 40 religious denominations are registered, Slovenia is overwhelmingly Roman Catholic. The 60 per cent of Slovenians who define themselves as Catholic dwarfs the second-largest religious group, the 2.3 per cent Muslim population.

The Church is treated with respect even among the less religious younger generation and religious services are broadcast regularly on national radio. It is highly insensitive to enter a church when a service is in progress and negative comments about religion may offend deeply, especially the elderly.

Travellers with Special Needs

Although awareness is improving, Slovenia still has some way to go to adapt to travellers with special needs. Public transport vehicles, except for international and modern intercity trains such as the service between Ljubljana and Maribor, usually have steps. Larger train stations can provide boarding ramps on request. Similarly, steps rather than ramps are standard in museums and only larger hotels have wheelchair-friendly rooms and lifts.

Change is slowly being made as buildings are modernized. Slovenia created the world's first footpath for the mobility-impaired; a 15-km- (9-miles-) wheelchair-accessible trail from Vodranci near Ormož. The most comprehensive source of information is the **Paraplegics Association of Slovenia** (Zveza paraplegikov Republike Slovenija), whose website has an English translation.

Gay and Lesbian Travellers

Educational campaigns have softened attitudes – the registration of same-sex partnerships was legalized in 2006 – and physical attacks are rare. Nevertheless,

Ornate altars of the church at Olimje Monastery

Fresh farm produce for sale at a farm near Šmartno

Slovenia remains deeply conservative in regard to the gay and lesbian communities. It is rare to see same-sex couples walking hand-in-hand. Similarly, sourcing gay-friendly accommodation can prove problematic – discretion is the best policy.

The focus of the nation's gay and lesbian community is in Ljubljana, which hosts the Pride Parade in June and the Festival of Gay and Lesbian Films in December. The capital also has a traditional Sunday get-together at a city-centre club. Internet resources include the Slovenian-language-only **Slovenian Queer Resources Directory** and **Out in Slovenia**, a sports and activities organizer.

Electricity

Mains voltage is 220V, 50Hz. British, Australian and Irish appliances require a standard two-prong, round-pin adaptor. North American appliances require a transformer.

Time

Slovenia operates Central European Time, so it is one hour ahead of Greenwich Mean Time (GMT), six hours ahead of US Eastern Standard Time, and 10 hours behind Australian Eastern Standard Time.

Responsible Tourism

Two-thirds of Slovenia is covered in natural forest, making it the second-most forested country in Europe after Finland. Over a third is protected by the European Union's Natura 2000 network of important habitats. There is a growing awareness of environmental issues, promoted by the government-aided Council for the Environmental Protection of the Republic of Slovenia and the sustainable development pressure group, Umanotera. The national tourist board has also declared its commitment to promote green and sustainable ethics.

Recycling is commonplace in urban centres, where there are separate bins for waste. Ecotourism is growing at around 20 per cent per annum. Under the Association of Slovenian Tourist Farms (see p190), there are 200 or so farmstays, concentrated in the north and west. They are small holdings practising low-impact agriculture and some are accredited "Eko" to signify their healthy environment and organic food. Organic farming has enjoyed a surge and the fresh fruit and vegetables at daily markets is generally produced without chemical sprays. Packaged organic produce is labelled "Bio".

Model soldiers decorate a clock on a public building in Stara Loka

DIRECTORY

Travel Safety Advice

Australia
Department of Foreign Affairs and Trade.
[w] dfat.gov.au
[w] smartraveller.gov.au

UK
Foreign and Commonwealth Office.
[w] gov.uk/foreign-travel-advice

US
US Department of State.
[w] travel.state.gov

Embassies and Consulates

Australia
Železna cesta 14, Ljubljana.
Tel (01) 234 8675, (01) 234 8676.

Canada
Trg republike 3, Ljubljana.
City Map C3.
Tel (01) 252 4444, (01) 252 3333.

UK
4th Floor, Trg republike 3, Ljubljana.
City Map C3.
Tel (01) 200 3910, (01) 425 0174.
[w] british-embassy.si

USA
Prešernova cesta 31, Ljubljana.
City Map B3.
Tel (01) 200 5500, (01) 200 5555.
[w] usembassy.si

Visitor Information

Slovenian National Tourist Office
Krekov trg 10, Ljubljana.
City Map E3.
Tel (01) 306 4575, (01) 200 5555.
[w] slovenia.info

Travellers with Special Needs

Paraplegics Association of Slovenia
Štihova 14, Ljubljana.
Tel (01) 432 7138.
[w] zveza-paraplegikov.si

Gay and Lesbian Travellers

Out in Slovenia
[w] outinslovenija.com

Slovenian Queer Resources Directory
[w] ljudmila.org/siqrd

Personal Security and Health

Slovenia is one of the safest European countries to visit. The capital, Ljubljana, is largely crime free – pickpockets are rare and violent crime almost unheard of. Slovenian public health services are also excellent and visitors to the country face no health risks. There are no endemic diseases and water is potable throughout the country. Instead, the most common ailments for visitors relate to the climate. Summers can be suffocatingly hot and sunburn can be an issue. Mountainous regions present the added danger of adverse weather, especially at high altitudes.

Police

Slovenian police, known as *policija*, have the task of providing public safety. Dressed in blue uniforms, they are generally courteous and able to communicate in basic English, especially the younger officers. All policemen have the right to request proof of identity from any citizen or visitor: it could be a driving licence, passport, a personal identity card or any other valid official document with a photograph issued by a government authority. While this power is rarely invoked – in practice, only by international border patrols and even then only in unusual circumstances – it is advisable to carry appropriate documents or a photocopy of your passport at all times.

Personal Safety and Theft

Slovenia enjoys one of the lowest crime rates in Europe, so public places are very safe. Mugging and violent crimes are extremely rare. Visitors might be approached by people begging for money in Ljubljana and Maribor, but they are not dangerous. Petty theft is uncommon, even in these cities. Nevertheless, it accounts for 90 per cent of all crime reported, so take the usual basic precautions to protect valuables. It is advisable to lock cars and close the windows. It is best not to leave cameras, wallets, bags, mobile phones or any other valuables in open view inside cars. Similarly, although street pickpockets are exceedingly rare, it is best to be alert at train and bus stations.

Theft from hotel rooms is rare, but in the highly unlikely event of anything being stolen, report the loss to the police to receive an insurance number.

By international agreement, any tourist detained for questioning or for any reason has the right to contact a diplomatic representative from their national consulate. The official will be able to advise on and source legal representation, hire a translator and contact family members if required. In the event of a lost passport,

inform your consulate or embassy immediately. It will issue a temporary replacement, usually for a small fee – a photocopy of your key information is helpful. Note that replacements must be collected in person at your embassy.

Security guard at the marathon in Ljubljana

Insurance

Citizens of the European Union with a European Health Insurance Card (EHIC) are eligible for emergency medical treatment in Slovenia. The EHIC application form is available in post offices.

Obtain a receipt to ensure reimbursement upon your return home in case you have to pay for any treatment. However, be aware that the reciprocal agreement does not cover medical repatriation, private treatment or dental treatment. Therefore, private medical insurance is a wise precaution for non-EU residents too, as it covers the cost of treatment and return home if required.

Check the small print on these policies to determine which sporting activities are covered, if any. Most insurers exempt "dangerous sports" such as skiing, rafting, climbing, paragliding, mountaineering and sometimes even hiking, from standard policies. Supplements or dedicated policies to cover these activities are more expensive but will refund the cost of services in case of any assistance by agencies or rescue services such as the **Mountain Rescue**

Blue-and-white police car

Association of Slovenia (Gorska reševalna zveza Slovenije), or an airlift to the hospital.

Medical Treatment

Trained staff at the *lekarna* (local pharmacy) offer over-the-counter advice, usually in fluent English, and can provide basic medicines for upset stomachs or bad colds as well as prescribe antibiotics. To buy your usual prescription medicines, it is advisable to bring a signed letter from your GP stating the medicine's generic name. Pharmacy hours are between 7am and 7pm from Monday to Friday and from 7am to 1pm on Saturday. All large towns have a duty pharmacy that is open 24 hours as well as on Sunday. This is organized by rota and a notice with the name of the current incumbent is posted on all pharmacy windows.

Tourist offices and hotel concierges are the best sources for information on the nearest pharmacy as well as the local doctor. Again, the standard of English is excellent. Consulates and embassies have a list of English-speaking doctors for more complex medical requirements. These should be your first ports of call in case of sickness.

Slovenian ambulance

Appropriately dressed visitors at Vršič Pass, northern Slovenia

A *bolnica* (hospital) is only for medical emergencies or in the case of a referral.

Health Precautions

Slovenian health standards are high and, accidents aside, the only precautions for visitors are likely to be concerned with the climate. Those caught in inclement weather on high alpine peaks are susceptible to hypothermia at any time of the year; heatstroke and sunburn are possible in summer. It is imperative to wear appropriate clothing for the terrain. To avoid sunburn, always use sunscreen and cover exposed skin; it is important to hydrate regularly, especially if taking part in strenuous activity.

British and American embassies warn of the dangers of tick-borne encephalitis in forested areas in summer. This potentially fatal brain infection is contracted from ticks that attach themselves to passing animals. Vaccination is advisable for hikers and campers who intend to stay in heavily wooded areas between May and September. Long socks are a good idea if walks and hikes are on the agenda.

Less dangerous are the mosquitoes, which drift in clouds near lakes, ponds and slow rivers in summer. None carry diseases, however, a mosquito repellent is handy to avoid uncomfortable bites.

Public Conveniences

In large cities, *javno stranišče* (public toilets) can be found without much difficulty. Often in the form of automatic cubicles with instructions in several languages on the door, these charge around €1 for use. Toilets can also be found at museums and in bars and cafés, although in the latter two, it is courteous to at least buy a drink rather than expect to use the facilities for free. Men should enter *moški*, women *ženske*, occasionally written as M and Ž; there is usually a picture on the door.

DIRECTORY

Emergency Services

Ambulance
Tel 112.

Fire
Tel 112.

Police
Tel 113.

Roadside breakdown
Tel 1987.

Insurance

Mountain Rescue Association of Slovenia
Tel 112.

Pharmacy on Ljubljana's Prešernov trg

Banking and Currency

On 1 January 2007, Slovenia woke up to a new year and a new currency when the euro replaced the tolar as the country's official currency. Although many locals complain that this also resulted in prices being surreptitiously hiked, the switch brought Slovenia in line with the bulk of the European Union nations. Consequently, visitors have the option of sourcing currency before they arrive in the country, something that was almost impossible before the switch. Once in the country, access to money is easy thanks to the abundance of exchange offices and ATMs.

An ATM, commonly known as a bankomat, in Slovenia

Banks and Changing Money

Money can be changed in a *banka* (bank) and at authorized *bureaux de change*. Banks operate between 9am and 5pm on weekdays, although some close for an hour at 12:30pm. *Menjalnice* (exchange offices) keep more flexible opening hours; in heavily touristed areas, such as on the coast, they may open until late in the evening in high summer. They are also located in larger post offices. More flexible still are the numerous other outlets at which to change money – travel agents and hotels in tourist areas, petrol stations on motorways near borders and even large shopping centres.

While banks will change cash for free or levy only a nominal fee on exchanges, other operators will charge a commission on all transactions. Typically this is between 1 and 1.5 per cent for *bureaux de change* and around 3 per cent for other operators, though some may charge up to 5 per cent. Hotels and camp sites tend to provide the poorest value for money.

Credit Cards and Prepaid Currency Cards

Major credit cards such as **Visa**, **MasterCard**, **American Express** and **Diners Club** are widely accepted in large towns, popular tourist centres and in large hotels. Outside of these, some small *gostišče* (inns), pensions and *gostilna* (restaurants) may demand cash – double-check if you are in doubt. All petrol stations accept cards. In the event of the loss of your card, it is essential to contact your card provider without delay, so that it can be blocked to prevent illegal use. ATMs are widespread, and traveller's cheques are largely redundant. A more useful alternative to traveller's cheques is a prepaid currency card, which can be topped up with euros in advance of travel and used to pay for goods or to withdraw cash from ATMs. This type of card is secure and operates with a PIN.

Credit cards used in Slovenia

ATMs

Ubiquitous throughout Slovenian towns and resorts, as well as in motorway petrol stations, ATMs accept international credit cards – usually Visa and MasterCard, and also, to a lesser extent, EuroCard, American Express and Diners Club. However, remember that interest accrues as soon as a transaction is made.

A moderately cheaper option is to use debit cards affiliated to recognized credit systems such as Maestro, Cirrus and Visa Electron Plus. Most card providers will charge a one-off fee at a set rate or one calculated as a percentage of the sum withdrawn; consult your bank before travelling. Every ATM will display the cards

DIRECTORY

Credit Cards and Travellers' Cheques

American Express
Tel (00) 44 1273 696 933.

Diners Club
Tel (01) 561 7800.

MasterCard
Tel (00) 1 636 722 7111.

Visa
Tel (00) 1 410 581 9994.

Façade of Banka Slovenije in Ljubljana

it accepts and all have an English-language option.

ATM crime, such as illegal "readers" mounted on to a card slot, which scan the cards' magnetic strip, or theft at dispensers, is unheard of in Slovenia.

Local Currency

The unit of currency in Slovenia is the euro, which is divided into 100 cents. The designs on the notes are generic architectural details and a European map common to all notes in the Eurozone. The coins feature a standard European design on one side and images of Slovenian cultural heroes or icons on the reverse. The uniform currency is a blessing to those travelling across Eurozone countries.

Bank Notes

Euro bank notes have seven denominations. The 5-euro note (grey in colour) is the smallest, followed by the 10-euro note (pink), 20-euro note (blue), 50-euro note (orange), 100-euro note (green), 200-euro note (yellow) and 500-euro note (purple). All notes show the stars of the European Union.

5 euros

10 euros

20 euros

50 euros

100 euros

200 euros

500 euros

2 euros

1 euro

50 cents

20 cents

10 cents

Coins

The euro has eight coin denominations: 1 euro and 2 euros; 50 cents, 20 cents, 10 cents, 5 cents, 2 cents and 1 cent. The 2- and 1-euro coins are both silver and gold in colour. The 50-, 20- and 10-cent coins are gold. The 5-, 2- and 1-cent coins are bronze.

5 cents

2 cents

1 cent

Communications and Media

Communications systems in Slovenia are of a high standard. There is a wide network of public services such as post and telecommunications, both of which function well. The news media is also well organized, although the near-absence of English-language publications presents a barrier for many visitors. Similarly, access to international print media is restricted to large cities and major resorts. However, a large quantity of English-language television and film is screened to compensate for the limited Slovenian output, and nearly all hotels and modern pensions subscribe to satellite channels.

Public telephone at the railway station, Ljubljana

Telephones

Public telephones in Slovenia are managed by Telekom Slovenije and are mostly found at bus and railway stations, hospitals, petrol stations and some government buildings. Generally in good order, they are operated using *telekartice* (phonecards) – public phones do not accept coins. These cards are sold at post offices and newsagent kiosks; prices range from 3 to 15 euros.

Hotels charge a premium for telephone calls made from rooms, so it is cheaper to use public or mobile telephones.

Mobile Phones

Slovenia employs a GSM (Global System for Mobile Communications) frequency that is standard for mobile phone networks, compatible with Europe and US tri-band phones, but not with the North American GSM. It is, therefore, advisable to contact your service provider to enable your "roaming" access before travelling to the country. However, providers charge inflated prices for using foreign networks, both to make and receive calls.

Phones set to roaming will automatically switch to the strongest local signal from Slovenia's mobile providers. **Mobitel**, **Debitel**, **Simobil** and

Vodafone are the largest national operators, supplemented by Austrian and Italian operators near their respective borders. Network coverage extends across 98 per cent of the country.

If your phone is not tied to a specific network, it is best to invest in a local SIM card – the electronic chip that links your phone to a network. Offered by service providers such as Mobitel and priced at around 10 euros, these SIMs give you a local telephone number and a sum of credit that can be topped up by prepaid cards sold in mobile phone shops, newsagents, post offices and often motorway service stations. Another option is to source a travel SIM card before travelling. This is a similar concept but it retains a telephone number from your home nation, so standard charges apply for incoming calls.

As elsewhere in Europe, it is against the law to use a mobile phone while driving.

Placard indicating Internet access at a tourist office

Internet

Slovenia has good Internet connectivity. Most hotels, restaurants, cafés and bars offer free Wi-Fi to their guests. Major cities have Wi-Fi hotspots where you can browse the Internet on mobile phones, tablets or computers free of charge for at least an hour. The **Wi-Fi Space** website lists free Wi-Fi access points throughout the country and pinpoints their locations on Google maps.

Some tourist information offices have a free terminal for Internet access. Public

Dialling Codes

- In Slovenia, telephone numbers have two-digit regional codes and seven-digit local numbers.
- To call Slovenia from abroad, dial the international code, then the country code (386) followed by the area code with the first zero omitted, and finally the number of the subscriber.
- Mobile phone numbers have a prefix of 031, 041, 051 or 040, followed by six digits. Dial first the code then the number when calling a mobile phone from a public or private local number; drop the zero if calling from abroad.
- To make a long-distance call, dial the two-digit regional code and then the local number.
- To make an international call from Slovenia, dial the international code (00), followed by the country code then dial the number, again omitting the first zero.
- For directory enquiries, dial 1188.

Post office with the distinct bugle logo, Škofja Loka

libraries also give free Internet access, although these are closed during weekends.

Postal Services

Carved out of the Yugoslav-era communications provider PTT and state-owned since 2002, **Pošta Slovenije** is recognized by its canary-yellow signs with a curled post bugle. There are post offices in any settlement larger than a village, which sell *znamke* (stamps) and *telekartice*, and have fax and photocopying facilities. Larger offices often offer money-changing facilities. Stamps are also available at newsagents.

The price of postage is determined by item and weight. International charges are €0.60 for a *pismo* (standard letter) up to 20 g (0.7 ounces); €0.56 for *razglednica* (postcard); 13.67 for a *paket* (parcel) within the EU and under 2 kg (4 lb); and €38.27 for *pakets* under 2 kg (4 lb) to the US and Canada. Letters can be deposited at the office or in yellow postboxes located at roadsides; parcels must be dropped off at the post office.

Post offices are open from 8am to 6pm, Monday to Friday and from 8am to noon on Saturday; the main branches in larger towns and cities open a few hours later. Larger hotels may accept post for visitors by prior arrangement. However, if staying for up to a month, it is more practical to use the poste restante services provided by post offices in the cities and larger towns. Correspondence is held for 30 days; carry proof of identity to collect your post. Ensure that all mail is marked poste restante and has the recipient's name clearly written.

Addresses

Slovenian street names make more sense when one understands the local names: *ulica* is street, *cesta* is road, *trg* is square. House numbers are written after street names. Numbers in smaller destinations often do not follow a logical order. To add to the confusion, villages generally dispense with street names and give each house a number, such as Ptujska Gora 36 in Ptujska Gora village.

Television and Radio

Slovenia has five domestic public service broadcast channels. Of the largest three, SLO 1 is a general broadcaster, SLO 2 is the main sports provider and SLO 3 covers politics. Unlike print media, large commercial broadcasters are owned by foreign companies, so the two American-owned Pop-TV and Kanal A frequently screen English-language content with Slovenian subtitles. Most hotels also subscribe to international satellite news stations such as BBC World and CNN. When radio frequencies were liberalized after independence, it resulted in a fragmented Slovenian radio service. Of interest to foreign visitors are the two channels of the national provider, Radio Slovenija.

Newspapers

Being a small market, Slovenia supports just five daily newspapers, which range from the serious *Delo* to sensationalist tabloid *Slovenske novice*. Foreign media is in limited supply outside Ljubljana, Maribor and premier resorts such as Lake Bled; imported publications are usually a couple of days out of date. Local English-language magazines include the fortnightly news-based *Slovenian Times* and *Hotel*, a bilingual tourism magazine published quarterly. Both are distributed free in upmarket hotels and tourist information centres.

DIRECTORY

Mobile Phones

Debitel
w debitel.si

Mobitel
w mobitel.si

Simobil
w simobil.si

Vodafone
w vodafone.com

Internet

Wi-Fi Space
w wifispc.com/slovenia

Postal Services

Pošta Slovenije
w posta.si

Newspaper kiosk in Ljubljana

TRAVEL INFORMATION

Most visitors to Slovenia from Europe, the US and Australia arrive by air. Jože Pučnik Airport puts the premier tourist destinations of Ljubljana, Lake Bled and Triglav National Park within an hour's travel of the arrivals lounge, and those travelling further afield will discover that the well-maintained and expanding transport network permits rapid transit across the nation. However, overland crossings from Austria, Italy, Croatia and Hungary are not uncommon. Visitors may choose to arrive in Slovenia by rail, sea or car. Rail travel takes longer and is more expensive than flying. Travelling by car is convenient and is cheaper in the long run. Catamarans, hydrofoils and cruise ships connect Piran to Venice and Trieste in Italy as well as to Poreč and Rovinj in Croatia.

Adria Airways flight at Jože Pučnik Airport

Arriving by Air

Slovenia has three international airports – **Jože Pučnik Airport** at Brnik, 23 km (14 miles) north of Ljubljana; **Edvard Rusjan Airport** in Maribor; and **Portorož Airport**.

National airline carrier **Adria Airways** operates direct routes from London, Birmingham and Dublin as well as from continental European hubs including Frankfurt, Munich, Vienna, Zurich, Brussels, Paris, Barcelona, Amsterdam, Oslo and Copenhagen. Budget operator **easyJet** also has scheduled services from London, Milan and Paris.

Other European airlines that offer scheduled services to Slovenia include Austrian Airlines, Air France, Finnair, Czech Airlines, Turkish Airlines and Vueling.

No airline currently operates direct routes to Slovenia from the US, Canada or Australia. Instead, travellers must fly to European travel hubs such as London, Paris, Frankfurt, Vienna or Budapest, and then take connecting flights with other European carriers.

Facilities at Jože Pučnik Airport, which is open daily from 6am to 10pm, include restaurants, ATMs and *bureaux de change*, a post office, a duty-free shop, free Wi-Fi Internet, tourist information offices and car rental agencies.

Air Fares

Fares on scheduled flights vary from airline to airline and season to season. Fares tend to be the highest during the tourist season in summer, but Slovenia's burgeoning reputation as a ski destination results in a second tourist season in winter. Booking tickets early saves money. However, budget airlines are no longer always the cheapest because major airlines have reduced their fares. It is wise to make a comparative analysis of prices on the airline websites before booking tickets.

Shuttle Services

Connecting buses operate from Jože Pučnik Airport to Kamnik and Kranj. Ljubljana presents the greatest number of options for onward travel within Slovenia, although Kranj serves as a convenient starting point to explore Triglav National Park. Tickets, which can be bought on boarding the bus, cost €2 to €4. Private minibus shuttles operate the same routes at regular intervals as well as one to Bled and Bohinj.

The **Ljubljana Airport Taxi Association** also has a stand here. Visitors can expect to pay around €41 to Ljubljana and €55 to Bled. Advance reservations can be made via its website, which also has a list of prices.

GoOpti is a shuttle service to airports and cities in Slovenia and neighbouring countries.

Shuttle bus from Jože Pučnik Airport to Ljubljana

Visitors outside the ticket office at the train station in Ljubljana

Rail Travel

Visitors can get to Slovenia by rail from the UK but the journey is about 20 hours and is expensive – around three times the price of a flight. The route involves changes in Paris and Munich to hook up with the EuroCity *Mimara* via Salzburg to Ljubljana. From Germany, daily EuroCity (EC) trains via Munich also connect Frankfurt and Stuttgart to Ljubljana. Austria has a regular Salzburg service, daily InterCitySlovenija (ICS) trains from Vienna to Ljubljana and frequent services between Graz and Maribor. From Switzerland, a daily EuroNight (EN) service links Zurich and Ljubljana. Croatia has several routes to the Slovenian capital: eight daily trains from Zagreb, two daily from Rijeka and a daily service from Pula. Italy has an overnight EuroNight connection from Venice to Ljubljana. Other trains to Ljubljana are from Prague, Budapest and Belgrade.

Arriving by Sea

The cruise companies **Kompas**, **Venezia Lines** and Dora operate up to three fast catamarans a week between Venice and Piran from April to late-October. The journey takes around 2.5 hours.

In addition, from late April to late September, the fast hydrofoil service of **Trieste Lines** skips along the north Adriatic coast, plying a daily return trip from Trieste in Italy, to Piran, then onwards to Poreč and Rovinj in Croatia.

Arriving by Car

Travelling to Slovenia by car (or motorbike) is popular with neighbouring countries. Routes are well marked and easy to follow – pan-European road routes have an "E" prefix and are highlighted in green on signs. As part of the European Union, Slovenia abides by the Schengen Agreement that permits free movement within partner neighbours Austria, Italy and Hungary. Major Slovenian frontier crossings such as those near Villach and Gorizia (Austria), Trieste (Italy) or Nagykanizsa (Hungary) are open 24 hours, year-round without border formalities. The police of the transit country may check departing motorists to ensure they comply with local road laws; Austria and Slovenia for example, require visitors to buy a vignette *(see p234)* to travel on its motorways.

Cycles lined up ready for hire at the tourist office, Ljubljana

DIRECTORY

Ariving by Air

Adria Airways
W adria.si

easyJet
W easyjet.com

Edvard Rusjan Airport
W maribor-airport.si

Jože Pučnik Airport
W lju-airport.si

Portoroz Airport
W portoroz-airport.si

Shuttle Services

GoOpti
W goopti.com

Ljubljana Airport Taxi Association
W airporttaxi.si

Arriving by Sea

Kompas
W kompas.com

Trieste Lines
W triestelines.it

Venezia Lines
W venezialines.com

Fast motorways also link Zagreb (Croatia) to Maribor and Ljubljana. All international drivers are required to carry a valid driving licence, the car's log book and a green card.

Green Travel

Travelling to Slovenia by train reduces the high environmental impact of flying. Within Slovenia, there are hardly any long car drives, as it is a small country. In addition, an excellent public transport network offers rapid links between major tourist destinations and cities. Bikes can be carried on all trains and provide a pleasant way to explore the country. Cycle hire is also available at cheap rates from tourist offices in popular destinations such as Lake Bled and cities such as Ljubljana and Kranj.

If you do not hike or cycle, exploring the remoter country-side without your own vehicle will be difficult as buses are generally slow and infrequent, especially at weekends.

Getting Around Slovenia

The public transport system in Slovenia is sufficiently widespread to make most destinations accessible. Relatively inexpensive by European standards, the rail network connects the regional centres; Slovenia's small size means travel times are generally short. But, touring beyond the network can prove problematic. While local bus companies operate routes in the countryside, some require careful planning or plenty of time due to a limited service at weekends. Most towns are small enough to be walkable. However, public transport comes into its own in the capital, Ljubljana.

Taxis standing in a queue outside Jože Pučnik Airport, Brnik

Travel in Ljubljana

Those travelling by bus need to buy an Urbana card, which costs €2, and you can then top it up with units. It is best to buy as many units as you think you will need in advance. Each unit, costing €0.80, covers 90 minutes of continuous travel time, including any changes of bus you might make during the journey. Swipe the Urbana card across an electronic card reader, situated near the driver's seat, when you enter the bus. These cards can be purchased and topped up at the tourist office and news-paper kiosks. Vending machines located next to principal stops accept both cash and credit cards.

Taxis cost €1–2 initial charge followed by €1.50–2 per km (0.6 miles). Always phone for a taxi if possible. Taxis picked up on the street, especially those parked outside the train station or central hotels, can be more expensive. Recommended taxi services include **Taxi Društvo Ljubljana** and **Taxi Metro**.

Trains

The national railway operator, **Slovenian Railways** (Slovenske železnice), is a model of efficiency compared to those of other former Yugoslav nations. Its 1,230 km (764 miles) of track snakes out from the transport hub of Ljubljana to most regions of the country. Carriages are invariably clean and tickets are generally cheaper than those of bus services. The network is also

Train arriving on a platform at Ljubljana's main train station

connected to pan-European routes to permit travel to neighbouring countries.

Prices vary according to the type of train. Top of the range are the express Inter-City Slovenia (ICS) trains. These operate to Maribor and Koper on international lines and reach the highest speeds; the shortest travel time between Ljubljana and Maribor is 1 hour 50 min-utes. First-class passengers receive a snack and non-alcoholic drink, which is included in the ticket price. Those in second class have access to a restaurant carriage. Irrespective of the class, all carriages are air-conditioned and comfortable. Naturally, ICS trains are the most expensive; a second-class ticket from Ljubljana to Maribor costs around €14.

Second to this are the InterCity (IC) or EuroCity (EC) trains, which pause at fewer stations than *regionalni vlaki* (regional trains) – these stop at every station on a line. The IC and EC are often faster to return to Ljubljana.

Prices are calculated on the basis of distance covered, and a *povratna vozovnica* (return ticket) costs double that of a *enosmerna vozovnica* (single ticket). First-class tickets cost around 50 per cent more than second-class tickets. Bicycles can be carried free of charge on all trains, except on ICS trains.

Special Train Services

Two alpine rail services deserve a special mention. A car train operates between Bohinjska Bistrica, near Lake Bohinj, and Most na Soči in the Soča Valley via a tunnel, thereby saving a long ascent over the Soriška planina Pass. A heritage steam locomotive known as the Muzejski vlak (Museum Train) operates between April and November up to three times a month. Coordinated by the tourism agency **ABC Tourism**, its vintage service travels through the spectacular scenery between Jesenice and Nova Gorica, via Lake Bled and

Tourist office in the main square of Koper, Slovenia's main port

Bohinjska Bistrica. Timetables are published on the agency's website, through which advance bookings can be made. Tickets can also be booked at local tourist information centres.

Tickets and Rail Passes

Tickets can be bought from the *železniška postaja* (train station), where yellow timetables list *odhodi* (departures) and white timetables list *prihodi* (arrivals). Slovenia's system of timetable symbols to represent days is difficult to understand for visitors – it is easier to source information directly from an official; information in English is available on Slovenian Railways' website. Credit cards are accepted in all stations. Tickets bought on the train incur a supplementary payment of €2.50. Timetables also list the correct *peron* (platform) for your train.

European Union residents are eligible to purchase an InterRail One Country Slovenia Pass. It enables unrestricted rail travel in Slovenia for three to eight days in a month and costs €50–119, or a third cheaper for travellers under 26. These are valid on all trains, including ICS trains. Non-EU residents qualify for the expensive Eurail Pass, which permits unlimited travel in 20 European countries, so is uneconomical for travel within Slovenia alone. The Turist vikend (Tourist Weekend) ticket offers 30 per cent discounts to passengers who make return journeys over the weekend.

Bus

Regional private companies operate the bus network in Slovenia. Buses are clean and rarely crowded outside of commuter hours. Departures are regular during the week but reduce dramatically at weekends – Saturday schedules are generally half of those of weekdays, and services on Sunday are almost nonexistent. Services to rural areas can be limited too. Conversely, popular routes from Ljubljana to mountain and coastal destinations can sell out on Fridays and public holidays in summer, so purchase in advance from computerized terminals is recommended.

On making a reservation, tickets should be collected two hours prior to departure for local bus lines, and six hours before departure for international lines. Otherwise, tickets can be bought directly before travelling from the *avtobusna postaja* (bus station) or from the driver on boarding. Fares are calculated on the basis of distance travelled, on a sliding scale, regardless of the bus company: €4 for 50 km (31 miles), €9 for 100 km (62 miles) and €17 for 200 km (124 miles). Luggage can be stored in the hold for a few extra euros, depending on size. Timetables are colour-coded to present an organized system of departures and arrivals.

DIRECTORY

Travel in Ljubljana

Taxi Društvo Ljubljana
Tel (01) 234 9000/1/2/3.
w taxi-ljubljana.si

Taxi Metro
Tel (080) 1190.
w taximetro.si

Trains

Slovenian Railways
Kolodvorska 11,
Ljubljana.
Tel (01) 291 3332.
w slo-zeleznice.si

Special Train Services

ABC Tourism
Celovška cesta 268,
Ljubljana.
Tel (05) 907 0500.
w abc-tourism.si

Cycling

Cycling is a popular pastime in Slovenia. The country's small size and the ability to transport bikes by train makes touring by bike feasible. As a rule of thumb, the terrain gets flatter the further east you go. Drivers are generally tolerant of cyclists but it is preferable nevertheless to seek the quietest country lanes. Cycling is not permitted on motorways. Helmets are obligatory for children aged 14 and under. Dedicated cycle lanes exist in most cities where cycling is prohibited in pedestrian areas.

Family cycling on a clear road in Žužemberk

Travelling by Road

Touring by car remains by far the most enjoyable and rewarding way to see Slovenia. Distances are short, the country roads are largely traffic free and a well-maintained and expanding motorway network permits rapid travel across the nation – it takes just three hours to traverse the 280 km (174 miles) from the Adriatic coast to the Hungarian border, for example. More than anything, your own car puts you right in the heart of Slovenia's stupendous scenery – indeed, a route like the Vršič Pass in the Triglav National Park is a destination in its own right. However, visitors need to be aware that snowfall can close high roads during winters.

Rules of the Road

Drivers are expected to have with them a full national driving licence and those driving their own car will be required to present on demand a vehicle registration document and a valid certificate of third-party insurance. Driving is on the right, overtaking on the left and seatbelts are compulsory for all passengers. Drivers are forbidden from using mobile phones at the wheel and dipped headlights are required even during the day. Carrying a reflective, breakdown-warning triangle is mandatory; it should be set up 100 m (328 ft) behind the vehicle if you pull over for anything other than the briefest halt. Other obligatory equipment includes a reflective vest, a spare set of bulbs and a first-aid kit. Between 15 November and 15 March cars must either be fitted with winter tyres or snow chains must be carried. Speed limits are 130 kph (81 mph) on motorways, 100 kph (62 mph) on secondary or tertiary roads and 50 kph (31 mph) in towns and villages.

Fair but determined, traffic police frequently mount radar patrols to snare speeding motorists, often on the outskirts of towns. Offenders are issued on-the-spot, fixed penalty fines for all driving infringements. These start at €40 and rise to €950 – standard fines are €120 for not wearing a seatbelt or using a mobile phone while driving. The maximum blood alcohol limit is currently set at 0.05 per cent.

Signboard for Vrsič Pass

Roads and Motorways

Slovenia has invested huge sums of money in its roads over the last decade. Most of this has gone into extending the *avtocesta* (arterial motorways) the east–west A1 and northeast–southwest A2. The two motorways cross at Ljubljana and are indicated by blue signs (green with an E number for international route numbers). The final sections of the motorway are nearing completion. Having dispensed with tollbooths in 2008, *vinjeta* window stickers are obligatory for all vehicles that use motorways. Purchased at large border crossings, motorway petrol stations and post offices, they cost €15 for a week, €30 for a month or €110 for a year. A one-year *vinjeta* (vignette) for motorcycles costs €55; a six-month one is €30 and a weekly *vinjeta* is €7.50. Failure to display a valid *vinjeta* can result in fines between €300 and €800.

Signage on all motorways and tertiary roads is excellent. Short cuts on uncategorized back roads – the white routes on a standard road map – often turn into long delays as you enter a maze of unsigned routes. On the plus side, you will experience a side of deep rural Slovenia

Beautiful mountain scenery viewed from a motorway

Parking outside the National Library, Ljubljana

that most visitors never see. *Bencinska črpalka* (petrol stations) dispense *neosvinčen bencin* (unleaded fuel) and diesel between 7am and 8pm on minor roads, have longer opening hours outside cities, and are open 24 hours a day on motorways. Some stations also offer liquefied petroleum gas (LPG). All accept standard credit cards.

Road Safety

Emergency roadside assistance is provided by national auto association, the **AMZS** (Avto-moto zveza Slovenije). In the event of an accident, you must call the police. It is illegal to move a vehicle before the police officers arrive.

Be aware that mountains and winters in Slovenia demand caution. Gradients in the Julian Alps can be up to 18 per cent and hairpin bends generally prevent towing of any sort. In addition, snowfall occurs throughout Slovenia during winters, with the possible exception of the coastal strip. While arterial routes are snowploughed, roads such as the Vršič Pass can be closed at any time between November and March. Winter equipment, such as snow chains, is required by law during this period.

Parking

Parking is the greatest problem in cities, especially in Ljubljana. Although the capital has dedicated car parks – follow the blue P to locate them – most parking in Slovenia's towns is on the streets, generally on roads on the periphery of pedestrianized areas and defined by a white line. Payment is on a "Pay and Display" basis, with costs being higher nearer to the centre. Parking in small towns and villages is free and generally easy.

Car Hire

Drivers must be over 21 years old (although some hire firms insist they are over 25) and must have held an EU or international driving licence

Car hire offices all in a row at the airport in Ljubljana

for at least two years. The major car hire companies operating in Slovenia include **Avis**, **Dollar and Thrifty**, **Hertz** and **Sixt**. Quotes from international hire companies fluctuate between firms and according to the season, but you can expect to pay from €50 per day for a modest two-door vehicle in summer. Long-term hiring generally brings more favourable day rates, but do check the unlimited mileage clauses. Prices include tax, personal accident insurance, and collision damage waiver (CDW); be warned though, the latter does not usually extend to tyres, wheels, the underside or the interior of the vehicle.

Shopping around with international firms (all of which operate bureaux at Ljubljana Airport) before you travel will turn up special deals; local outlets are usually cheaper still if you are not too concerned with appearances. All hire companies require drivers to present a passport, driving licence and credit card (sometimes two) as a deposit upon collection of the car. Double-check whether restrictions apply when crossing international borders, especially if this was part of your travel plans.

General Index

Acknowledgments

Dorling Kindersley would like to thank the many people whose help and assistance contributed to the preparation of this book.

Main Contributors

Jonathan Bousfield was born in the UK and has been travelling in Central & Eastern Europe for as long as he can remember. A student of East European history and languages, he has lived at various times in Belgrade, Sofia, Zagreb, Riga, Vilnius and Cracow. His first travel-writing job involved researching a guide to the former Yugoslavia in 1989. Since then he has authored the *DK Eyewitness Travel Guide to Bulgaria*, the *DK Top Ten Guide to Talinn*, and co-authored the *DK Eyewitness Travel Guide to Eastern and Central Europe*. He is also the author of the *Rough Guide to Croatia*, the *Rough Guide to the Baltic States* and a co-author of the Rough Guides to Austria, Poland and Bulgaria. He has also been a magazine editor, feature writer and rock critic.

James Stewart has been a travel journalist and guidebook author for over 10 years. He writes for several international publications including *The Times*, *Guardian*, *Telegraph*, *Independent*, *Sydney Morning Herald* and *Wanderlust*. He is the author of the *Rough Guide to Tasmania*, the Cadogan guides to *Slovenia* and *Croatia and the Adriatic*, the co-author of *DK Eyewitness Back Roads Germany* and the *Rough Guide to Germany*. He has contributed to Rough Guide's *Make the Most of Your Time on Earth* and *Clean Breaks*.

Fact Checker Ales Fevzer

Proofreader Sandhya Iyer

Indexer Hilary Bird, Zoe Ross

Editorial Consultant Scarlett O'Hara

Design and Editorial

Publishing Director Clare Currie
Publisher Vivien Antwi
List Manager Christine Stroyan
Project Editors Michelle Crane, Sadie Smith
Project Art Editor Shahid Mahmood
Senior Cartographic Editor Casper Morris
Senior DTP Designer Jason Little
Senior Picture Researcher Ellen Root
Production Controller Louise Minihane

Cartography Credits

Regional mapping supplied by JP Map Graphics, www.jpmapgraphics.co.uk

Additional Photography

M. Balan, Jens Eriksen, Britta Jaschinski, Hanne and Dave King, Shikha Kulkarni, Andrew de Lory, Ian O'Leary, Shruti Singhi, Jonathan Smith, Antony Souter, Linda Whitwam.

Revisions Team

Ashwin Adimari, Umesh Aggarwal, Subhashree Bharati, Andrew Bishop, Samantha Cook, Cincy Jose, Sumita Khatwani, Rahul Kumar, Jude Ledger, Darren Longley, Bhavika Mathur, Alison McGill, George Nimmo, Susie Peachey, Rada Radojicic, Hollie Teague.

Photography Permissions

Dorling Kindersley would like to thank the following for their assistance and kind permission to photograph at their establishment.

Bogenšperk Castle, Brewery Museum, Celje Regional Museum, Cerkno Museum, City Museum of Ljubljana, Kobarid Museum, Museum of Underwater Activities, Nace's House, National Gallery of Slovenia, National Museum of Slovenia, Olimje Monastery, Open-air Museum at the Pleterje Carthusian Monastery, Orthodox Church of Sts Cyril and Methodius, Plečnik House, Predjama Castle, Preseren House, Ptuj Regional Museum, Rogatec Open-air Museum, Seminary, Slovene Ethnographic Museum, Slovene Museum of Contemporary History, Snežnik Castle, St Florians Church, St Nicholas's Cathedral, Technical Museum of Slovenia, Trebnik Manor, Trebnje Gallery of Naive Artists, Tržič Museum, Turjak Castle, Velenje Museum, Veno Pilon Gallery Ajdovščina.

Picture Credits

Key: a-above; b-below/bottom; c-centre; f-far; l-left; r-right; t-top

The publisher would like to thank the following for their kind permission to reproduce their photographs:

4Corners: Guido Cozzi 109b, SIME/Guido Baviera 47tl, SIME/Johanna Huber 104–105.

akg-images: 37br.
Alamy Images: Pat Behnke 107tr, imageBROKER 86, Philip Game 196b, Ladi Kirn 70clb, Lonely Planet Images/Jonathan Smith 198cl, Cro Magnon 26c, Ian Middleton 23cr, 79tr, 204tl, Mitja Mladkovic 26br, North Wind Picture Archives 40br, PjrTravel 43tc, Realy Easy Star / Tony Spagone 191tl, David Robertson 15bc, 21br, Stoz 31br, Ken Welsh 112cl.
Antiq Hotel: 192bc.
AWL Images: Alan Copson 146-147.

Bunker Productions/Festival Mladi Levi: Urška Boljkovac 211tl.

Cajna Hisa: 201tr.
Corbis: Bob Krist 108, Design Pics/Lizzie Shepherd 205cb; Jacques Langevin 43crb, William Manning 51br.

Dreamstime.com: Giuseppe Anello 13tr, Sergii Figurnyi 48, Janos Gaspar 14tr, Jojjik 14br,

Matej Kastelic 10cla, 50bl, Isso Marovich 13bc, Mikolaj64 113tl, Mildax 12br, Petrlouzensky 11br, Arseniy Rogov 112br, Serrnovik 130, Matic Štojs 190cl, Niko Vukelic 71crb

Petra Draskovic: 158bl.

European Central Bank: 227 (all images).

Festival Ljubljana: Miha Fras 33c.
Festival Seviçc Brežice: 33br.
Ales Fevzer: 26bl, 30cl, 30bl, 31tl, 106cla, 106clb, 125br, 126cla, 213tl, 218–219.

Getty Images: Bongarts 43cb, Hulton Archive/Handout 38t, Photographer's Choice RF/Connie Coleman 199tl.
Golden Fox: 32cl.
Gostilna Lectar: 203br.
Gostilna Mihovc: 202tr.
Gostilna Pec: 206bc.
Gostilna Raduha: 203tr.
Grad Otočec: 197br.

Robert Harding Picture Library: J.D. Dallet 15tr.
Hotel Kovač: 107bl.

Javni Zavod Kinodvor: Nada Zgank 99tl.

Jazz Cerkno: Marko Čadež 98bc.

Kavarna Q: 207br.
Koroška Galerija Likovnih Umetnosti Slovenj Gradec, Slovenia, http://www.glu-sg.si/: Jože Tisnikar, The Flute Player, Oil and tempera on canvas, 1971, 45 x 35 cm 176br.

Ljubljana Tango Festival: Branko Čeak 32br.
Lutkovno Gledališče Maribor: Boštjan Lah 210bc.

Mary Evans Picture Library: 41tl.
Majerija: 205tl.
Moderna Galerija, Ljubljana: Matija Pavlovec/ Gabrijel Stupica, The Large Self-Portrait in Light Hues, 1959 © Marlenka Stupica 29bl.
Mulej Tourist Farm: 190bl.
Muzej in Galerije Mesta Ljubljana (MGML): Janez Pukšič 77crb.

Muzikafe: 195bl.
Na kluk: 194tr.
National Gallery of Slovenia: Bojan Salaj 28cr.

Pavus Grad Tabor: 206tl
Penzion Mayer: 193tr
Photolibrary: 39tr, 107tl, 107crb, Age footstock/Tibor Bognár 172–173/JD. Dallet 21tc, Morales Morales 23cla, Art Media 41crb, Alberto Campanile 27crb, William Cleary 74t, Guy Edwardes 44–45, 128–129, Borut Furlan 216br, Christian Handl 8-9, John Warburton-Lee Photography/Christian Kober 20bl, Lonely Planet Images/Grant Dixon 117cra, Martin Moos 34b, 35cr, Rainer Mirau 116br, National Geographic Society 27tr, Steve Ogle 30tr, Peter Schickert 188–189, Science Photo Library/Philippe Psaila 23bc, 155br, Lizzie Shepherd 68–69, Martin Siepmann 117bc.
Proteus: 204br.

Škocjan Caves Park: Borut Lozej 5clb,142tr, 142cla, 142br, 143tl, 143br.
Špajza: 200bl

Turistično Društvo Solčava: 2-3, 20t, 212b.
Turizem Bled: 113cr.

Wikipedia: 38bc, 39bl, 40tc, 41bl.

Zdravilišče Radenci: 214tr.

Jacket images
Front and spine: AWL Images: Ken Scicluna.

Front Endpapers
Alamy Images: imageBROKER fbr, Corbis: Bob Krist t; Dreamstime.com: Serrnovik bl, Photolibrary: William Cleary cb.

All other images © Dorling Kindersley. For further information see: www.dkimages.com

Phrase Book

Pronunciation

c – "ts" as in rats
č – "chi" as in church
g – "g" is a hard g as in get
j – "y" as in yes
š – sh
ž – shown here as "zh", sounds like the "J" in the
French name, Jacques

Emergencies

Help!	**Pomóč!**	pomochi
Stop!	**Stóp!**	stop
Call a doctor!	**Poklíčite zdravníka!**	poklichiite zdrawnika
Call an ambulance!	**Poklíčite rešílca!**	poklichiite reshilca
Call the police!	**Poklíčite policijo!**	poklichiite policiyo
Call the fire brigade!	**Poklíčite gasílce!**	poklichiite gasilce
Where is the nearest telephone?	**Kjé je najblížji telefón?**	kye ye nayblizhyi telefon
Where is the nearest hospital?	**Kjé je najblížja bólnica?**	kye ye nayblizhya bolnitsa

Communication Essentials

Yes	**Dà**	da
No	**Nè**	ne
Please	**Prósim**	prosim
Thank you	**Hvála**	hvala
Excuse me	**Oprostíte**	oprostite
Hello	**Živio**	zhivyo
Goodbye	**Nasvídenje**	nasvidenye
Good night	**Láhko nóč**	lahko nochi
Morning	**Jútro**	Yutro
Afternoon	**Popóldan**	popoldan
Evening	**Večér**	vechier
Yesterday	**Včéraj**	vchieray
Today	**Dánes**	danes
Tomorrow	**Jútri**	yutri
Here	**Túkaj**	tukay
There	**Tàm**	tam
What?	**Káj?**	kay
When?	**Kdáj?**	kday
Why?	**Zakáj?**	zakay
Where?	**Kjé?**	kye

Useful Phrases

How are you?	**Kakó ste?**	kako ste
Very well, thank you	**Zeló dôbró, hvála**	zelo dobro, hvala
Pleased to meet you	**Me veselí**	me veseli
See you soon	**Kmálu se vídimo**	kmalu se vidimo
That's fine	**Odlíčno**	odlichino
Where is/are…?	**Kjé je/so…?**	kye ye/so
How far is it to…?	**Kakó dáleč je do…?**	kako dalechi je do
How can I get to…?	**Kakó láhko prídem do…?**	kako lahko pridem do
Do you speak English?	**Govoríte anglêško?**	govorite angleshko

I don't understand	**Nè razúmem**	ne razumem
Could you speak more slowly please?	**Láhko govoríte počásneje?**	lahko govorite pochiasneye
I'm sorry	**Se opravíčujem**	se opravichiuyem

Useful Words

big	**vêlik**	velik
small	**májhen**	mayhen
hot	**vròč**	vroch
cold	**hláden**	hladen
good	**dóber**	dober
bad	**slab**	slab
enough	**dovòlj**	dovolj
open	**odpŕt**	odprt
closed	**zapŕt**	zaprt
left	**lévo**	levo
right	**désno**	desno
straight on	**narávnost**	naravnost
near	**blízu**	blizu
far	**dáleč**	dalechi
up	**gôr**	gor
down	**dól**	dol
early	**zgódaj**	zgoday
late	**pôzno**	pozno
entrance	**vhòd**	vhod
exit	**izhòd**	izhod
toilet	**straníšče**	stranishchie
restaurant	**restavrácija**	restavratsiya

Shopping

How much does this cost?	**Kóliko stáne to?**	koliko stane to
I would like…	**Želím…**	zhelim
Do you have…?	**Ali imáte…?**	ali imate
I'm just looking	**Samó glédam**	samo gledam
Do you take credit cards?	**Jêmljete kreditne kártice?**	yemlyete kreditne kartitse
What time do you open?	**Kdáj odpréte?**	kday odprete
What time do you close?	**Kdáj zapréte?**	kday zaprete
This one	**To**	to
That one	**Tísto**	tisto
expensive	**drágo**	drago
cheap	**pocéni**	potseni
size (clothes)	**velikóst (oblačíla)**	velikost (oblachiila)
size (shoes)	**velikóst (čévlji)**	velikost (chievlyi)
white	**béla**	bela
black	**čŕna**	chirna
red	**rdèča**	rdechia
yellow	**ruména**	rumena
green	**zeléna**	zelena
blue	**ódra**	modra
bakery	**pekárna**	pekarna
bank	**bánka**	banka
bookshop	**knjigárna**	knyigarna
butcher's	**pri mesárju**	pri mesaryu
chemist's	**v lekárni**	v lekarni
market	**tŕžnica**	trzhnitsa
hairdresser's	**pri frizêrju**	pri frizeryu
newsagent's/ tobacconist	**raznášalec časopísa/ trafikánt (trafikántka)**	raznashalec chiasopisa/ trafikant (trafikantka)
post office	**pósta**	poshta

shoe shop	**trgovína za čévlje**	*trgovina za chievlye*
supermarket	**súpermárket**	*supermarket*
travel agent	**potoválni posrédnik**	*potovalni posrednik*

Sightseeing

art gallery	**galerija z umetnínami**	*galeriya z umetninami*
bus station	**ávtobusna postája**	*avtobusna postaya*
castle	**grad**	*grad*
cathedral	**katedrála**	*katedrala*
church	**cérkev**	*cerkev*
closed for holiday	**zapŕto za práznike**	*zaprto za praznike*
forest	**gòzd**	*gozd*
garden	**vŕt**	*vrt*
island	**ôtok**	*otok*
lake	**jézero**	*yezero*
mountain	**gôra**	*gora*
museum	**muzêj**	*muzey*
railway station	**žéleznիška postája**	*zheleznishka postaya*
tourist information centre	**cénter za turístične informácije**	*center za turistichne informatsiye*
waterfall	**slap**	*slap*

Staying in a Hotel

Do you have a vacant room?	**Imáte prosto sôbo?**	*imate prosto sobo*
double room	**Dvópósteljna sôba**	*dvoposteljna soba*
single room	**Enópósteljna sôba**	*enoposteljna soba*
Is breakfast included?	**Je zájtrk vključén?**	*Je zaytrk vkljuchen*
porter	**portír**	*portir*
key	**kljúč**	*klyuchi*
I have a reservation	**Imám rezervácijo**	*imam rezervatsiyo*

Eating Out

Have you got a table for…?	**Imáte mízo za …?**	*Imate mizo za*
I want to reserve a table	**Želím rezervírati mízo**	*zhelim rezervirati mizo*
The bill please	**Račún, prósim**	*rachiun prosim*
I am a vegetarian	**Sèm vegeterijánec/ vegetarijánka**	*sem vegetariyanets/ vegetariyanka*
waiter/ waitress	**natákar/natákarica**	*natakar/ natakaritsa*
menu	**meni**	*meni*
wine list	**vínska kárta**	*vinska karta*
glass	**kozárec**	*kozarets*
bottle	**stekleníca**	*steklenitsa*
knife	**nòž**	*nozh*
fork	**vílica**	*vilitsa*
spoon	**žlíca**	*zhlitsa*
breakfast	**zájtrk**	*zaytrk*
lunch	**kosílo**	*kosilo*
dinner	**večérja**	*vechierya*
main course	**glávna jéd**	*glavna yed*
starters	**prèdjédi**	*predyedi*
dessert	**sladíca**	*sladitsa*

Menu Decoder

krúh	**kruh**	*bread*
sól	**sol**	*salt*
pôper	**poper**	*pepper*
pásta	**pasta**	*pasta*
soláta	**solata**	*salad*
krompír	**krompir**	*potatoes*
krúhovi cmòki	**kruhovi tsmoki**	*potato dumplings*
zélje	**zelye**	*cabbage*
rèpa	**repa**	*turnip*
góbe	**gobe**	*mushrooms*
jábolka	**yabolka**	*apples*
hrúške	**hrushke**	*pears*
slíve	**slive**	*plums*
svinjína	**svinyina**	*pork*
klobáse	**klobase**	*sausages*
šúnka	**shunka**	*ham*
ájdova káša	**aydova kasha**	*buckwheat porridge*
njoki	**nyoki**	*gnocchi*
rižóta	**rizhota**	*risotto*
gólаž	**golazh**	*goulash*
telétina	**teletina**	*veal*
govédina	**govedina**	*beef*
divjáčina	**divjachiina**	*venison*
fazán	**fazan**	*pheasant*
zájec	**zajets**	*rabbit*
postŕv	**postrv**	*trout*
máslo	**maslo**	*butter*
piščánec	**pishchianets**	*chicken*
ríž	**rizh**	*rice*
ravióli (slovenske vrste)	**ravioli**	*ravioli (the Slovene type)*
mesné króglice	**mesne kroglitse**	*meatballs*
dúnajski zrézek	**dunajski zrezek**	*wiener schnitzel*
čevápčiči	**chievapchiichii**	*čevapčiči*
dágnje	**dagnje**	*mussels*
môrski rákci	**morski raktsi**	*shrimp*
kalamári	**kalamari**	*squid*
štrúklji	**struklyi**	*štruklji*
potíca	**potitsa**	*potica*
gibánica	**gibanitsa**	*gibanica*
zavítek	**zavitek**	*zavitek*
sladoléd	**sladoled**	*ice cream*
popárjeno	**poparyeno**	*steamed*
zavréto	**zavreto**	*boiled*
ocvrto	**otsvrto**	*fried*
zapéčeno	**zapechieno**	*roasted*

Drinks

bélo víno	**belo vino**	*white wine*
čáj	**tsay**	*tea*
rdèče víno	**rdeshie vino**	*red wine*
gazírana	**gazirana mineralna**	*sparkling*
minerálna vôda	**voda**	*mineral water*
negazírana minerálna vôda	**negazirana**	*still mineral*
	mineralna voda	*water*
kava	**káva**	*coffee*
žgana pijača	**zhgana peeyatsa**	*spirit*
voda	**vôda**	*water*

Numbers

0	**nič**	*nichi*
1	**êna**	*ena*
2	**dve**	*dve*
3	**tri**	*tri*
4	**štíri**	*shtiri*
5	**pét**	*pet*
6	**šést**	*shest*
7	**sédem**	*sedem*
8	**ósem**	*osem*
9	**devét**	*devet*
10	**desét**	*deset*
11	**enájst**	*enayst*
12	**dvánajst**	*dvanayst*
13	**trínajst**	*trinayst*
14	**štírinajst**	*shtirinayst*
15	**pétnajst**	*petnayst*
16	**šéstnajst**	*shestnayst*
17	**sédemnajst**	*sedemnayst*
18	**ósemnajst**	*osemnayst*
19	**devétnajst**	*devetnayst*
20	**dvájset**	*dvayset*
21	**ênaindvájset**	*enaindvayset*
22	**dvaindvájset**	*dvaindvayset*
30	**trídeset**	*trideset*
31	**ênaintrídeset**	*enaintrideset*
40	**štírideset**	*shtirideset*

50	**pétdeset**	*petdeset*
60	**šéstdeset**	*shestdeset*
70	**sédemdeset**	*sedemdeset*
80	**ósemdesèt**	*osemdeset*
90	**devétdese**	*devetdeset*
100	**stó**	*sto*
101	**stoena**	*stoena*
102	**stodve**	*stodve*
200	**dvesto**	*dvesto*
500	**petsto**	*petsto*
700	**sedemsto**	*sedemsto*
900	**devetsto**	*devetsto*
1,000	**tisoč**	*tisochi*
1,001	**tisočena**	*tisochiena*

Time

One minute	**Ena minuta**	*êna minúta*
One hour	**Ena ura**	*êna úra*
Half an hour	**Pol ure**	*pól úre*
Monday	**Ponedeljek**	*ponedéljek*
Tuesday	**Torek**	*tôrek*
Wednesday	**Sreda**	*sréda*
Thursday	**Četŕtek**	*chietrtek*
Friday	**Pétek**	*petek*
Saturday	**Sobóta**	*sobota*
Sunday	**Nedélja**	*nedelya*

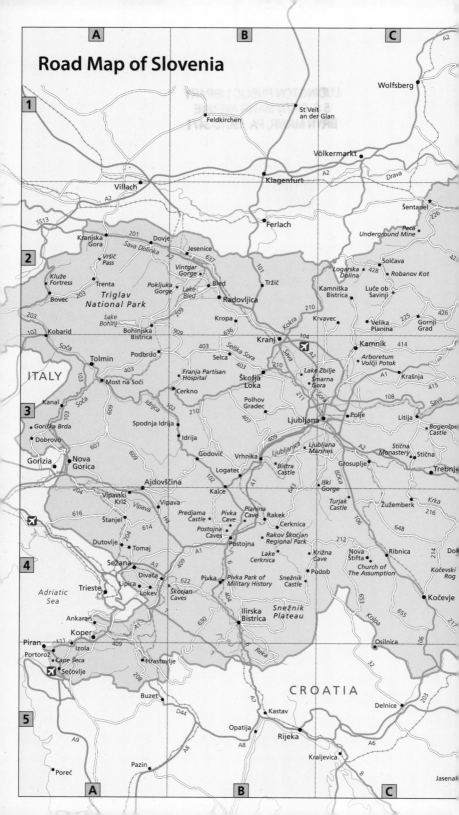

Road Map of Slovenia

A **B** **C**

1

Wolfsberg

St Veit
an der Glan

Feldkirchen

Völkermarkt

Villach

Klagenfurt

Drava

A2

SS13

Ferlach

Šentanel

Peca
Underground Mine

2

Kranjska
Gora

Dovje

Jesenice

Sava Dolinka

Vršič
Pass

Vintgar
Gorge

Logarska
Dolina

Solčava

Robanov Kot

Kluže
Fortress

Trenta

Pokljuka
Gorge

Lake
Bled

Bled

Radovljica

Tržič

Kamniška
Bistrica

Luče ob
Savinji

Bovec

Triglav
National Park

Lake
Bohinj

Bohinjska
Bistrica

Kropa

Krvavec

Velika
Planina

Gornji
Grad

Kobarid

Soča

Podbrdo

Selška Sora

Kranj

Kamnik

Arboretum
Volčji Potok

Krašnja

3

Tolmin

Most na Soči

Selca

Franja Partisan
Hospital

Škofja
Loka

Lake Zbilje

Šmarna
Gora

Polje

Litija

Bogenšpe
Castle

ITALY

Kanal

Cerkno

Polhov
Gradec

Ljubljana

Stična
Monastery

Stična

Goriška Brda

Spodnja Idrija

Idrija

Godovič

Vrhnika

Ljubljanica

Ljubljana
Marshes

Grosuplje

Trebnj

Dobrovo

Gonzia

Nova
Gorica

Logatec

Bistra
Castle

Iški
Gorge

Turjak
Castle

Žužemberk

Krka

4

Ajdovščina

Kalce

Predjama
Castle

Pivka
Cave

Planina
Cave

Rakek

Cerknica

Nova
Štifta

Ribnica

Do

Vipavski
Križ

Vipava

Postojna
Caves

Postojna

Rakov Škocjan
Regional Park

Lake
Cerknica

Križna
Cave

Church of
The Assumption

Kočevski
Rog

Štanjel

Dutovlje

Tomaj

Sežana

Divača

Pivka

Pivka Park of
Military History

Snežnik
Castle

Pudob

Kočevje

Adriatic
Sea

Lipica

Lokev

Škocjan
Caves

Ilirska
Bistrica

Snežnik
Plateau

Trieste

Ankaran

Koper

Osilnica

5

Piran

Izola

Portorož

Cape Seča

Sečovlje

Hrastovlje

Buzet

CROATIA

Delnice

Poreč

Pazin

Kastav

Opatija

Rijeka

Kraljevica

Jasenai

A **B** **C**